FORESEEING THE FUTURE

Evangeline Adams and

Karen Christino

One Reed Publications

Cover design by Barbara Peterson

One Reed Publications 2002
Copyright 2002 by Karen Christino
ISBN 0-9628031-6-2
Printed in the United States of America

Publisher's Cataloging in Publication

Christino, Karen.
    Foreseeing the future: Evangeline Adams and astrology in America
/ by Karen Christino
    224 p.
    Includes bibliography and index.
    ISBN 0-9628031-6-2
    1. Adams, Evangeline, 1868 - 1932. 2. Astrologers -- United States -- Biography. 3. Astrology -- History -- 20th century. I. Adams, Evangeline, 1868 - 1932. II. Title.
133.5 [B]

Printed in the United States
10 9 8 7 6 5 4 3 2 1   07 06 05 04 03 02

For Al H. Morrison, whose extreme dislike of Evangeline Adams was only exceeded by his desire to see this book in print.

Acknowledgments

Research for this project was supported by a grant from the New York City Chapter of the National Council for Geocosmic Research.

My warmest appreciation to Edward L. Dearborn, Adam Kraar, Adele Stein, Judith Werner and Norman Winski – the book would not have been complete without their tremendous help.

Many others in the astrological community and elsewhere were helpful during the long research and editing phases. I thank each of them for their interest, time and assistance:

Lina Accurso, Steve Bass, Hymenaeus Beta, Nick Campion, Walter Coleman, Joann Caponigro, Don Christino, Diane Cramer, Donna Cunningham, Eldeeta Curry, Edith Custer and the *Mercury Hour*, Raul daSilva, Brian Diemert, Rabbi Joel C. Dobin, Larry Ely, Meira Epstein, Kathy Fleck, Bill Heidrick, Madelyn Louise Hillis and the *NCGR Memberletter*, Susan Luck Hooks, Glen Houghton and Weiser's, Ken Irving, Mary E. Jarvis, Michael Lutin, Ken Kimball, J. Lee Lehman, John Marchesella, Anita Marshall, Maurice McCann, Adele McCormick, Frances McEvoy, Michele McKee, Ken Negus, Arlene Nimark, Dorothy Oja, Joan O'Neill, Jack Petty, Alison Picard, Steve Pincus, Nona Press, Renee Randolph, Lois Rodden, James Santa-Mo, Joanna Shannon, Susan Sheldon, Barbara Shrager, Joseph Silveira deMello, Scott Silverman, Sarah Levinson Slosberg, Gloria Star and the *AFAN Newsletter*, Edwin Steinbrecher, Abby Strauss, Henry Suzuki, Noel Tyl, Valerie Vaughan, Julia Wagner, Wesley Wallace, Henry Weingarten, John Weiser, Lorraine Welsh and the *Astrologers Newsletter*, Lawrence Arthur Williams, Bonnie Wilson, Pat Winski and Robert Zoller.

Contents

	Introduction	5
1.	New York, 1899	6
2.	Looking Backwards	12
3.	Andover Days	19
4.	A Whole New World	26
5.	The Lure of the Occult	44
6.	On Her Own	54
7.	New York, New York	63
8.	Problems and Publicity	77
9.	Evangeline and the Law	85
10.	The Magician	101
11.	Here Comes Mr. Jordan	111
12.	Big Business	124
13.	Onward and Upward	143
14.	Boom and Bust	152
15.	Superstar	160
16.	Fading Light	171
17.	Epilogue	181
	Appendix	187
	Notes	188
	Bibliography	201
	Index	215

Introduction

The astrologer Evangeline Adams was one of the most popular personalities in America in 1931. Thousands of listeners gathered near the radio three nights a week to listen to Adams' soft Yankee twang and hear about her many celebrity clients and her feats of prognostication. More importantly, they wanted to get a glimpse of what the future held in store for them. Evangeline's radio sponsors reported receiving upwards of 4,000 letters a day requesting horoscopes, and she employed more than twenty-five assistants in her New York City offices. Adams had already written several bestsellers on astrology, but she had originally established herself by giving personal consultations, for which she charged $50 per half hour – a sum that would purchase a full dining room set at the time.

Evangeline Adams popularized astrology in America, bringing it to the middle classes and beyond. Before she began practicing in Boston in 1896, astrology enjoyed a limited vogue among homeopaths, esoteric philosophers and disreputable fortune tellers. Through her untiring efforts, intelligence and social status (she was related to the presidential Adamses), Evangeline raised the level of the public's perception of astrology. She turned her several arrests for fortune-telling in New York City to her favor and garnered much publicity. In 1914 a New York City magistrate declared for the record that she "raised astrology to the dignity of an exact science."

In coordinating her book releases, radio show and personal appearances, Adams was as savvy as any multi-media star today, creating a striking public persona that made her legendary. Astrologers, in particular, have been eager to repeat the myths and stories about Adams again and again, until the tales reached epic proportions; unfortunately, there have been endless distortions and exaggerations. I became intrigued with Evangeline's story in my quest to find the truth about her life. Though not all of my original questions have been answered, it has been an engrossing journey, the likes of which I'm sure I will not find again. If readers experience some small measure of my own fascination with Evangeline and her stellar life, I will be delighted.

Karen Christino
April 2001   Brooklyn, New York

Chapter 1: *New York, 1899*

In March of 1899, Evangeline Adams was one of the few women in the world making a living reading horoscopes. Thirty-one, single and ambitious, Evangeline had come to New York to make her fortune. She was relieved to leave the Boston area, her family's home for generations. Her relatives were not sorry to see her go: she had not only broken an engagement to a wealthy merchant and struck out on her own in business, but had pursued, they thought, a bizarre way of life. Evangeline's mother, once one of her closest confidantes, had passed away a few years earlier; and in the last few months, her close friend and astrology teacher, Dr. Smith, had also died. It was time to move on.

Astrologically, Evangeline believed it was a good time for the long journey from Boston to New York. Planetary conditions promised unexpected surprises and exciting opportunities. So she had packed her bags to come to New York at just this time and had optimistically installed herself in Fifth Avenue's luxurious Windsor Hotel.

By the afternoon of March 17, 1899, Miss Adams was well aware of just how lucky she had actually been. The magnificent and renowned Windsor had been completely destroyed by fire, and she had escaped unharmed. And this was to be Evangeline's first big success story in New York: she claimed to have forecast the disaster the day before.

Before the nineteenth century turned, New York's Fifth Avenue was still a real neighborhood, with a spaciousness that has long since disappeared from this part of town. You could see the sky here, down the block, over the brownstones and beyond. One could still promenade on the broad slate sidewalks framing the cobblestoned avenue. Horse drawn cabs and carriages rambled up and down the street. Here, as in most other city neighborhoods, the services of a traffic cop were not yet necessary.

Above 42nd Street, Fifth Avenue became an exclusive area, with block-long town houses and huge mansions patterned after European castles. Warren Leland's Windsor Hotel was located in this affluent area and was designed exclusively for those who aspired to a royal way of life. The hotel attracted the best class of people and had already eclipsed its former rival, Madison Square's Fifth Avenue Hotel. As industrialists Jay Gould and William H. Vanderbilt lived nearby, they had naturally brought the Wall Street crowd closer to home after hours. The Windsor was soon dubbed the "Wall Street Club" and "Night Stock Exchange." Celebrities who had stayed at the hotel included J. Pierpont Morgan, Andrew Carnegie, General Ulysses S. Grant, Presidents McKinley and Arthur, and celebrated artists like Adelina Patti and Nellie Melba.

The Windsor took up an entire block across 47th Street from the heiress Helen Gould's impressive home. Built of seven brick and brownstone stories, it was larger than most of its neighbors. Inside, there were marble and mosaic floors, terra cotta walls, wide halls, a newsstand and telegraph office. All the latest gadgets and conveniences had been eagerly installed, including elevators, full electric lighting, and a complete telephone system. Fresh palms and other greenery decorated the lobby; lacy curtains and rich drapes fell from every window. At the head of a tremendous central staircase was a circular reception room, mirrored from floor to ceiling. A domed roof beautifully flooded the space with natural ambient light.

Evangeline Adams and her secretary, Emma Brush, occupied a first floor suite. They were grateful to proprietor Warren Leland for his hospitality, as the Fifth Avenue Hotel had refused to allow businesswomen in their line to practice within its doors. Coming here had been a risk – their suite was exclusive and expensive, running $84 a week. A skilled secretary like Emma could earn about $10 a week – a good salary at the time, yet not enough to pay for even a night's stay at the Windsor! But the gamble seemed to be paying off, as Leland had already recommended Adams to several guests. She had seen clients and done astrological readings till long after midnight on Thursday, March 16, and began appointments early Friday morning. But Friday was a holiday, and the ladies were soon taking a much-needed rest. Thousands would be streaming up Fifth Avenue in the St. Patrick's Day parade; spectators had been clamoring for over an hour outside the ladies' first floor window, anxiously awaiting the event. Nearly 350 Windsor residents were guaranteed great views from the windows of the hotel.

It was a warm, clear day for New York in March. Police officers were having a tough time keeping sightseers on the sidewalks. This was an event! In the days before television, radio and film, the spectacle of a parade held an even greater attraction than it does today. At around three o'clock, drums were heard to approach. Seventy-five horse and carriages followed, riflemen passed in uniformed troops, and an immense allegorical float featuring girls in flowing gowns drifted by. Finally, members of the Ancient Order of the Hibernians, costumed specially for the event, ended the parade. The brass band played, hundreds of horses' hooves clattered on the cobblestone streets, carriages lurched, and the crowd exclaimed with delight. In the hotel, a gray-haired gentleman watched from a bay window on the second floor. Lighting a cigar, he casually tossed the match out the window. At that moment, a breeze rustled the sash, and it was instantly ignited. Horrified, the man ran away as the head waiter, John Foy, tried to beat out the flames. But the fire quickly spread to the heavy drapes and then the wall. Foy dashed downstairs and out the building towards a firebox across Fifth Avenue.

In an age when papers carried a daily "Yesterday's Fires" column, accidents like this were a real and constant danger. Foy forced his way through the thick crowd. Reaching the curb, he was stopped by the cop who had been assigned to keep order; his shouts were drowned out by the celebrants and music.

Across 47th Street, David Dudley, Helen Gould's African American chef, came out of the house with his friend Fred Johnson. They could see a thin line of smoke rising from the flagstaff of the hotel. Dudley eluded the double-rows of police and ran into the Windsor, shouting "Your hotel's on fire!" Seeing nothing wrong, the clerk, Leland's nephew Simeon, blandly observed "You must be crazy." Deciding to take matters into their own hands, Dudley and Johnson raced upstairs to warn the guests, but were met with a thick cloud of smoke. They were forced to turn and run, for the lower floor now burst into a mass of flames.

The fire streamed to the top floors only five minutes after the blaze had started, spreading up the center of the building and towards the rear. The tinderbox-like construction of the dried out, almost thirty-year-old hotel gave the flames every opportunity. Proprietor Warren Leland had just left his family in their fourth floor apartment. Coming downstairs, he was shocked to see the front parlor ablaze, and he, too, found the way back upstairs blocked by smoke and flame. No alarm had yet been rung within the hotel.

Outside, fancy parade carriages were passing the Windsor's front. Clouds of smoke could now be seen, and shouts of "the Windsor's afire!" rang out from the crowd. The spectators pushed down towards the hotel from all sides, completely breaking up the parade. Police Commissioners, fortuitously passing the Windsor as part of the procession, immediately tried to control the mob.

Frightened guests on lower floors got out quickly. But many residents, observing the parade or quietly resting in upper story rooms, were not aware of the blaze until too late. A Russian bath establishment adjoined the hotel. Bachelor E.J. Nellis got the shock of a Victorian lifetime as six wet and naked women burst into his room, crying for aid. He quickly helped them dress and get safely to the street.

The Duncan family was conducting a dancing class in Parlor 40 at the time. Keeping cool heads, the young teachers Isadora and Elizabeth got the thirty children, clad only in flimsy dresses and satin slippers, safely out of the hotel.

Evangeline Adams and Emma Brush were startled by noises from outside their apartment. Opening the door, they found the floor dense with smoke. A man in the hall advised them to hurry and not bother locking up. Wary of the stranger, the ladies quickly gathered up their most important belongings, and Evangeline locked not only her wardrobe, but the front door as well. Then the two walked out of the building unharmed.

Noisy fire wagons had begun to arrive, but were impeded as their horses shied from approaching the mob at the front of the building. As firemen finally rushed into the lobby, Simeon Leland set off the fire gongs on every floor.

The head porter got out the emergency hose on the first floor. Suddenly, a huge, fat man wearing the costume of the Ancient Order of the Hibernians rushed in, gesticulating and giving orders. In his drunk and very excited state, he became entwined with the hose, which threatened to interrupt fire fighting efforts. But the porter and police were soon able to bundle him out the door.

The qualities which had made the Windsor an elegant showcase now contributed to its demise. Wide corridors all around the building made for a strong draft which fed the flames. The fire leapt through elevator shafts, consumed wide expanses of wall, fed on window hangings, and raced up wooden stairways. The immense domed skylight allowed the fire easy access to upper stories. Flames soon burst out of front windows on every floor. A *New York Times* reporter wrote:

Women turned pale and screamed, little ones shrank back sobbing, and men felt the sweat break upon their brows, as the heads of panic-stricken people protruded from the hotel windows, turning now toward the flames and now toward the sidewalk, and calling for help in tones that made the hearers sick.

Within fifteen minutes of the alarm, fire fighters had run up ladders and were helping people down from upper stories; but the fire was spreading too quickly.

Leland's daughter, Helen, panicked, and was the first to leap from the sixth floor, where the flames were fiercest, striking the pavement headfirst; she died instantaneously. The crowd watched horror-stricken as a mother threw her child to the street, dashing it to pieces, and then jumped to her own death.

Many guests, who had the presence of mind to use the rescue ropes in their rooms, slid or dropped from them on their descent. Iron fire escapes were red hot, and fire fighters avoided spraying them with the cool water, lest they'd crack and come away from the wall.

Outside, Evangeline Adams watched the victims, blackened by smoke and soot, dropping from above. She noted a woman in a delicate tea gown hugging a kitten to her, apparently in a state of shock as she walked unconsciously across bodies laid out in the street. From her astrological point of view, Adams had a sense of destiny and fate as well as free will. She could see that this horrible event affected everyone involved. Some, like herself, had simply been lucky. Others had no control over their situations. And although some victims of the fire might have had an opportunity to save themselves, their emotional states led to injury or even death.

People's responses to the awful situation often sealed their fates: if those above had only waited, most could have been saved. Firemen were already reaching upper stories with scaling ladders hung from window sills. But the flames and smoke were so intimidating that many gave in to the impulse to leap to probable death below, rather than face what appeared to be a certain demise from the raging fire.

The hysteria of many was matched by control in others. A middle-aged man from North Dakota first lowered his daughter and wife carefully down to the street with an escape rope. Then he coolly wrapped his hands in towels and shot down the rope himself, drawing cheers from the transfixed crowd as he landed unharmed. Nurse Frances Troup, bound by duty, incredibly carried her helpless, fainting patient, an invalid daughter of Leland's, down five flights of the fire escape to safety.

A Miss Wheeler, twenty-four, had been so nervous about her health that she typically had a physician call from four to six times a day. When she and her mother found their hallway exit blocked by flame, Miss Wheeler underwent a miraculous recovery. She ably lowered the safety rope to the ground and deftly swung from the ledge, proceeding hand over hand to the street like a trained athlete. Her mother followed suit.

The fire was the worst hotel disaster New York had ever seen. In the end, over sixty people would lose their lives, with an inestimable loss of property and valuables. Within an hour of the fire's discovery, the Windsor was completely gutted. Evangeline and Emma safely watched from the steps of Helen Gould's home as the hotel's walls fell stupendously, crashing to the ground with an enormous cloud of smoke and ash that shattered the plate-glass windows in stores opposite.

Miss Adams later said she had read Warren Leland's horoscope only the day before and had seen a very difficult planetary combination. She also felt there were danger signals in his palm. Twenty-four hours later, Leland had lost all that he valued the most: the Windsor itself, and the lives of his wife and favorite daughter. To witness such a level of destruction and loss of life must itself be a difficult life experience; to have emerged unscathed prompts one to re-examine life. For Evangeline, philosophical reflection about the ultimate cause of the disaster only strengthened her belief in astrology.

Did Evangeline Adams really predict the disaster? In later years, she'd also claim to have forecast the stock market crash of 1929 and the deaths of King Edward VII and the great opera singer Enrico Caruso. Legend had it that Adams made astrology legal in New York State and that she also predicted World War II long before her death in 1932. Just what is true and what is exaggeration, sensationalism or story? Over a hundred years later, can we possibly learn the truth?

Evangeline Adams often boasted of being descended from the famous New England Adams clan. At times she even gave the impression she was a direct descendant of President John Adams, in order to gain credibility and impress her celebrity clients. But while Evangeline is not directly descended from the presidential Adamses, she is, in fact, related to them, being born of a common ancestor. This places her firmly within one of the first families in the United States.

Many of Evangeline's forebears shared qualities which would later be evident in her own character. A number of her father's family held strong religious convictions and beliefs. As some of the first U.S. settlers, they were also vital and hard-working, brave and courageous.

The first settlers of the Massachusetts Bay Colony were Puritans, who had fled England to escape religious persecution. When Henry Adams decided to come to America with a family of ten in 1636, the high cost of living for a farmer in Somersetshire also contributed to his decision. It seemed to be a good choice, as the family prospered in Massachusetts. They were also strong and healthy: despite many hardships, most of Henry's sons lived well into their seventies and even eighties.

It is with Henry's sixth son John Adams that we shall concern ourselves (seventh son Joseph would begin the presidential line). John returned to England with his mother several years after arriving in Massachusetts at the age of twelve. By the time he came back to America in 1652, he was a millwright with a wife and daughter. This family became one of the first to settle Menotomy, now Arlington, Massachusetts.

Early genealogies typically contain a few distinctions which set them apart from modern histories. The first is that children were born to most married couples with almost shocking regularity. The mortality rate was high, so that even if most families had ten or twelve children, many died in youth or infancy. Early death was the rule rather than the exception. Many women's lives were shortened by the difficulties of continuous childbearing, coupled with the hard work necessary to raise and support a large family in a rural setting. Thus, John's eldest grandson, Joseph, born in Menotomy in 1688, would have two wives.

Colonial American communities were small, self-supporting, and tightly knit, as the families were dependant upon each other for their survival. Settlers and Native Americans were still reeling from the culture shock of exposure to one another, and conflicts were not uncommon. Thus the local militia was next in importance to religious and educational life in the early villages of Massachusetts. Joseph Adams distinguished himself in the militia, becoming a Lieutenant, and his son William, also born in the growing town of Menotomy, would become an Ensign in 1771. But, by this time, it was not the American natives but the colonists' mother country that William's regiment was prepared to resist.

Following 1763, British soldiers had been stationed in North America to enforce tighter tax and import and export restrictions, with many staying in Boston proper. Evangeline Adams' great-great-great grandfather, Captain William Adams, participated in the famous battle that would rout the British from Boston once and for all in 1776.

Captain Adams marched with his men to Dorchester on General Washington's order. Moving in with heavy artillery on the anniversary of the Boston Massacre, the patriots seized the highland. By nightfall, some 2,000 men began to fortify Dorchester Heights. Even the elements were with the colonists, as a full moon provided light for their efforts, and a low mist shrouded them from view. To the eyes of British General Howe and his fleet the next morning, two forts had seemingly appeared out of nowhere. The British had been outmaneuvered, and, as a result, Howe and his men soon quietly left the city. Captain William was now free to return home to his family, where he maintained a prominent place in the community.

Although William had done quite well for himself, he wanted something better for his eldest son, John, born in 1750. He had thus educated and prepared him for a life in the clergy. In colonial Massachusetts, this was the safest and surest route to success. The close association of church and state still dictated some form of worship of all Massachusetts citizens, and churches were an important part of village life. Our latest John Adams was subsequently chosen Deacon at Menotomy in 1792. The Adamses had been improving their lot.

Unfortunately, Deacon John did not fare so well in marriage as in his career, and in conceiving eleven children, would go through three wives. John's eldest son, John Jr., was born in the town of his forefathers, newly renamed West Cambridge, in 1774. Growing up as the first son of a prominent clergyman, he was no doubt expected to follow in his fathers' footsteps. But John Adams Jr. elected to strike out on his own. Here is where our story takes a turn. After five generations of Adamses born and bred in the same town, John would marry at the age of twenty-four and settle down in North Andover, situated twenty miles north and west of his home, not far from the Merrimack River towns of Lowell and Lawrence. Along with this propitious move, the century turned as well, and we come closer to the real characters in our story.

John III fell even further from the family tree, as he contented himself with the profession of shoemaker. When he met Elizabeth Allen Stevens at the age of twenty-three, he must have fallen head over heels in love. Although they quickly registered their intentions with the local clerk and were married in January, 1827, first son George Adams was born on April first of that year. However family and friends may have felt about this impetuous affair at the time, it worked. John III lived in North Andover and remained a successful shoemaker all his life; he and Eliza raised a family of ten.

Young George Adams graduated from Phillips Academy, a well-known Andover school for boys, in 1846, and went on to Dartmouth College in New Hampshire. Eventually, he would also become the father of a little girl named Evangeline.

It's an interesting coincidence that Evangeline's mother was also named Adams. Her people, however, form a contrast to the paternal Adamses (and they don't appear to be related). At the time the latter were achieving rank, status, and social position, the former were simply trying desperately to eke out a living.

The maternal Adamses lived some fifty miles north of Andover, close to the Maine border in Rochester, New Hampshire. Some accounts describe the family of Benjamin and Elizabeth Horne Adams as poor or even poverty stricken. Certainly there was no opportunity for them to send their son Isaac, born in 1803, to school. Yet, as the pace of industrialization in the mills of Lowell, Massachusetts was quickening and no child labor laws existed, it was relatively easy for a boy to get a job. Isaac Adams did so, as an operative in a cotton mill.

Isaac stayed in this position for some time, enjoying a new feeling of financial independence. Although he loved the machinery and was fascinated by its efficiency and power, a cotton mill is no place for a teenaged boy. The twelve hour days, stifling atmosphere, low pay, and dullingly repetitive tasks soon took their toll. Adams was young and strong; although his education was limited, he was bright. At the age of eighteen he moved to the hills and forests of

Sandwich, where he apprenticed himself to a cabinet maker. He would learn a trade and become a self-supporting artisan.

While carpentry offered the kind of satisfaction no factory work could provide, Isaac eventually became unhappy with his newly chosen profession. Some part of him missed the hum of the engines, the clatter of metal on metal, the excitement and progress the new-fangled machines represented in the 1820's. At the age of twenty-one, Isaac put down his lathe and saw and once more set off to make his fortune, swearing not to return to Sandwich till he could buy the whole town. He was now a craftsman who knew how to use tools and had a knack for figuring how best to get a job done. It was with these qualifications that he presented himself to a Boston machine shop and landed a position. During his years there, Isaac developed an interest in printing, becoming intrigued with how machines had begun to help spread the printed word to more people than ever before.

Printing presses had remained virtually unchanged in the three and a half centuries since Gutenberg's day. Hand presses utilized platens, in which a heavy plate impresses type against paper. But the nineteenth century brought many developments. In 1814, *The London Times* became the first newspaper printed with cylinders on a steam-driven power press, bringing the printing industry into the industrial revolution.

In America, printing had not kept pace. After the upsets of the revolution, it took some time for craftsmen to develop their own type and presses. At the age of twenty-five, Isaac Adams suddenly realized what needed to be done. A standard wooden platen could be combined with power. It would increase speed while maintaining a high-quality output. Isaac soon invented the Adams Power Press.

Isaac Adams' life was incredibly changed by his invention. His press design was introduced in 1830, and improved and adapted over the next few years. In 1836, Isaac and his brother Seth set about manufacturing the presses, which came into almost universal use in the United States, particularly for book printing. For more than fifty years the Adams Press continued to be the preferred machine, and it was exported to many countries around the globe. Sales of the Power Press soared, and there seemed to be, for the moment at least, no end to the burgeoning Adams fortunes.

Isaac became well-known, respected and prominent. His wealth allowed him to purchase much land and raise a family in the grandest style. One estimate placed his estate at between one and two million dollars at a time when there were no income taxes!

Evangeline's mother Harriet (Smith) Adams grew up in this world of wealth and prestige, knowing only luxury and finery. Her middle name was always a parenthetical note, and perhaps relates to her children's claim of relation to Abigail Smith Adams, wife of U.S. president John. As Harriet's father's printing business was directly linked to books and reading, she was probably better educated than most women of her day. But not much was demanded of her. Born in 1829, Harriet lived in a world where servants took care of her needs. Her father's money insured that most of her wishes were also granted. When Harriet was only eleven years old, Isaac Adams was elected to the Massachusetts Senate, making her a little girl with big connections. While she may not necessarily have been spoiled, she was certainly protected, fussed-over and petted. Although Harriet must have heard her father's fabulous rags to riches story repeated hundreds of times, she herself, blissfully ignorant, did not have the experience to understand what it was really all about. A girl who is invited to the most exclusive balls nearly every week in season can hardly be expected to be practical about life. But before very many years would pass, she would have to learn.

Andover-bred George Adams and Harriet probably met while he was attending Dartmouth College. It is hard to imagine these two together. Sweet, shy, sentimental and idealistic Harriet, with a faraway look in her eyes, did not seem quite the ideal partner for the somewhat brash and aggressive George. But George was charming as well, and his talk of his ambitions could well have won over the sheltered girl's heart. They were married in February of 1853; the groom was almost twenty-six and the bride twenty-three.

George Adams had clearly had too much of his family's shoe business and their settled life in Andover. He had big plans: he knew he could be a great success, and he was eager to travel and see the bigger cities outside New England. He wanted money and he knew where the opportunities lay: in Dunkirk, New York.

Dunkirk was a small village on the shores of Lake Erie. It had been selected as the western terminus for the new railroad to the Great Lakes, which would replace the Erie Canal. By 1848, Dunkirk had become a boom-town, as investors, speculators and entrepreneurs hurried in to take advantage of the great opportunities promised by this new route to the west. While George revelled in the local opportunities for his wholesale coal and foundry business, the heiress Harriet must have been horrified to find herself in such a place. The town had been hastily and shabbily built. Immigrants who had worked on the railroad greatly outnumbered the original settlers.

In 1853 Dunkirk was squalid, ugly and unsanitary. There were many seedy boarding houses, no churches, and most roads were unpaved. Harriet was pregnant as well: she delivered a boy in the dead of winter, January 1854.

Things were soon looking up. The volume of the new railway quickly surpassed the dreams of its projectors, demanding expansion and improvements. George was doing well financially and soon tired of Dunkirk. Grander prospects beckoned from the other end of the line: Jersey City, New Jersey, just across the Hudson River from New York City.

An Adams daughter was born in 1856, and after the birth of second son John D. Adams in 1859, the family settled down to a real home life. Although the first two children tragically died within a year, Charles Francis was born in 1861, and William Lincoln in 1864, at the height of the Civil War.

Evangeline Smith Adams came into the world on February 8, 1868; her mother was nearly forty. Evangeline was a popular name in that day. But the name Evangeline Adams somehow unites in harmony those disparate forces from the Garden of Eden: Eve and Adam, woman and man, unconscious and conscious, and implies a zealous spirit and salvation by faith. It would certainly become an appropriate name for a woman who would try to comprehend the Infinite.

Astrologers are always hungry for accurate birth data in order to draw up horoscopes. One of Evangeline's enduring mysteries is that there is no birth certificate available for her. As a result, several different birth years have been suggested, although only one horoscope was consistently referred to in Evangeline's autobiography and later published by her husband. Yet, since a birth certificate is available for her brother Charles, which corroborates the information in the Adams family genealogy, and brother John's obituary also repeats the same birth year this volume lists, it's likely that the rest of the information it contains is correct as well, including Evangeline's birth date of 1868.

Evangeline's father, George, always on the lookout for a new investment, was soon enthralled with an idea. A radical idea, a wonderful idea! In his mind, it would have rivalled that of his father-in-law's printing press, and he must have fully expected it to bring similar results, making him wealthy for life: paper railroad car wheels!

The idea of the paper wheel was greeted with some derision and ridicule, but was essentially a sound one. Various wrought-iron or steel-tired wheels had been used with success almost twenty years earlier, and most utilized some wooden parts for cushioning. The creators of the paper wheel simply substituted highly compressed paper for wood. George Adams looked upon the wheel as revolutionary, realizing that it was cheaper to produce, would provide greater safety and quiet, and perhaps even improve mileage. He was willing to make the investment in the new product, and immediately set about manufacturing the wheels.

But was the United States ready for the paper wheel in 1869? Apparently not. As Evangeline tells us in her autobiography, "Father, through no fault of his own, had lost most of his money just before his death." George Adams died suddenly in May of 1869 at the age of forty-two, leaving his wife, three young sons, and infant daughter to fend for themselves. Ironically, the paper car wheel soon became a staple of the industry, and was enthusiastically utilized by Pullman on his famous sleeping cars. This would be no consolation to George's family. The Adamses had planned on the children attending school in Andover, and we must imagine Harriet only too happy to get back to familiar surroundings. With John, now ten; Charles, eight; William, five; and baby Evangeline, she returned to Andover, Massachusetts.

Chapter 3: *Andover Days*

Andover was the perfect place for the family to recover from their loss. Located only twenty miles north of Boston, it was still something of a haven from the outside world; Andover Theological Seminary and its Christian ideals dominated the scene. One of the few places relatively untouched by the Civil War, Andover provided a quiet country setting, but was not at all rustic.

Men dominated Andover Hill, as the seminary was dedicated to training future ministers. But many maiden ladies chose to live alone and participate in the intellectual life of the community. And even though Evangeline's home life was dominated by her three older brothers, Harriet Adams never re-married. She was able to remain independent, no doubt having an income from her father, who had only recently retired. Evangeline grew up in a world in which she was quite special, being not only the youngest, but also the only girl in the family. She typically had to stand up to her older brothers, and seems to have felt competitive with them, while also learning a great deal from their experiences. Her only real authority figure was her mother, with whom she formed a strong bond.

Evangeline Adams wrote her autobiography *The Bowl of Heaven* in 1926. By that time she was famous, and the book quickly sold out many editions. She fondly recalls her Andover days, and we get a feeling that she was happy there. Interestingly, the childhood incidents she recounts all have lessons attached to them. Orthodox Congregationalists, the successors to the Massachusetts Colony's Puritans, held sway at Andover, and Evangeline received a strict Christian upbringing.

An early photograph shows the little girl all dressed up in skirts, jacket, riding cape and hat, and clearly not happy. She has the aplomb to sit still, but her little fist is clenched and her chubby cheeks are frowning. There is a forlorn and almost antagonistic look in her big eyes, but she is otherwise quite composed. Despite this momentary displeasure, Adams' reminiscences of Andover point to a secure and indulged childhood. The family home was a large two-story affair with a white picket fence on a beautiful tree-lined street.

Evangeline's earliest recollection is of a family circus organized by her brothers, and inspired by the acquisition of Jockey, a circus horse who'd been put out to pasture. The children commanded a local audience. Evangeline had been assigned the role of bareback rider, and was to make her entrance astride a large Newfoundland dog named Jack. Not one to acquiesce to such a gross indignity, little Eva insisted on mounting Jockey the horse. The boys were up in arms, with Harriet immediately enlisted to right matters; but Evangeline was triumphant. She stole the show with Jockey, loved being in the limelight, and would never forget it. Her mother's indulgence had nevertheless begun to nourish a willful streak in the girl.

After she had shown herself capable of keeping saddle, Evangeline says she was allowed to ride Jockey nearly eight miles to school every day. Perhaps she exaggerates in retrospect some fifty years later, yet she does seem to have had the privilege of independence at an early age. She always loved animals, and took the best care of the old horse, parking him in a nearby woodshed in inclement weather. Unfortunately, the little freckle-faced janitor's son had a crush on her and Eva did not return his interest. The boy retaliated by sneaking out and hitching Jockey to the schoolyard fence in nasty weather. Evangeline claims to have fought back, legitimately, going to the school board to get an official permit which entitled Jockey to residence in the shed.

This story demonstrates many personal qualities which would continue to reverberate throughout Evangeline Adams' life. Even at an early age, her personal dealings with the opposite sex were not always easy. She showed great compassion, particularly for harmless creatures or those who needed her help, but she knew an injustice when she saw one, and was not afraid to fight. By nature a sweet girl brought up with Christian ideals, she appears to have been willful about getting her way. She also knew how to enlist the help of those in authority, and her forcefulness carried the day. Much later when she was on trial for fortune-telling in New York City, Adams would find a similar fight for justice necessary.

By the age of nine, Evangeline had become somewhat spoiled and indulged by Harriet, but an accident would change everything. A beautiful day in January of 1877 promised wonderful sledding. Accustomed to doing whatever she liked, Eva got her sled and prepared for an assault on the hills. Harriet could see that the conditions were bad; she advised her daughter not to take the sled. But Evangeline was stubborn, she *would* take the sled, no matter what. Harriet was not a forceful woman, and she realized that her daughter must learn by experience. She let her go, and Eva lost control of the sled and broke her leg. Adams later recalled that this was probably one of the most significant events in her life. It would be the basis for her ultimate philosophy of life: to avoid willfully opposing wise counsel or larger forces. Intelligent non-resistance, for her, would become the greatest power in the world.

Eva's few other allusions to her childhood are somewhat poignant and imply a lonely existence. She lost her best friend to another, but, ever the philosopher, she tells us in her autobiography that, "If anybody could rob me of a friendship, it was because the friend did not really belong to me." A book she read at ten made a big impression, as it brought to life and corroborated her orthodox upbringing. In it, an evil man was dragged out into the woods by his enemies. Unknown to them, he had murdered his father, dragging him to the same hiding place. Suddenly he cried out, "Haul me no further! This is as far as I dragged my father!" Andover's strict Christianity had made its mark: the concept of retribution caught Evangeline's fancy and become to her the law of action and reaction. Through it, she perceived an orderly universe. Serious thoughts for a fourth grader!

Eva had never gotten along particularly well with her brothers, and she was only twelve when John and Charles left home for good. They escaped to bigger cities and marriage, while Evangeline stayed at home. But there was so much going on in Andover that she couldn't miss their presence much.

Raised to respect the Bible, Andover girls were different. Everything in their environment stressed the development of character, mind and spirit. Waltzes, parties and pointless socializing were not part of their life. Sheltered from the harsh realities of the outside world, they were somewhat innocent and cloistered. A girl surreptitiously kissed by a young Academy boy was seen as a unique victim. The legends of the village included a woman who had turned down nineteen offers of marriage, and one who declined the suit of nine theologues in one season. Andover was rather unusual as a post-Civil War Massachusetts town where men greatly outnumbered women; but many women still chose to remain single.

Abbott Academy and other private schools for girls and young ladies benefitted from the experience and example of the Theological Seminary, and provided a similar curriculum. Evangeline was inquisitive and enjoyed study. She particularly loved mathematics, ancient history and philosophy; these would help her with her astrology studies later on. Although she confessed to not caring for languages, she probably had to study some Latin, German or French, as well as Shakespeare, English literature, physiology, Euclid, Racine and Schiller.

There were other goings-on up the hill. Lectures, concerts and prayer-meetings were open to all, and many activities were designed exclusively for women. There were literary clubs, debating societies, and orations in Greek and Latin delivered by young seminary students. Anniversaries and exhibitions allowed for much socializing and discussion. Professors often held receptions, opening their drawing rooms to students and local families. One could hear popular preachers argue theological points at chapel. The Young Women's Bible Study Group was in reality a theological seminar given by a senior professor. Religious experience was all-encompassing, and was even given a romantic aura by the many impassioned theologians on the hill. It was a gentle, graceful and cultivated upbringing, and one which offered great advantages to a thoughtful girl like Evangeline Adams.

Eva was particularly taken with the teacher who taught her Congregational Sunday School class, Elizabeth Stuart Phelps, who was a local celebrity. Phelps had written an international best seller, *The Gates Ajar*, a number of years before, and was considered something of an upstart, albeit a devout one, by the local populace, as she was the most famous feminist writer of the day. Adams vividly remembered many long walks among the campus elms, deep in discussion with her teacher: Phelps was a role model of an independent and self-supporting woman.

Elizabeth Stuart Phelps was a true Andover product, as her father was a strict seminary professor. Her mother had died when Elizabeth was only eight, and Austin Phelps soon married his wife's tubercular sister. In another two years she, too, was dead, and he soon married again. Elizabeth thus became a young woman in a household with many children and was responsible for much around the home. Engaged in her teens, her fiancé was killed in the Civil War. She began *The Gates Ajar* while only twenty, and it became the story of a woman much like herself, recovering from the loss of a loved one. An instant hit upon publication in 1868, it offered consolation to the many Americans who had suffered similar losses. The book was famous enough to be parodied by Mark Twain, but was attacked by the press, some considering it blasphemous and heretical, others feeling it was simply immoral. This may have been because of Phelps' almost spiritualistic insistence on life after death, or because of the portraits of a deacon and minister as well-meaning but incompetent authority figures. But Elizabeth Phelps never strayed from her Bible, only the traditional approach to it.

At times an invalid (a generic Victorian-era term for someone not well enough to participate in an active life), Phelps was a prolific author who supported herself through writing. Her short stories were published in such popular magazines as *Harper's*, *McClure's*, and *Scribner's*, and she regularly produced novels as well. Much of her work combines Christian with feminist ideals: if Christianity worked at all it would be seen through an equality of the sexes.

While her early books for children stressed learning to be proper, *The Silent Partner* featured a factory worker turned evangelist and an heiress with a preference for helping those less fortunate than herself. In *The Story of Avis*, a weak husband and the inevitability of children destroy a brilliant woman's painting career. A little later on, Phelps' book *Dr. Zay* featured an independent and successful female doctor who later married. Phelps' own life mirrored those of her heroines: she was self-supporting, lived a life of service to the community, and did not marry until the age of forty-four, when she had already established a reputation as a writer and was past child-bearing age.

Elizabeth Stuart Phelps was an inspiration to Evangeline Adams. While Phelps' subjects are commonplace today, they were hot topics in the 1870's and 1880's, when most women had few rights outside of marriage. Phelps was one of the first American novelists to consistently address the social problems of the Industrial Age through her work. Evangeline was not only lucky enough to be brought up in an intellectual community, but her Sunday school teacher was famous. Eva loved books and discussions of the universe and was always attracted to celebrity; and her teacher was as much of an animal lover as she. Phelps, however, also introduced Evangeline to something even more intriguing: the occult. Evangeline tells us in *The Bowl of Heaven* that Phelps' house "was the center of discussion and investigation of all sorts of *isms*."

Spiritualism was prevalent in the later nineteenth century, understandable in an age when many died young. If Darwin had killed faith with his theory of evolution, it was resurrected in the popularity of so-called "scientific" investigations into paranormal phenomenon. Seances and evenings of mesmerism and spirit rappings became extremely popular in the northeast, with mediums garnering great publicity. Even before that, Dr. Eliakim Phelps, Elizabeth's grandfather, had claimed to live in a haunted house. A Congregational minister, member of the underground railroad and organizer of one of the first temperance societies, Reverend Dr. Phelps was serving as a secretary of the American Education Society in Connecticut in 1850 when he experienced a spiritual visitation which lasted seven months. His granddaughter recounted his experiences in her autobiography:

How the candlesticks walked out into the air from the mantelpiece and back again; how the chairs of skeptical visitors collected from all parts of the country to study what one had hardly then begun to call the "phenomena" at the parsonage at Stratford, Connecticut, hopped after the guests when they crossed the room; how the dishes at the table leaped, and the silver forks were bent by unseen hands, and cold turnips dropped from the solid ceiling; and ghastly images were found, composed of underclothing proved to have been locked at the time in drawers of which the only key lay all the while in Dr. Phelps's pocket; and how the mysterious agencies, purporting by alphabetical raps upon bed-head or on table to be in torments of the nether world, being asked what their host could do to relieve them, demanded a piece of squash pie.

Phelps, however, came short of publicly espousing spiritualism. Unlike Swedenborg, who had based his doctrine on a spiritualist revelation in the previous century, Eliakim's experience with his poltergeists certainly did not provide him with any great insight into the world beyond. But Elizabeth betrayed her own interest in the spirit world in her work. *The Gates Ajar* promised that the dead were present with us, and Phelps' short stories capture Eliakim's experience and deal with the predictions of mediums and clairvoyants, as well as a ghost who avenges his own death. Life beyond death was presented as a natural and simple progression of earthly life.

This was what Evangeline Adams was fascinated with as an adolescent, and this is why she developed such an attachment to her mystical, magical Sunday School teacher. When Phelps preached, Eva listened. She listened so well that she learned the biggest lesson of all: how to learn from another's experience. Phelps had had the experience of running a household and raising a family without becoming a wife and mother; she could see that for married women, the inevitability of childbearing made it a tough job. She wrote about women resigning themselves to difficult situations, of the infidelity of men and the moral superiority of women. Phelps made an independent life dedicated to humanity seem glamorous. And Evangeline's life seems at times patterned after her teachers': she, too, would work to support herself independently in a humanitarian profession, understood the impact of publication, and would later marry a much younger man, as had Phelps.

Elizabeth Stuart Phelps stated that her chief interests lay in "Heaven, homeopathy and women's rights." Homeopathy in the 1870's and '80's was the preferred alternative to traditional medicine, with almost one in five medical schools dedicated to this system of healing. As a reaction to the earlier heroic medical practices which consisted primarily of bloodletting and purgatives, homeopathy stressed natural methods of healing. As it relied upon the connection between the spiritual and material planes, most homeopaths had something of a philosophic background. They believed in exercise, a healthful diet and fresh air, and prescribed infinitesimal dilutions of simple, natural drugs to stimulate the body's natural forces.

Evangeline Adams, through personal experience, would come to espouse the system as well, as she fell dangerously ill sometime between the ages of sixteen and seventeen. We don't know exactly what she suffered from, but it could easily have been diphtheria, meningitis or even tuberculosis, diseases which were common at the time and demanded a long period of recovery.

The Adams family doctor was Lewis Whiting, one of the first homeopathic physicians in the country, and he treated Eva throughout her long illness. One of the nicest things about nineteenth century medicine was that doctors made house calls, and homeopathic cures necessitated a careful watch on the patient, with a close study of progressing symptoms. During her solitary months of illness, Evangeline got to know Dr. Whiting well. The familiar black leather bag with its rubber clasp, the many bottles, vials and powders, the tablespoon and glass by her bedside provided hope. About the only activities Evangeline was capable of in her weakened state were reading and thinking. She pondered the things which troubled her, she thought about Elizabeth Phelps and her lessons, and she read and re-read her books. When Dr. Whiting came, she asked him what he thought about the big questions, about life and death and the world beyond. The two had many discussions during Eva's long recovery, and became friends.

Chapter 4: A Whole New World

Evangeline did eventually struggle slowly and painfully back to health, but she was a changed person. She had taken a long, hard look at reality during her lingering illness. It was now 1886, and Eva was eighteen. Her eldest brother, John, now twenty-seven, had recently married, and was established in Chicago, as was youngest brother William, aged twenty-two. There must have been medical bills to think about. Despite grandfather Isaac Adams' death several years before, the Adams Power Press was still the preferred machine for bookbinding, providing some income for Harriet, but it was not enough. As Evangeline tells us in her autobiography:

I found myself facing the double problem of supporting myself and providing most of my mother's livelihood. This was no sacrifice to me, for my mother had given herself to the last limit of her strength for her children.

Harriet was now approaching sixty. The two women decided to leave their large home in Andover. They had spent some time with their relatives in the West, but would return to Boston. The big city offered advantages: it was still a literary mecca, and there were many job opportunities available. The Adams ladies soon moved into a town house, and Evangeline began her job search. Their home was an early nineteenth century Georgian style row house, well-placed around the corner from the Boston Common and the beautiful Public Garden, and in easy walking distance to busy Beacon and Boylston Streets. Although today an exclusive locale, a century ago it was simply suitable for the well-to-do. The neat and lovely three-story brick home appears today very much as it would have then, with a gas lamp in front, small columns flanking the front door, flower boxes, shuttered windows, and upstairs dormers for servants. Looking out on quiet suburban Chestnut Street, its proximity to its many neighbors and local shops would have provided the easy companionship common to a life in town.

None of Evangeline's autobiographical material ever specifically mentions her home on Chestnut Street, but it is an important fact, as it places the Adams women in the fashionable Beacon Hill neighborhood of Boston. Evangeline always talked a lot about herself, but she typically concealed more than she revealed. She never mentioned that one grandfather was a successful shoemaker or the other a millionaire inventor (although at times Evangeline alluded to Isaac Adams' mathematical ability, which she felt she had inherited). What she chose to highlight instead was her link with the famous Adams clan – something which at once confers dignity as well as a classic pedigree, easily understandable to the most simple American. She emphasized the fact that she and her mother didn't have much money ("Even the cost of a book was a big thing to consider, when it meant going without a new hat"), which necessitated her entry into the work force. But this story simply cannot be that accurate with the two women living in Beacon Hill: they could have easily lived more cheaply elsewhere. The Adams ladies were clearly keeping up appearances: they felt their social position and standing demanded a better neighborhood and they made sure they got it. Possibly Evangeline was also providing herself with an excuse for working. She remained an independent woman who chose to work, but in the 1880's this was viewed by many with some concern or even disdain.

Evangeline Adams always shed only the best light on her situations and experiences, so that whenever possible, it is important to compare her accounts with the public record. She also told a very good story, and almost mythologized her life through her descriptions of important events in her autobiography and publicity material. She romanticized the events of her life, making it more poetic and symbolic. Adams often avoided or overstepped explicit facts, but she seemed keenly aware of being in the public eye. She was a natural publicist of herself, almost brilliant in this regard, and knew instinctively how to reach the public. But her storytelling does at times make us wonder just how much truth there is to the tale. Adams' youthful experiences from her autobiography, for instance, are clearly drawn to both entertain and foreshadow future events. In these and many other cases, Evangeline's account is the only one available.

In the late 1880's, almost twenty percent of women over sixteen were part of the work force. Although nearly half of them worked as domestics, ladies like Evangeline had to look elsewhere or risk declassing themselves. Times were changing rapidly, however, and although not encouraged, it was socially acceptable for women to work if the necessity presented itself. Work as a schoolteacher or dressmaker was possible, as were positions in stores or offices, with the telegraph, telephone and typewriter opening up many opportunities for women in business. Evangeline could probably still hear Elizabeth Stuart Phelps' insistent voice saying, "Don't teach, don't sew... go into business." And she was lucky – her aunt, Mrs.

Webster, was married to a successful flour and grain merchant in town, who just happened to need a private secretary. She landed the job and settled into a new routine at Lord & Webster.

Always a serious girl, Eva had grown into a very serious young woman with responsibilities. She had fine taste, always dressing in a very feminine manner, but was not typically attractive. A picture at about age nineteen shows a young woman who clearly cares about her appearance: a beautiful brooch and lace grace her throat, with hair fashionably curled across her forehead. But she was on the short side and somewhat stout, and could probably best be described as plain. No doubt espousing healthful dress, Evangeline avoided the tight, wasp-waist corsets so popular in her day. She had a chubby face, large prominent nose and thin lips. The perfect, prized, ivory complexion was not hers, and she needed to wear eyeglasses. Yet Evangeline had a likeable countenance and her blue-gray eyes were alert, intense and alive.

Evangeline Adams always liked to work, and loved to feel useful. Her first position was likely quite exciting for her, and especially now that she considered herself the breadwinner of the family. Elizabeth Phelps had presented fictional women who supported their mothers, and Evangeline, finding herself in this position, too, must have conjured up a romantic image of self-sacrifice. She was bringing art to life; and if she sometimes became bored, frustrated or tired, she could console herself with the fact that she was, after all, doing her Christian duty.

Before long, however, she could distract herself with something infinitely more entrancing: romance. Soon her boss, Mr. Lord, apparently influenced by his partner, Uncle Webster, offered the girl his hand in marriage. She accepted.

At first glance, it seems unusual for a bright and independent young woman, greatly influenced by the feminist Phelps, to so readily consider marriage. But Eva had a mother to support, and Mr. Lord had become a big part of her life. Although Andover had been intellectually stimulating, it was still a small town. When most girls were out socializing, Eva had been either studying or sick, and did not have much experience with romantic relationships. Since her move to Boston, she spent most of her time at work. Lord was distinguished, courteous, and attentive. If quite a bit older, he still flattered with his interest. A plain, unusual girl doesn't get many suitors, and it was common in the nineteenth century for women to marry older and established men. Lord was successful and stable; and she was attracted to him. Her life had probably not fallen out exactly as she had hoped. She often daydreamed, and was something of an outsider with oddball ideas. Here was an opportunity to be realistic and practical.

In the meantime, many other things were going on. Her favorite among the faculty at Andover Theological had been Professor Egbert Coffin Smyth, a kind, middle-aged man, who was now on trial. Smyth had been a fixture at Andover for many years. President of the faculty, he was also extremely popular with the students, and well known outside of town. He had only recently declined the presidency of Bowdoin College when Andover's board decided to make an example of him.

To teach at Andover one had to agree to follow an explicit Christian creed, that of the Trinitarian Congregationalists. The arrival of Darwin's theory of evolution in 1859 was literally ignored at Andover, but the growing popularity of more liberal interpretations of the Bible could not be overlooked. Harvard had recently embraced Unitarianism, which stressed the individual use of reason, not adherence to a particular creed. When Dr. Smyth and his colleagues published some progressive articles, the board had an opportunity to fight against doctrinal nonconformity, and hoped in so doing to put an end to the schisms that existed between liberal and conservative members of the faculty.

The board brought five professors, including Smyth, up on charges. The details of their violations would strike us as minor points today, but went to the heart of what made Congregationalists special. All would have been well if the offending faculty had apologized, recanted, or resigned, but they were firm in their belief in moving ahead with the times. They retained counsel and fought the board.

This created a furor and gained great publicity. The students were overwhelmingly on the side of their teachers, and letters in the *Boston Journal* and *Christian Union* made the wider area aware of the controversy. Evangeline Adams followed it all with keen interest. There would actually be a public trial, held in Boston at the request of the faculty, shortly after Christmas. She made sure she was there and would soon completely change how she looked at religion.

If Dr. Smyth could espouse the non-traditional, and be as good and kind as she knew him to be, surely he would not be damned for it. The trial lasted for several days, and provided many dramatic episodes. For Evangeline, it was terrifying, as her beloved Dr. Smyth was the only one convicted! She now doubted the narrow Andover creed and could not see any part of God in the persecutors of Smyth.

(Ironically, Smyth continued to serve on the Andover faculty for many years, being re-appointed each year by the Trustees as their president. His appeal was delayed many times as the more conservative members of the board died off. The case was finally dismissed six years later.)

Evangeline's attachment to a man on trial did not sit well with the Adamses. She had already annoyed some of them with her unorthodox tendencies, and they must have hoped her engagement and eventual marriage and children would put her back on the right track. This was not to be the case.

It wasn't long before Evangeline became uncertain about her engagement as well. Once again, however, all of our information on the affair with Mr. Lord comes from Evangeline herself, through her autobiography *The Bowl of Heaven*. Here, she clearly presents mixed feelings about the relationship. On one hand she says "I was in love with the wrong man." Later on, she tells us "I was totally unresponsive," and "I did not love him." We are given no real details, typical turn-of-the-century decorum would see to that. So we must assume that at one time Mr. Lord really did appeal to her, and at another, she felt quite differently. She probably began to see her future husband as part of the authoritarian and orthodox set. He was conservative: would he support her various intellectual interests? She also perceived that the marriage may have been arranged by her relatives as a way of snapping her back to normalcy, which she hotly resented. Yet, she had made a commitment. An engagement in 1887 was taken quite seriously, since a young woman couldn't even think of kissing her beau unless they were engaged, and this meant they would soon surely marry. One did not break an engagement. Even in the obvious cases where the man was found to be a drunkard or profligate, the woman's reputation was never the same. Evangeline would wait and see.

Eva's friend Dr. Whiting was a long-time member of the Massachusetts Homeopathic Society, whose president was Dr. J. Heber Smith. As Whiting had found Eva to be a young women with unusual ideas, he provided an introduction to Dr. Smith in Boston. Smith had studied Sanskrit and Eastern religions and had taken to the use of astrology as a diagnostic tool. Evangeline subsequently arranged for an interview in which he would read her horoscope.

Everyone loved J. Heber Smith. Evangeline's constant admiration of him is reinforced by many other glowing reports. Besides being an educator, diagnostician and family physician, Smith was an active member of many medical societies, worked with prison inmates, and wrote about medicine for publication. He also had a strong interest in occult and metaphysical topics. No wonder Evangeline was eager to meet the good doctor!

Born in Maine to a well-known Methodist clergyman, Smith attended private schools in Massachusetts, hoping one day to enter the ministry as his father and grandfather before him. Unfortunately, his studies were interrupted by ill health and he continued with a private tutor, later entering Harvard for a classical course of study. Once again, however, illness interrupted his plans and he was obliged to give up theology. When Smith was again well enough to return to school his goals had changed and he now enrolled at Hahnemann Medical College in Philadelphia, graduating as Valedictorian of his class. He soon returned to Melrose, Massachusetts, just north of Boston, and settled down to marriage and a successful practice of homeopathic medicine.

Dr. Smith had probably been introduced to astrology through his early classical and theological studies. Perhaps he had also learned something about it during his years in Philadelphia, where the prominent homeopathic astrologer Dr. Luke D. Broughton and his brothers were then practicing. Astrology had from ancient times been used as a diagnostic tool; until the eighteenth century it was still taught in universities as a routine part of physician's training (even Galileo's formal duties as a teacher, for example, were instructing medical students in casting horoscopes). One of the ways in which astrology had survived since ancient times was through scientific use, in medicine. Homeopathy relied heavily upon supplying the precise remedy to suit a patient's symptoms. Some felt that in difficult or confusing cases, an accurate birth chart, or horoscope, of the patient could help pinpoint the root cause of an illness. It seemed to work for Dr. Smith, as his diagnostic skill soon led him to consultations in Boston proper and later a large practice in that city. Yet, it must be said that Smith's patients probably never knew of his astrological expertise: he never actively pursued astrology as an end unto itself.

Smith's devotion to duty, as well as his magnetic personality and courage (he is said to have braved lifelong infirmity) made him extremely popular. When the Boston University School of Medicine was founded in 1873, Dr. Smith became one of its original faculty members, holding the position of Professor of *Materia Medica* (homeopathic remedies) until his death nearly thirty years later. His manner was quiet, but his cheerfulness and good humor were often commented upon. Students later remembered him as a silver-tongued orator with a gift for infusing his lectures with wit.

After hearing so much praise for J. Heber Smith, Eva must certainly have been surprised to meet such an unpretentious and unprepossessing man. In his mid-forties, with thinning hair and drooping eyes and moustache, his gaze nevertheless conveyed an understanding of the many sad cases with which he had come into contact. Evangeline was drawn to the doctor's kind and forthright manner. She recounted in her autobiography that hers was a special case, as Smith never practiced astrology outside of his medical work. The doctor sat down across from her at a table and asked for her date, time and place of birth. These would enable him to construct a symbolic map of the heavens above Evangeline when she was born. Writing this in the center of a wheel-like horoscope chart, Smith consulted various books, made some careful calculations, and finally entered all of the positions of the planets on the chart. Evangeline was fascinated already, as she had always enjoyed math.

While almost anyone can be taught to erect a birth chart, it is the interpretation which makes the astrologer. Smith was of a highly philosophic bent, but also benefitted from his regular dealings with many people and use of astrology as a practical tool on a day-to-day basis. His chart reading amazed the young listener. "Didn't you break your leg when you were nine years old?" he asked. Evangeline recalled the memorable incident but couldn't quite place the year. And Smith was bothered by something: Eva had given him a birth time of 7:00 a.m., but the doctor noted that a person born that early would be slim and fairer of complexion. "If you had been born at that time," he said, "you would have been very beautiful." He corrected the time to 8:30, which coincided with Evangeline's unexceptional appearance. She in her turn was both shocked as well as impressed by the doctor's professional bluntness. She would later recall,

I suppose I experienced during this first interview with Dr. Smith the same excitement which so many of my own callers and correspondents tell me they get out of their first realization of the powers of astrology. I remember how amazed I was to see my whole life, past and present, spread out on the table between us.

And the future, too. Dr. Smith's reading continued,

You are not only a born astrologer, and should take up the study of the science, but you should go a long way with it.

Flattered into total belief, Eva was now completely open to whatever Smith would tell her next. He went on,

When you come before St. Peter, I will tell him that the fact you have no children is not to be held against you. Your horoscope denies you offspring of your own. But it indicates that you are better able to rock the cradle of the world then the cradle of one child.

No children; the thought had perhaps crossed her mind before. Smith also told her that she had an influential planet in the house of travel, promising many journeys.

Evangeline was then bold enough to ask the question which had already troubled her, and Smith responded in quite a matter of fact way, that no, she would probably not marry the man to whom she was then engaged. Could astrology really predict the future? Smith also said that she could expect a proposal from a much richer man within the year: Uranus influencing her house of partnerships, a once-in-a-lifetime planetary transit, would see to that. And before she left, he showed her his procedure, explaining the pie-like chart with its twelve slices of houses.

Eva had had an extraordinary experience with a sane, rational and respected man, and had been told that if not pretty, she could, after all, be a talented astrologer. Harriet would later confirm that the broken leg had occurred at age nine, just as Dr. Smith had said. Her father's diary would also later verify the 8:30 a.m. birth time.

It's well to bear in mind that Evangeline's story of the interview with Dr. Smith is supported by no outside documentation. There is no way for us to know exactly how accurate he was, and as Evangeline's account was written almost forty years later, her own imagination could easily have added to or heightened many of the details. There is no doubt, however, that J. Heber Smith was a thorough professional; recognized, admired and respected by all who knew him. And there is no doubt he made a lasting impression on Evangeline Adams. She was hooked. Dr. Smith's influence would change the entire course of her life.

Eva's secretarial work provided her with greater independence of movement – she was no longer tied to the home and could come and go much as she pleased. Lord & Webster took up much of her time, but she couldn't forget her experience with Dr. Smith. The little she could find out about astrology on her own revealed it to be a very old subject, and Evangeline had always loved ancient history. The philosophic aspect which Smith gave to his interpretation appealed to her as well. And, of course, there was the lure of the occult: Eva's experiences with Elizabeth Stuart Phelps and her long illness had made her interested in the mysteries of life and death, and Smith's astrology seemed to illuminate some of them. But Dr. Smith was a busy man, and even though Evangeline was persistent, it took quite some time before he could give her lessons.

Smith also loaned Eva books which explained the history and philosophy of astrology. She learned how astrology began with the ancient Egyptians and Chaldeans, and how the constellations gave rise to the twelve signs of the zodiac. The ancients based their predictions on the positions of the sun, moon and five visible planets, gearing them toward leaders and their kingdoms. Soon the Greeks had adopted astrology and added a new innovation: the calculation of horoscope charts for the moment of any individual's birth. It was this technique of drawing up a birth chart, purely dry and mathematical and little changed since the heyday of the Greeks and Romans nearly 2,000 years before, that Evangeline first learned from J. Heber Smith.

But her studies gave her much more, a new religion in fact. She had been disillusioned by the Congregationalists, the persecutors of Dr. Smyth, and would later say,

I am not disdainful of conventional religion. But I am impatient with some of its camp-followers. Especially difficult is it for me to maintain my own tolerance in the presence of people who attribute to God the petty attributes which they themselves possess. No such inverted egoism would be possible if they studied the teachings of astrology. The first thing they would learn is how small they are in comparison to the universe. I know it wasn't until astrology that I found any basic relation between myself and the universe. And from that moment, I found not only contentment, but inspiration.

Astrology filled the void. The system placed the individual not only at the center of his or her own personal universe, but also linked one inextricably with the larger cosmos.

The most interesting thing about a birth chart is seeing its influence on human life; Eva's friends and family were the first to be astro-analyzed. Evangeline soon so entertained and perhaps amazed her friends that they brought their friends in for chart readings. The practice and experience were just what she needed. Soon properly introduced strangers insisted on paying the young woman for her services. She accepted the pay, reserving it for new books and astrology lessons.

But there was trouble in paradise. From the very beginning, Evangeline noted that the Adams family "opposed my connection with astrology by every means within their power." They were not only upset but outraged, and although they knew nothing of the subject, considered she was "dabbling in heathenism." Most people at the time equated astrology with beggars, the lower classes and superstition. While some wealthy and eccentric characters might support astrology, its practitioners were, for the most part, viewed with suspicion, and seen as little more than thieves, preying on a gullible public. The more Evangeline studied astrology, the more upset her relatives became – and there were many of them in Boston. Chief among these was Mrs. Webster, Evangeline's aunt and the wife of her employer, who wrote to John, the eldest Adams brother in Chicago, saying Eva was "going to the dogs," and demanded that something be done about it. (John just let the matter be.)

Evangeline's fiancé, Mr. Lord, so closely linked to her aunt and uncle, must certainly have agreed with them. He was a conservative man and in those days astrology was an uncommon subject. He must've been at a loss, hoping his betrothed would soon regain her senses. But she had found a study that was just right for her and was determined to learn all about it. Astrology was slowly turning her into an independent professional – one who didn't have to rely upon an older businessman for support. The more she involved herself with astrology, the weaker Lord's hold on her became. She had also compared their horoscopes. After studying individual birth charts, Dr. Smith introduced her to the art of chart comparison, or "synastry," which analyzes how two people will interact. He had soon shown her how the horoscopes of she and Mr. Lord had a superficial physical attraction, but lacked stronger connections on the mental or spiritual plane. As Evangeline always took both astrology and Dr. Smith quite seriously, this knowledge could not have been without its impact; and finally, the relationship just seems to have gone nowhere.

J. Heber Smith hadn't the time to continue tutoring Evangeline on his own, as he had many pressing obligations. He referred her to one of the most prominent practicing astrologers in Boston. Catherine Thompson, only ten years older than Adams, had already lived through much adversity. Born of well-to-do English parents, her mother had died when she was just seven years old, her twin brother at sixteen, and her father when she was only nineteen. But Catherine had the best European education available, studying music, literature and art in Germany, London and Paris, and she received a diploma from Cambridge. Cultured and sophisticated, she soon married a wealthy businessman and moved to America. They set up sumptuous homes in New York and Newport, where Mrs. Thompson became a well-known hostess. Although hugely successful, her husband developed a fixation on outdoing financier

Jay Gould. When this proved impossible, Thompson snapped – abandoning his wife and two children and disappearing without a trace. Catherine was left to fend for herself and found a position as a hostess to a widowed Washington Senator for a time. She finally took up astrology, studying in New York with the prominent astrologer and homeopath, Dr. Luke Broughton, and later settled in Boston. Through her husband and friends she had met many men working in financial areas and concentrated her efforts on market forecasting.

Catherine Thompson brought culture and class to the then-disreputable art of astrology. A consummate professional, she reached an intelligent clientele, and raised the level of public perception through her own forceful personality and many newspaper write-ups. Evangeline met her in 1888, and she was the ideal teacher for Adams at the time, helping her fill in all the details she needed in her horoscope readings. Unlike Dr. Smith, Mrs. Thompson was practical rather than philosophic, concentrating on life cycles and the interpretation of appearance, business success, marriage and children in the horoscope. Although well-educated and well-bred, Evangeline was at this time in every respect inferior to her teacher. From Thompson's example alone, she learned how to operate as a businesswoman, how to deal with clients, and how to properly price her services. She also learned how astrology was practiced in real life: what astrological indications would point towards a happy marriage, who should succeed in what type of career, where luck or hard work were indicated, if investment was advised now, later or never. She also learned how to judge the general financial climate, based on the day-to-day movements of the planets, sun and moon: to businesspeople and speculators, this was worth a good deal.

Dr. Smith had also referred Evangeline to another of his colleagues, Dr. George S. Adams (who was no relation). Dr. Adams, a former mechanic and director of the Westborough Insane Hospital, was also a homeopath and faculty member at Boston University. The Westborough Hospital was one of the first and largest state-owned institutions in the country that was run according to homeopathic principles. Dr. Adams was a great innovator, using his mechanical background to bring the latest technical advances to the hospital. He gave clinical lectures on insanity to senior university students, supported by his clinical work with the patients. But, Evangeline tells us, he was also an expert astrologer:

Everything in that institution from the care of the most violent patient to the purchase of the best kind of hens to lay the breakfast eggs was done according to the stars.

Dr. Adams, like Dr. Smith, based his treatment on the patient's birth chart whenever possible. As he treated many patients who were considered incurable, he must have had quite an intriguing collection of horoscopes, and was said to obtain excellent results.

Evangeline was intrigued by Dr. Adams' work. If the horoscope revealed not only personality and character tendencies, but also medical problems that were likely to arise, what could be more instructive than to see unbalanced individuals along with their birth charts? She had no hesitation in approaching Dr. Adams, and joining his clinical students in observing the inmates of the violent ward. Eva found this work so fascinating that she made the hour-long trip to Westborough again and again.

If Mrs. Webster and the Adams clan had been disturbed by the studies with Dr. Smith and Mrs. Thompson, at least these teachers were people of some standing in the community. At the time, however, general opinion held that the mentally ill were best locked away and forgotten. No one in polite society would allude to such things, much less become involved with them. So it came as a great shock when the family found out about Evangeline's visits to the asylum. Poor Mr. Lord must certainly have been scandalized.

Evangeline was young and headstrong, and her mother had never really been able to control her. Harriet, for her own part, had supported her daughter's new interest in much the same way she supported most of her children's pursuits. Harriet had recently developed heart problems, necessitating the hiring of a live-in nurse. This gave the Adams family greater cause for concern, as they disapproved of the nurse being Catholic. While Evangeline was away, various relatives would drop by, making their critical feelings known and upsetting the patient. Evangeline herself felt they "attacked me on all sides": here was another example of her relatives' intolerance. Feeling torn, she met with the family's attorney to discuss the matter. He confirmed what she probably already suspected: that she, as the primary wage earner, was technically the head of the household and could do whatever she chose.

This created another schism, as Eva informed the family they were no longer welcome. As her aunt, Mrs. Webster, was the wife of one of her employers as well as "the ringleader of the family circus," Eva was also forced to resign her secretarial job. She was thus compelled to pursue astrology in greater earnest in order to supplement her mother's independent income, an ironic situation since astrology was the main cause of the family's objections.

But what of the engagement? We may never know, as Evangeline omits any real details from her autobiography. Characteristically, the incidents are only told to illustrate astrological principles, and not to reveal personal experience. This the author rarely, if ever, did. Probably she, herself, broke off her commitment at the same time, with the words of another of Elizabeth Stuart Phelps' characters firmly in mind:

No bounding impulse cried within her: That is happiness! There is rest! But only: It were unreasonable; it is unwise... "If I married you, sir, I should invest in life and you would conduct it. I suspect that I have a preference for a business of my own. Perhaps that is a part of the trouble."

Yet again, she had brought literature to life; and certainly both parties at this point felt well rid of one another.

Evangeline always made her mother a priority, and Harriet's health was not improving, so the nurse remained a necessity. But they probably learned to get along with a little less than before. Evangeline recalled that,

Even the cost of a book was a big thing to consider, when it meant going without a new hat. I remember distinctly having to decide on one occasion between a much-needed Easter bonnet to replace one of three years' service and an old, rare book on astrology. It is needless to add that I used the old bonnet a fourth year, and purchased the book.

Evangeline eventually earned a more regular income through teaching. She was well-read and educated. Mrs. Edwards' School for Young Ladies in Andover had a curriculum which practically matched men's college courses; one of the few exceptions was trigonometry. But since her studies with Dr. Smith, Adams had some familiarity with this topic as well, and was unusually well-suited as an educator.

Evangeline was pleased that the printer who turned out her astrology business cards approved of her enterprise, but he was virtually the only one to do so. There was not much beyond her own somewhat grim determination to back her entrance into the world of astrology as a real profession. However, she did join a local Unitarian church, which inspired her. Unitarianism was ideally suited to the young astrologer's needs. It challenged its members to develop their own concepts of God, had no set religious doctrine, and stressed the unity of all things; thus the use of reason and personal preference predominate over a particular creed. Unitarianism's liberal and intellectual underpinnings were a much more positive and uplifting influence than Congregationalism, which assumed that most people had a naturally sinful bent. Unitarians were traditionally open to new ideas, and had the confidence to allow their parishioners plenty of freedom to pursue their own spiritual goals.

Eva's pastor was the Reverend Minot J. Savage, whose thoughtful, clear-cut and convincing sermons were some of the most popular in the city. Ever curious but not gullible, he was another spiritualist, and an active member of the Society of Psychical Research, along with Harvard Professor and psychologist William James. The group felt communication with spirits was possible and that science could demonstrate the nature of life after death. Reverend Savage was also the author of many books and magazine articles on philosophy, religion and spiritualistic phenomenon. Evangeline would also soon convince him of the validity of astrology. He wrote her,

I confess that I do not see how the planets can be the rulers of human life; or why Mercury should determine one quality in man and Saturn another. But you have predicted things which have come true and told me most remarkable things about myself. How you found them out, I do not know; but I feel sure of your good faith and wish you all success.

Adams would save and quote this letter, as she would do with many others. The natural publicist in her understood the value of a testimonial.

Although Evangeline Adams had taken many lessons from Catherine Thompson, it's at this point that her studies with the grand lady came to an end. It is probable that they argued or disagreed and went their separate ways. Nowhere in all of her books and numerous interviews does Adams ever mention Mrs. Thompson, crediting Dr. Smith alone with introducing her to astrology, supporting her interest and teaching her the practice. Yet other writers have assured us that Thompson was a most important influence, and likely a more significant one. Catherine Thompson was reputed to be one of the best astrologers of her era. She was not much older than Adams and firmly ensconced in Boston; she could not be eclipsed. Adams, herself, has said that second only to taking care of her mother, the most important thing was to establish herself as "the best-known astrologer in America." This was the only way to outdo Catherine Thompson, whose reputation was limited to the Boston area and within astrological circles.

Thompson would later, for a few years around the turn of the century, edit and publish an astrology magazine called *The Sphinx*. In it, she expressed the desire to popularize astrology in America, the very phrase Adams would often later repeat as her own wish. Thompson also included many testimonials and reviews of her work in the magazine; Adams had already begun to collect her own. Catherine Thompson's real claim to fame lay in her popularity with an exclusive clientele and ability to use the media for publicity. Evangeline Adams would follow her lead and do it all on a grander scale in New York City. It does appear that she not only felt competitive with her teacher, but that she quite successfully emulated her, following her good example in both business and career.

Mrs. Thompson was no doubt a difficult personality. As a result of her husband's desertion, she reputedly hated men. A Shakespearean scholar, she also firmly believed herself to be the reincarnation of Queen Elizabeth of England. This in itself implies an autocratic person; at the very least, she was quite sure of herself. As an astrological authority, she probably also felt very much at ease in telling her students exactly what to do. And Evangeline, as we have seen, had her own ideas and resisted anyone's commands, including those of her mother. Could she listen to a woman who referred to herself using the royal "we"? (This excerpt is from Thompson's advertisement in *The Sphinx*.)

We hold diplomas from the University of Cambridge, and have been carefully trained by the best masters, and have confidence, therefore, that our work will always command a high price from anyone capable of appreciating a good thing. And the day will come when our time will be so valuable that we shall have to ask even more.

Ultimately, Thompson was incorrect in placing so much confidence in herself. *The Sphinx* magazine would soon be out of business. The English astrologer Sepharial had invested in it, and admitted his shares had become worthless:

Although a shareholder I never received any balance sheet of this august company. I hold thirty shares of face value ten dollars each, fully paid and non assessable. Any of my readers can have the scrip of three hundred dollars for 6d.

In *The Bowl of Heaven*, Evangeline Adams says she usually made notes in blue pencil throughout her astrology books. In a 1900 issue of *The Sphinx*, the following notes are added, also in blue pencil, to Thompson's articles: "utterly incompetent," "silly liar," and "dam' rot," among others. Although the handwriting is not similar enough to Adams' to be an exact match of samples available thirty years later, these could well have been her thoughts. Obviously, Catherine Thompson was not exactly everyone's favorite astrologer, and we can understand why Evangeline stopped studying with her.

More rewarding, however, was Evangeline's relationship with Dr. J. Heber Smith. Smith was always happy to lend his books, and the young woman eventually felt he was more than just a teacher, a "great benefactor and friend," in fact. He possibly employed her part-time to help him draw up the charts of his patients. In *The Bowl of Heaven*, Evangeline writes, with typical effusiveness, that,

The great physician allowed me to spend hours and days in his office; and between callers we would prepare and interpret their charts, a practice which helped him in his diagnosis and gave me the benefit of his medical knowledge as well as his lifetime of astrological research.

Smith's influence would be a lasting one. Although never a medical student *per se*, Adams learned much about the horoscopic indicators of various ailments, and utilized these throughout her career, as can be seen in her books and surviving typed readings from the 1920's and 1930's.

Dr. Smith felt astrologers should concentrate on broad principles and avoid getting caught up in insignificant details. The study of astrology rests both on the technical ability needed to erect a chart, as well as the interpretation of symbolism. Smith felt that the spiritual perception should predominate over the literal. This was no problem for Eva: her mind naturally tended to the symbolic, the figurative and suggestive. This quality was helpful to her astrological work, but detracted from her autobiography. Again and again we find embellishments and inconsistencies. Yet, she always told a good yarn and easily dramatized her experiences.

Though she already practiced professionally, Evangeline was still a journeyman astrologer at this point. Her work with Dr. Smith had exposed her to a wide variety of horoscopes and solidified her technical skills. Through Smith, she truly began to believe in the infallibility of astral influences. Whenever she doubted, Dr. Smith provided evidence to back up his convictions, either from personal experience or library references. Most importantly, J. Heber Smith encouraged Evangeline's interest. Over forty years later, she was still speaking of him in a letter:

Dr. Smith was right when he told me that if I landed in the Sahara Desert, things would begin to move and I would gather the world around me.

Her fondness for him lasted a lifetime.

Smith had already told Adams that her engagement might not last. But, according to her account, he had also noticed that within the year, upcoming planetary transits suggested an offer from a much richer man. Evangeline recalled in her autobiography that this, too, soon came to pass.

Evangeline Adams presents the saga of the sculptor Franklin Simmons, like all of her stories, in impressionistic style. In one account it seems she met him shortly after her introduction to Smith; in another she already appears to be settled in New York City during their association. But, as Simmons had moved to Rome by the time Adams was born, and visited here in 1888, we can say with some accuracy that Eva knew him at about the age of twenty or twenty-one, while she was still living with her mother in Boston. Simmons first came to her for a chart reading at the suggestion of a friend.

Sir Franklin Simmons was another older man: much older. Born in 1839, he was nearly thirty years Evangeline's senior. He had grown up in Maine, studied sculpture in Boston, and quickly succeeded in his profession. Before he was thirty, he had spent two years in Washington modelling the busts of such Civil War heros as Abraham Lincoln, William T. Sherman and Ulysses S. Grant. Other works included classical, Bible and equestrian studies in marble and bronze. Simmons left the United States in 1867 to work on a statue in Rome, and decided to stay on. He eventually received an Italian knighthood.

Evangeline gives us a charming account of their relationship in *The Bowl of Heaven*:

In as much as he had for many years been a student of astrology, we recognized at once the points of common interest in our horoscopes. Before we knew it, friendship deepened – and, on Sir Franklin's part, into love.

I don't know what might have happened on my side if it hadn't been for two things, both of them connected with astrology. The first was Sir Franklin's mid-Victorian idea about women and their jobs. He wished to take me away to his beloved Rome, to install me as chatelaine of his beautiful palazzo, and introduce me to a life of pleasurable leisure. And leisure didn't appeal to me. But the man did attract me. I might have succumbed to my gallant suitor – if it hadn't been for his Moon!

I saw, the first time I looked at Sir Franklin's chart, that his Moon, governing his relations with women, was badly afflicted, a condition which suggested that our relationship would probably end either in my death or my unfaithfulness. I found either alternative most undesirable.

So Simmons would return to Rome, alone; but here we have more evidence that Evangeline was well-to-do, and perhaps even technically part of society. Simmons was wealthy, successful and celebrated. His marriage proposal implies that she moved in a similar social sphere. Oddly, Evangeline never mentions their great age difference. Mr. Lord was also older and that, in itself, doesn't seem to have bothered her either: to Evangeline, age was not that important.

Once more, astrology played a pivotal role in her decision-making process. In her first relationship she believed it had alerted her to problems and reinforced her decisions. In the next, she felt it helped her avoid a possibly disastrous liaison.

*Evangeline's mother
Harriet Adams*

*Evangeline's father
George Adams*

Evangeline as a little girl

Elizabeth Stuart Phelps

*Evangeline's home on
Chestnut Street*

Evangeline at about nineteen

*Physician and educator
Dr. J. Heber Smith*

"The Great Cheiro"

Chapter 5: *The Lure of the Occult*

People in the nineteenth century felt they were in a great age of enlightenment. Towards the end of the century, there was evidence everywhere of man's mastery of the elements. The telephone and telegraph miraculously allowed immediate long-distance communication. The phonograph and gramophone had been invented, automobiles (much *cleaner* than horses) were beginning to come into use, and experiments were already underway which, if successful, would even allow man to fly. Scientific discoveries were providing comfort and convenience for all, and so began to be trusted and relied upon. The magical effects of electricity were already beginning to light some homes. Railroad travel was extremely popular, and trolleys provided comfortable and cheap travel. Great progress could be seen in manufacturing as well, and there seemed no end to what Americans, in particular, could accomplish. Idealism was predominant: there would always be new frontiers to tame and new opportunities presenting themselves. The pursuit of wealth had great value, as it was seen to intrinsically represent a life well-lived.

Nowhere were these assumptions more obvious than at Chicago's Columbian Exposition of 1893, which featured evidence of man's technical triumphs from across the country and many foreign lands. Nearly 600 acres of swampland had been transformed into a city-within-a-city along the lake front. Exhibits on agriculture, manufacturing, invention, the liberal arts, education, and even the women's movement were on display. The idea of progress infused it all, with recently developed notions of humanitarian social reform and the supremacy of the mind perceived as making it all possible.

Evangeline Adams claimed in a 1915 brochure to have spent part of her early life in the West, and two of her brothers were now married with families in Chicago. Oldest brother John had been there for nearly fifteen years; youngest brother William had lost his first wife and had already married for a second time and settled in Chicago as well. So we can assume Eva spent some time visiting them and must have attended this great World's Fair. She was always drawn to the exotic, and the many foreign expositions would have attracted her attention. There was an Eskimo Village, Arabian encampment, Egyptian shoe store, French café, and many more. The world was still a very wide place at this time, and most attendees would never again get a chance to see such cultural diversity. The women's building, the astounding Yerkes telescope, and Palace of Fine Arts would also have had enormous appeal for Evangeline.

The World's Parliament of Religions was held at the fair; one of its delegates was the Swami Vivekenanda, a Hindu monk from India. He attracted great attention with his lectures on Bhakti Yoga, Realization, the ideal of a Universal Religion, readings from the Sanskrit, and his interpretation of the orthodox Vedanta philosophy. Vivekenanda would spend the next two years lecturing and teaching in Chicago, Washington, New York and Boston. Evangeline Adams reportedly studied with him, and as esoteric philosophy and religion had become her special interests, it was a natural match. J. Heber Smith had already introduced her to some of these topics. But the fact that Vivekenanda was an immediate favorite both socially and professionally made him even more attractive. The swami drew great crowds and his lectures were filled to overflowing capacity. Another celebrity, and a religious one at that! Evangeline was now twenty-five years old. Although she had already been giving professional astrology readings, she was still not a self-supporting professional. She always hungered to learn more. Vivekenanda represented another guide and teacher along the way, one who could instruct her in a spiritual and religious system that fully accepted the value of astrology.

The Hindu Vedanta stresses spiritual self-reliance and strength. Through discriminating between the eternal and the temporal, we have the ability to liberate ourselves from suffering and to perfect our souls. As an individualist who was carving out a life stressing spiritual goals, Evangeline found these ideas inspiring. Reincarnation in the Hindu philosophy is part of an underlying belief in cycles: everything is in flux, continually becoming and then falling away again. Astrology is essentially based on the cyclic motion of the planets, so we find an obvious parallel between the two studies. Another key concept in Vedanta is the existence of "prana" or the power of vibration in the universe, along with "akasa," the fundamental physical material. To believe in astrology, there must be an acknowledgement of not only the material presence of ourselves within the planetary system, but also our interrelatedness on some higher vibratory level. So the tenets which Vivekenanda presented fitted themselves very nicely into Evangeline's world view, and almost explained why it worked. Eva would later incorporate these and other important beliefs into her own unique philosophy of life.

Although Swami Vivekenanda was an orthodox religious teacher in India, his popularity in America soared. Interest in the occult and mysticism was flourishing in the 1890's, and with it a curiosity about eastern doctrines. There were countless experiments, demonstrations and lectures on topics such as spiritualism, clairvoyance, telepathy and psychic phenomenon. Theosophy had been introduced some years before, but now gained greater popularity, and Christian Science also spread, as did various forms of evangelism and revivalism.

Astrology, too, was swept forward in the United States during this notable period of interest in the metaphysical. When Catherine Thompson's teacher, Dr. Luke Broughton, had come to this country in the mid-nineteenth century, he reported that there were only about twenty people who could competently erect a horoscope. None of these were American-born. Yet, interest in astrology increased as Broughton and his brothers published some astrological magazines and more books on astrology became readily available. James Wilson's *Dictionary of Astrology* was reprinted in Boston in 1885, the American-born W.H. Chaney published his *Primer of Astrology* in 1890, and J.G. Dalton's *Spherical Basis of Astrology* came out in 1893. British astrology was also flourishing, and with this movement came many imports from England, including ephemerides of the planets' positions, textbooks and almanacs.

With confidence in science at a high point, most occultists strove to base their beliefs on scientifically proven facts. Science became a buzz-word for legitimacy. Spiritualists continued to seek proof of physical manifestations, and astrologers, too, felt their study to be a science. If they could calculate and time the length of an influence, base a prediction on the actual motions of a planet, and then wait and see the manifestation of events on the physical plane, they assumed they were indeed operating in a scientific manner. Evangeline Adams always felt this to be the case.

Adams also studied many other metaphysical, mystical and occult topics, chiefly spiritualism and palmistry. Although she would later espouse astrology as the best, she claimed to have studied the occult in many forms and in many lands. She had experience with,

...yogis, swamis, rhythmical dancers, table-tippers, spirit-photographers, and mediums generally. I am eternally interested. As for phrenologists, physiognomists, graphologists, numerologists and the many others who work in the daylight, I have no feeling except continued interest that their findings so often agree with my own strictly mathematical calculations.

Boston was a center of much liberal thought, and in the Transcendentalist spirit of the mid-nineteenth century, occult interests were enthusiastically taken up there. Advertisements and literature on the various philosophical movements could be easily found. As each group believed they had a monopoly on the truth, they often campaigned for initiates with great fervor. The prominent socialist, Mrs. Ole Bull, had Swami Vivekenanda speak on reincarnation at her home, where one could meet other well-known individuals who were interested in the East Indian teachings. Annie Besant, clad in the flowing white robes of an Egyptian seeress, gave talks on Theosophy and Christianity, Theosophy and Social Problems, Theosophy and Present Social Conditions. Lectures and meetings on New Thought, Buddhism and the Bahai movement were also accessible to open-minded students.

Count Louis Hamon breezed into town in the winter of 1894. He had already been in the United States for a season, following tremendous success in London. Dubbing himself "The Great Cheiro" (pronounced as in chiromancy), he had been making a fortune by reading palms, utilizing his own system of predicting dates, numbers and timing. If Swami Vivekenanda drew followers with his kind, sedate and wise manner, Cheiro created a furor through sheer charisma. Evangeline would later say of him,

Poor Cheiro! His life, as I soon found by a consultation of his horoscope, was destined to be a stormy one. His palm, too, indicated the same thing. But he was – and I daresay still is – one of those daring, dashing, handsome fellows for whom the journey through life is just one high adventure after another. Women were "crazy about him." And, in many ways, he was a spoiled child. But he could read palms.

An immediate social hit in London, Cheiro had received threats of blackmail and had nearly been shut down by the authorities. He claimed that a jilted lover in New York would've stabbed him to death but for the shield provided by a cigarette case in his breast pocket and a pistol he had taken from a suicidal client the day before.

His conspicuous life had begun in Dublin only twenty-eight years earlier, when he was found to have the mark of the mystic cross on both palms. Born William Warner, his father was English and his mother French. The boy's mother was a palmist herself, and tutored him in the occult art. He did so well with it that he soon surpassed her, writing his own published treatise on the subject by the age of eleven. Training for the clergy, he was forced to leave school when his father lost a fortune in speculation.

According to his own account, Hamon subsequently travelled to Bombay to study the hand with Brahmins, became a foreign correspondent, and inherited a great deal of money, which was soon stolen by his manager. At some point he changed his original name and added the title of Count. He returned to London and continued to write before becoming "The Great Cheiro" and reading the hands of such notables as Madame Melba, Oscar Wilde, Sarah Bernhardt, Lillie Langtry, King Edward VII and Mark Twain. From all his famous clients he obtained hand prints and endorsements. Cheiro would later claim to have met Rasputin (they tried unsuccessfully to hypnotize each other), to have been kidnapped by bandits in Soviet Georgia, to have spent a few evenings in the company of Mata Hari (who he felt had "no heart"), and to have helped to break the bank at Monte Carlo by employing the natural correspondences between the roulette wheel and astrology. He was an avid traveller and journalist, who visited Japan, China and South America in a day when most people were not used to leaving their home towns. He also allegedly used his skill as a hypnotist to seduce women across the globe. So eventful was his life that he deemed two autobiographies necessary to relate all of his escapades in detail.

Charming, handsome and popular, Cheiro had worked on his book, *The Language of the Hand* while in New York in 1893, and had gone to Boston to kick off a lecture tour of the states. Yet he was so successful there, he ended up staying for over a year. It's a good bet that Evangeline attended his lectures, where he expounded on the Oriental philosophy of the hands; but she could have just as easily been influenced by the following reviews in the Boston papers:

Cheiro is a scientist and furthermore makes no mystery of his science. He has proved by his life and experience that it can be used for the help and advancement of the human race, both morally and mentally. (Journal, April 7, 1894)

His occult knowledge is vast and genuine, and the true seeker after the higher life cannot but find in his aid the most potent stimulus. (Boston Budget, June 3, 1894)

In spite of the hot weather, the large hall was filled to the doors with fashionable and distinguished people, and at the close of the lecture Cheiro was greeted with enthusiastic applause. (Herald, June 16, 1894)

Establishing himself in a suite in the luxurious Hotel Brunswick, Cheiro draped a room with Egyptian hangings and mystic emblems, and drew up to twenty Bostonians a day, all eager to pay $10 for a twenty-minute palm reading. Many were turned away daily. The fee was an exorbitant sum, as many Americans only earned about $10 for a sixty-hour work week at the time. Palmistry on this level was something new, and Cheiro stressed that his practice was also a science, backed up by the latest medical discoveries. Evangeline was so taken with what the palmist had to say that she was soon studying with him and would continue doing so throughout the winter. She learned much about chiromancy during this season and must have had a gift for this art as well, for she continued to use it as part of her practice for many years.

Palmistry had possibly an even greater history of derision than astrology, being immediately linked with wandering gypsies and vagrants. While astrologers could point to the reputations of such renowned believers as Ptolemy, Francis Bacon and Kepler, Cheiro also insisted that the likes of Aristotle, Pliny, and Paracelsus were disciples of his art, and quoted chapter and verse as proof of palmistry's lasting influence ("God caused signs or seals on the hands of all the sons of men, that the sons of men might know their works" – Job 37:7).

Like astrology, Cheiro felt palmistry could reveal character, health and disease, potential, and even, although less accurately, the timing of future events. Yet as a living part of the subject, the hand immediately demonstrated where a person was in his or her life development at that particular moment. Astrology, because it rested so heavily on a life-long birth chart, was less accurate in this regard. As exact birth times were often hard to obtain a century ago, an accurate chart could also be difficult to cast. It was helpful, then, to turn to a client's hands for further information.

While Evangeline's association with Hamon appears to have been a productive one, she had some conflicts with this teacher as well. Although she clearly sought to emulate him, there appears to have also been a competitive spirit. "The Great Cheiro" was earning about 150 times the average working man's hourly wage; his fees were enormously high. Adams felt he overcharged her for lessons. She even shares a mischievous anecdote, after she had begun practicing palmistry herself:

I found my distinguished callers not only fascinated by the study, but quite willing to have their hands smeared with printer's ink so that I could make a perfect impression of their lines and mounts. The method was my own. At the time, Cheiro was using lampblack, which was far from satisfactory; but he was not too proud to adopt my plan. He even asked for my "secret method" of removing the ink stains. I told him he had charged me well for my lessons in palmistry

*and I saw no reason why I should give away my great "discovery."
He then offered me five dollars for a small package of the mysterious
preparation. And I sold it to him. I didn't know whether to feel guilty
or not – and I don't now. The preparation was Gold Dust.*

"Gold Dust" was a common household cleanser! Here, the well-to-do resident of Beacon Hill reveals herself as somewhat more down-to-earth than her rich and famous teacher!

Like Cheiro, Evangeline had begun to keep a collection of palm-autographs – proof positive of the support and confidence of famous clients. It was not only socially unacceptable but considered a breach of confidence to reveal the personal birth information upon which a horoscope chart was based, giving Adams another reason to include palmistry in her practice.

Although the relationship with Cheiro did not last long, it was extremely significant in the development of Evangeline's career. She had perfected another skill which might give greater accuracy to her readings and help her immediately analyze anyone, correct birth data or not. And Cheiro was soon on his merry way, next becoming a press correspondent for the Japan-China war.

Evangeline Adams was in the midst of a great period of excitement, discovery and growth, for she continued to study astrology and other metaphysical and occult subjects. Yet she also had big responsibilities at home: her mother's health had continued to decline. Harriet needed rest and quiet for her heart trouble, and a nurse was hired to look after her. But for the past several years, her mental and emotional condition had been slowly deteriorating as well.

Harriet had always been somewhat forgetful and absentminded, but soon there were definite lapses in attention. Periods of drowsiness, confusion, and odd behavior could have been attributed to complications in her condition or just plain old age, since she was in her mid-sixties. Harriet was becoming more of a character, doing and saying things she would have held in check in earlier times. For the past year, it had become painfully obvious that Harriet Adams was beginning to lose her mind. "Dementia" was the clinical phrase then; today her condition might be diagnosed as Alzheimer's Disease or senility. There was nothing that Dr. Smith or anyone else could do. Harriet's speech went from confused and blurred to incoherent. Her memory was soon mostly gone and she lived primarily in the moment, with delusions increasingly encroaching on her sanity. To make matters worse, occasional violent or emotional episodes, a symptom of Alzheimer's, put a great strain on her heart: one condition aggravated the other. Many patients with Alzheimer's also experience a general feeling of euphoria and delusions of grandeur, so Harriet was probably spared much of her own suffering.

But what about her daughter? Evangeline was only twenty-five when her mother began to fall ill. Her brothers were in Chicago, leaving her personally responsible for everything. A live-in nurse was there to help physically, and the immediate family would have helped financially. Nevertheless, the emotional strain must have been enormous. Evangeline deeply loved and respected her mother; to watch her sink deeper into hopeless dementia could have been nothing other than incredibly difficult and painful. Being woken up in the middle of the night, having to physically restrain her at times, help feed and bathe her, take her to the toilet, and watch lest she escape in some delusion and hurt herself, were all part of the regular routine, as was the realization that a still living and breathing person was no longer herself at all.

At least Evangeline's strong beliefs supported her and gave her outlets for her energies. She threw herself into her studies and was lucky enough to continue doing professional readings. She studied with Vivekenanda and Cheiro, read much, and attended lectures (Theosophist Annie Besant, she reported, was the only notable who refused to give her a palm autograph). Adams became deeply immersed in spiritualism. Her pastor, the Reverend Minot J. Savage, was very much involved with the study, and Evangeline was soon attending meetings and seances regularly. A small group would meet in the evening, perhaps have some light refreshment, then dim the lights as they heard a prayer and concentrated their energies. Sitting around a dark table, all would join hands as a medium or other sensitive individual would enter a trance and attempt to contact the other side. Raps, table tippings, automatic writing, spirit appearances, or even the voice of a dear departed speaking through the medium were all hoped-for events. Late at night the group might seek visions by gazing into a large crystal ball. Evangeline tells us in *The Bowl of Heaven* that, *"I myself had the most extraordinary experiences at seances and spirit demonstrations."*

As open-minded as Adams was, others engaged in metaphysical inquiry often lacked such tolerance. She disagreed with Professor Hyslop, head of the Society for Psychical Research:

I remember spending a whole evening explaining the astrological interpretation of the law of vibrations, how the different planets operate, and how they affect the lives of the individual. "For instance," I said, dropping into astrological phraseology, "Uranus never fails to bring about a new epoch when it transits or aspects the radical Sun" – " Wait a minute," he interrupted, "what proof can you give me that Uranus or the Sun is in the heavens?"

So ended the discussion, and apparently the association, but Evangeline continued her own spiritualistic investigations. She had met and become close friends with an Englishman named William Wilberforce J. Colville. She called him an "intimate friend," but from her accounts, it appears that the relationship was strictly platonic, and that the two were together engaged in exploring the beyond.

Colville was about eight years older than Adams, and very much in touch with those he referred to as his invisible helpers – teachers, counselors and guides from other planes. His mother had died when he was an infant, and besides seeing and hearing her for many years thereafter, he claimed to be able to predict coming events through prophetic dreams while still a child. After attending a psychic demonstration at the age of thirteen, Colville found that he could speak inspirationally. He and a psychologist friend experimented with mesmerism, and Colville, dubbed the "kitten orator," made his first public performance in London at sixteen. Billed as "one of the marvels of the nineteenth century" while still a teenager, Colville travelled and lectured all over England, while also investigating spiritualism.

A typical W.J. Colville evening went like this: a hymn was sung, Colville recited a prayer and followed with another hymn. Then the audience was consulted for a topic, upon which Colville would speak inspirationally for about an hour. At the close he would ask for a phrase from a member of the audience and compose an impromptu verse. Audiences were usually charmed and astonished.

Evangeline introduced Colville to some of her Harvard friends, who attempted to trip him up by having him speak on obscure mathematical topics. As usual, even though the speaker had no personal knowledge of this complex subject, Adams says he was equal to the challenge and discoursed for an hour.

Colville stayed in the United States for over ten years, lecturing across the country. He was a prolific author, and wrote on various occult and metaphysical topics. He claimed to practice automatic writing daily, hold crystal-gazing sessions, and act as a physical medium, regularly conducting private seances from midnight till 2:00 or 3:00 a.m.

Much of Adams' experience with spiritualism came through her association with Colville. She was exposed to his wide range of talents, and accompanied him on many of his local engagements.

Still, she considered him "in private life a rank eccentric": at a dinner they attended hosted by the fashionable Mrs. Ole Bull, Colville suddenly crawled on his hands and knees under the table for no apparent reason. Evangeline was fascinated with him nevertheless. Here was a man who claimed a direct channel to the Infinite, and she had the opportunity to listen in!

Evangeline at this time was meeting many new and exciting people. Her own astrological and social background made her, for many, a unique dinner companion, and she actively sought out new ideas and experiences. These, in turn, gave her entrées to various social circles, while helping her expand her client base at the same time. She was becoming more and more immersed in the things she loved, and able to introduce her services to the increasing number of people who were interested in them. Many have categorized Adams as a naturally shrewd Yankee businesswoman, but behind this was simply her love of the work.

The year was 1896. Evangeline was now twenty-eight and Harriet Adams had lost so much of her memory and reasoning power that in the main, all that was left were her delusions. Although her heart condition continued to be a problem, the dementia took a greater toll. By the end of June, emaciated and skeleton-like, Harriet died.

Although this was a tremendous loss for Evangeline, it certainly must have also been something of a relief. For years she had had to support and look after her mother, manage a large home, and oversee the nurse and other domestic helpers (it was typical of the time to have "girls" to cook and clean). That was over. Evangeline had by now become an experienced teacher, developed a growing astrology business, and was estranged from most of her family members, either through disagreements or geographic distance. She was absolutely free to do whatever she liked, and keeping up the appearances necessary in a fancy neighborhood didn't seem that important anymore.

Even though Beacon Street was full of writers, reformers and metaphysical explorers, these were out of the mainstream. Queen Victoria of England was still very much in power, and society in general, even in America, followed her lead, being polite, considerate and careful of accepted norms. Women were still rigidly corseted and ensconced in feathers, lace, wide hats, puffed-out hair and gloves. Stockings were available in two colors: white and black. Heads were covered and ankles kept out of sight; clothes were made to last. Typical bedrooms still had washstands, a pitcher and basin, and chamber pots. Although the first automobiles had recently appeared, victorias, barouches and the smell of horses were everywhere. Horse-drawn omnibuses, cabs and streetcars provided the main source of public transportation. More people were living in cities than ever before, and most well-to-do families escaped the heat during July and August by vacationing at a beach or lake.

Evangeline decided to take an apartment in the Copley Hotel. Apartment living was a new and sensible way of life, and although not exactly fashionable, was seen as a necessary alternative for middle-class people living alone without a great deal of money. The Back Bay location was in a completely modern part of town, created through landfill. Churches already dotted the area, and many of the new hotels and apartment buildings featured indoor plumbing and central heating. Evangeline's aim was primarily to set up her astrology studio. She didn't need much room, had only her books and a few possessions, and could live and work in the same space. Like many, she probably had an Irish immigrant to take care of household chores.

Copley Square was a magnificent site, large, open and imposing compared to the quiet and tranquil, tree-lined Chestnut Street home. A new library had opened across the street a year before, and on the other side of the plaza rose Trinity Church. Its famous rector, Phillips Brooks, was also from Andover, and Evangeline often stopped by to hear his vital, inspiring sermons. She must've revelled in having such a fine library and church so close at hand. This area was cosmopolitan, with many schools, hotels and apartment houses in the vicinity. Symbolically, the move signalled Evangeline's official entry into the world-at-large.

The Copley Hotel housed many other professionals. Among Adams' immediate neighbors were several other teachers, as well as physicians, salesmen and attorneys. Smaller apartments were inhabited by middle-class working people. While Evangeline still officially earned her living as a teacher, more and more of her income was generated from horoscope and palm readings. She charged $2 per visit, which probably lasted from thirty minutes to an hour. When we compare her rates to Cheiro's $30 an hour, they are quite reasonable. But with regular bookings, Evangeline could earn almost ten times as much as she did through teaching. The work was becoming lucrative, and she was good at it: many clients returned for updates and more information.

While Evangeline Adams was a skilled astrologer and palmist, she possessed several other qualities which insured her success. Most importantly, she continued to be absolutely fascinated with her practices, and was genuinely curious to find out exactly how the horoscope and palm indicated events in her clients' lives. Her belief in what she liked to call "the science" was profound. Adams was, above all, known for her sincerity. She prayed every night that she might be guided to counsel her clients wisely. Because of the strength of her own beliefs, Evangeline convinced a great number of people of astrology's validity. If she might fail to convince, she never failed to impress one with her own convictions.

Unlike Cheiro and other occult practitioners, Adams was, first and foremost, a well-bred Boston woman. She did not generally go in for eastern trappings, costumes, veils or evocative perfumes.

Clients were reassured by her sensible and direct approach and practical efficiency. Her teaching experience helped her explain mysterious occult influences in a realistic manner. Sitting across from her at a sturdy desk was more like studying with a private tutor than consulting an oracle. Evangeline made one feel comfortable, secure and confident.

Although not yet thirty, Adams had maturity. Her judgement, coming from one so outwardly serious, polite, and well-dressed, seemed sound. Something in her person was already reminiscent of a formal but kindly maiden aunt, who wisely counsels without condemning. Clients turned to her in times of trouble, pouring out their hearts or revealing secrets. Adams treated them with common sense and empathy and was also trustworthy and discrete. She always enjoyed socializing, but was not a gossip, and made a point of keeping her clients' confidences.

Evangeline's own idea of astrology was cosmic; she felt it illustrated one's place in the cosmos. But Adams had a bigger draw: she predicted the future. This, of course, was what brought the distressed, downhearted or simply curious to her. No matter how conventional and even matronly Adams appeared, she was still an astrologer and palmist. These things were not the norm in the gay 'nineties. As she shared in *The Bowl of Heaven*,

People came to me in those days with hat brims down and coat collars up, and lied scandalously as to their real names and stations in life.

Part of the attraction, perhaps, was also the thrill of doing something a little illicit or risque.

Evangeline put out a promotional pamphlet called "Astrology and Palmistry" at this time. Although no author is specifically cited, the writing style is quite intellectual, sounding very much like J. Heber Smith's work. The pamphlet explained astrology in part by saying,

The physical body through which man functions brings him within the radius of planetary influences and although his mind is not impelled, it is nevertheless conditioned by these influences toward certain definite modes of expression... It is in the province of the Astrologer to compute the advantages or hindrances which every human being must some day meet by reason of the planetary positions, inherited tendencies, natural proclivities and environment consequent at the moment when he enters by the fact of his birth into the universal harmonies of nature and the limitations imposed by time and space upon human existence.

At the end of the pamphlet, Evangeline advertised her services: "Office hours from 11-3 or by appointment." With telephones yet to typically appear on the scene, many clients simply dropped by during the day. Adams also advertised her services for fund-raising events, where she would indulge her taste for drama by dressing up as a gypsy to read palms! The following is a charming example of late nineteenth century marketing. We can also notice the obvious difference in writing style from the main part of the pamphlet: this piece was probably written by Evangeline herself.

The undersigned takes this method of calling attention to her novel way of providing interesting amusement at Church and Society Fairs, Afternoon Teas, Soirees, etc., in a way that combines attractiveness, entertainment, variety and profit – in fact all the essential features for which such affairs are usually held.

For some years past, Scientific Palmistry has been steadily growing in favor as a means of affording refined and interesting entertainment at social gatherings, and when presented by an expert in the science offers an amusement equally interesting to young and old, besides affording an opportunity of obtaining needed information upon the more vital questions of life, which is likely to prove of great service in after years.

In response to the numerous and repeated requests that have been made by the Ladies and Committees having charge of the arrangements for Fairs, Entertainments, etc., to add to my palmistry readings the characteristic costume and other features peculiar to the Zingari of the East, I have adopted the garb of a Gipsy Queen and in this role, with the addition of my Oriental Tent, form an attraction that is unique and at once interesting, instructive and picturesque, and lucrative as well; for unlike most attractions, especially at Fairs held with the object of adding to the revenue of some organization – mine is not only self-supporting but also yields a good return to the Fair Fund.

In furnishing my own equipments another advantage is gained in the saving of expense beside the trouble and annoyance usually experienced in providing suitable fittings and other necessary adjuncts, the Oriental Tent being not only an attraction in itself, but also portable and readily placed in any part of the hall desired, or in a carpeted room.

– Evangeline S. Adams, Scientific Astrologer and Palmist

Adams shows in the pamphlet that she knew how to nicely legitimize her services for public consumption.

Evangeline had clients from all walks of life, but many were artistic and literary types. She was an avid theater-goer, and counseled numerous actors, actresses and musicians. These people certainly were more open to astrological advice than the average working person. One important client was Isaac B. Rich, a major Boston theatrical manager. Evangeline's clientele also included magazine editors, writers such as the popular author Lillian Whiting, and many others who wanted answers to their problems of life. The head of a detective agency and a reputable surgeon both consulted her regularly for practical advice which they felt helped them do their jobs better. Adams could always analyze character, provide general forecasts, compare charts for relationship potential, and select the best days for important activities.

One of her most famous clients was the investment broker and financier Thomas Lawson. By the time he consulted Adams, Lawson was worth about $50 million. With one of the stormiest careers in the market, he could surely use Adams' advice, though she could not keep him from losing most of his fortune before he died in 1925.

As open and enlightened as Evangeline felt herself to be, she had heretofore moved in a limited sphere. Her earlier readings were usually for acquaintances or those introduced socially, who were respectable, middle-class or well-to-do. When she opened her doors to the public, however, anyone could call in answer to her advertisements. We get an idea of how sheltered Evangeline had been from this account:

A modestly dressed young woman, slightly inclined to blond plumpness, presented herself at my door, mumbled something about having been recommended to me by a mutual friend, and gave me her dates. There was nothing in her appearance or manner to indicate that she was a "professional," but her horoscope had informed me and something I said suggested that I was not wholly unaware of her nature. She came right out with the astounding statement that she ran the best "house" in the Back Bay. I could have fainted if I had been the fainting kind..

I can't say this revelation lessened my surprise, but it loosened some of my inhibitions. After I recovered from the shock of this interview – and it wasn't a quick recovery, either – I tried to take the conventional view of the incident. I tried to blame this young woman for her first wrongdoing. I tried to be glad that she had not succeeded in ensnaring this socially eligible young man. But I couldn't honestly do so. Not after what I had seen in her chart – and his. So I resolved that in the future, whenever a woman of this class came to me I would deal with her impersonally as with any other client, and if she displayed an honest desire to raise herself out of the pit into which her tendencies had urged her, I would not let squeamishness or prudery prevent me from giving her every bit of help in my power.

That first interview prostrated me. I wasn't myself for weeks. And I have the same reaction even now on a less violent scale. But no cases give me greater satisfaction when they go right; and I am convinced after long experience that almost anybody – to use an evangelist's phrase – "can be saved." But only through knowledge! The line between good and bad is a thin one. We must know the forces with which we are dealing. And we must use them to keep us on the right side. Knowledge is the thing. And astrology is knowledge.

Evangeline Adams was nothing if not respectable and ethical. Unconventional, yes, but she could not condone what she considered immorality on any level. She hoped to help every client who she felt had gone astray. Her Christian forebears would've been proud, and so would her Unitarian minister and even Dr. Smyth, the kind professor who had stood against the conventional Congregationalists of Andover. And yet, there were things which were even worse than prostitution:

The most shocking experience of my early years was the first time all three parties to a divorce suit came to me at different times and unbeknownst to each other to get my prediction as to its result.

This was initially shocking, as people did not customarily divorce in those days. But Eva would have many opportunities to study what she referred to as "the seamy side" of life. At the turn of the century she was a lady who found herself in a unique situation. Meeting with a man alone behind closed doors, as her private interviews so often demanded, was in itself a scandalous prospect to many respectable people. In every way it appears that Evangeline's break with her family was absolutely necessary, as they would never have accepted her ignoring such established social norms.

Of course, there were many unmarried women at work in the 1890's, and it was characteristic of the time for women to be forced to choose between career and marriage. Birth control was not generally heard of, understood or available, and was also viewed as immoral: married women had children, and many of them (the medical men's wives appear to be the exceptions to the rule: Dr. Adams had only one child and Dr. Smith, two). Women that were like Evangeline, who chose to remain single, were generally dedicated to their work.

Certainly Adams led a crowded, busy life. By 1897 she listed herself in the Boston City Directory as an astrologer. Besides teaching and doing readings, she visited the library, studied astrology, attended the theater, went to lectures and church services, and had many friends and invitations. Within a certain enlightened facet of Boston society, she even became popular. She was, after all, still an Adams. Now that her mother was gone and her family distant, she could spend more time socializing with friends and networking with prospective clients.

An important early client was B.O. Flower, editor of the intellectual journal *The Arena*. Some of J. Heber Smith's writings appeared in this journal, and we can assume that it was a publication that Adams read. Billed as "a monthly periodical of social advance" and purported to include "the best thoughts of world makers," it included articles by Susan B. Anthony, Josiah Quincey, Leo Tolstoy and Goethe. Topics included philosophy and metaphysics, politics, fiction, poetry, theology and health. *The Arena* strove to be a journal for both sexes, and its forward-looking perspective was revealed in such features as "A Girl's Age of Consent" and its support of women's suffrage. *The Arena* strikes one as just the type of thing Adams enjoyed, combining a somewhat radical intellectual outlook with the metaphysical. Flower himself wrote on reincarnation, clairvoyance and mysticism.

Many of Evangeline's friends were at least a decade older than she, and in addition to Dr. Smith, she often discussed astrology with the brilliant Oliver Ames Goold. A kind and generous man, he had a thriving astrology practice, and the two shared their thoughts and experiences.

Adams was extremely proud of her close friendship with the famous author and naturalist John Burroughs. He had come to her first as a client, for advice on a domestic crisis. His son's enrollment in Harvard, as well as speaking engagements, brought the popular writer to the Boston area. As a philosopher interested in the natural world, Burroughs had many things in common with Adams. His books reached a wide audience in the 1890's; once again we can see Evangeline attracted to celebrity. A gregarious man, Burroughs typically made himself available to his readers, and Adams was among the many who visited him at his Slabsides, New York, retreat. They also spent time together in her studio as well, seeking "the truth about life."

One of Evangeline's closest friends in Boston at this time was Louise Chandler Moulton. This charming lady was over thirty years the astrologer's senior, and had already written her most important works: collections of poems, short stories, novels and books for children. A cultured *grande dame* known for her integrity, she had married a Boston publisher and was long the Boston literary correspondent for the *New York Tribune*. She and her husband spent part of every summer in London and Paris, where she wrote pieces on European society and literature.

Adams' social sphere widened through her work, and she recalled rubbing elbows with H.G. Wells at a Beacon Street dinner. Charles Fleischer, the liberal humanitarian Rabbi of the Congregation Adath Israel, was also in attendance: he would become an editor of the *New York American* and a radio commentator, and was also a lifelong client and friend.

All of these friendships point towards Evangeline's continuing interest in philosophy, religion and literature. She was educated, cultivated, and had taste. She found others stimulating and was always hungry to learn something new, hear the unique point of view, or introduce astrology to a new acquaintance. She described her first years alone as "hard," and between her work and studies there was probably not enough time to do all that interested her. Her consistent attraction to older people attests to her continuing role as a student herself.

While her work was most important, Eva still took time for pure recreation. As most middle-class Americans, she did leave town for the summer, spending the time in a cooler environment in the mountains or near lakes in Massachusetts and New Hampshire. Riding was always an important pastime as well, and many early photographs picture her on horseback. Alone or with friends, she seemed quite happy when in the saddle.

Adams' first few years alone in Boston were busy and full, and she began to reap the rewards of her efforts. If anything held her to memories of Andover, it was her paternal grandmother, who died in the summer of 1898. Although her ties to most of the Adamses had been severed years earlier, she still resented their continued disapproval. Evangeline was moving ahead in her profession, but could only go so far in Boston. Catherine Thompson attracted most of the businessmen interested in astrology, and other respected practitioners, such as Oliver Ames Goold, provided competition. Evangeline was ambitious and she wanted to do more. When Dr. J. Heber Smith died of heart disease in October of 1898, there were no longer any strong bonds keeping Evangeline in Boston. The Great Cheiro reported of Dr. Smith that he,

Two years in advance, predicted his own death. When the appointed time came, he "put his house in order," every paper and document was in its place; and so he met his death as calmly for himself as he had often studied it for others.

Evangeline's sentimental attachment to Smith probably had something to do with her staying in Boston. She had always been uplifted by his confidence in her success and never ceased to be grateful for his patient instruction and wise counsel. Dr. Smith left Evangeline his astrological library, as well as all of his notes, manuscripts and research papers. Many of the volumes were already familiar, as she had often borrowed them during their ten-year association.

Evangeline felt that her horoscope indicated her greatest success would come through expansion and travel, and she began to think about relocating to New York.

Chapter 7: *New York, New York*

Evangeline consistently practiced what she preached. When making any major decisions, she always consulted her horoscope and selected a good time in which to act. As she surveyed her upcoming planetary indications, she noticed that March, 1899 held excellent influences for both her career in general and astrological work in particular. Eva's favorite planet, Jupiter, was also significant, making it a good time for travel and expansion. She had wanted to visit New York and now planned a trip. If she was successful enough on this visit, she hoped to concentrate her energies on her astrology and palmistry practice, and leave teaching behind.

The Adamses had been visiting New York City for generations, and usually stayed at the fashionable Fifth Avenue Hotel in Madison Square. The hotel was located at the intersection of Broadway, Fifth Avenue, and West 23rd Street, one of the busiest places in town, full of shops and people. The wide stone plaza was alive night and day with yellow electric trolley cars and trotting hansoms and carriages. Women in floor-length walking skirts and wide, ornate hats, as well as men in business suits and bowlers, all passed by. Plenty of clients would be available, and should be pleased to come to this up-scale address.

Yet, even though Evangeline had foreseen great things for herself, they soon seemed to be going all wrong. After completing the tiring day-long journey from Boston by rail, she and her secretary were welcomed by Mr. Vinal, the Fifth Avenue's proprietor. As he showed her a room, Adams mentioned her plans. Vinal was horrified, and flatly refused to allow any occult readings on the premises. Evangeline, for her own part, had learned the value of non-resistance many years before. She accepted Vinal's judgement and went on her way:

Although, in perspective, I smile over this first encounter with provincial prejudice in supposedly broad-minded New York, I didn't do much smiling when I found myself suddenly homeless on the sidewalk of Madison Square. The dignity of my beloved science had been insulted. I had been insulted. I was what my ancestors would have described as righteously indignant. In short, I was mad clear through. And I must have made a neat picture of youthful determination as I staggered along under the weight of my carefully overpacked portmanteau. Of course, I didn't know that I was com-

mitting a social error by carrying my own bag in so fashionable a neighborhood; but I should have experienced a certain wicked pleasure if I had known it. I was in a mood to defy assistance – and the world.

But where would she go? In her account of these events in *The Bowl of Heaven*, Evangeline telescopes time in order to make for the greatest dramatic impact. She reports that she immediately walked over to the Windsor, luggage and all, registered, did a reading for the proprietor that very night, and predicted the disaster which would occur on the morrow. This was probably not the case. The Windsor was nearly a half hour's walk uptown; and in a magazine account from 1921, Adams would say that, "A personal friend gave me a letter to Mr. Leland." She was not one to rush into things: her actions were typically the result of forethought and planning. We can safely assume that Adams and her secretary stopped at the Fifth Avenue Hotel for at least a day or two.

Evangeline's secretary was Emma Brush, originally from Orange, New Jersey. A fifty-year-old with a teenaged daughter to support, Mrs. Brush no longer had a husband. She would be Evangeline's faithful assistant for a number of years. Her very presence is a reminder that Adams always did things in an extremely professional manner, and usually enjoyed the support of committed employees.

Adams' several reports of what happened at the Windsor Hotel are generally consistent. As luck would have it, the Windsor was even more upscale than the Fifth Avenue, and the proprietor, Warren Leland, was thrilled to have an astrologer in the hotel.

Leland, aged fifty-three, was one of the best known and most popular hotel men in America. His grandfather had opened a tavern in Vermont in 1818, and the family had since been identified with some of the most famous hotels in the country. Leland, himself, had already sold his hotel in Chicago for over a million dollars, was credited with securing the 1893 World's Fair for that city, and fought the railroads in court in order to keep them from destroying the beauty of Chicago's lakefront. He had taken over the Windsor Hotel in 1896, and already it, too, was making a huge profit.

Leland hosted many financial giants, and was also a great speculator himself. People who play the market are interested in one thing: maximizing their investments. As a group, they fall into two categories: those who respect the tried and true routes to solid financial growth, and those who are eager to try new and unusual methods to make a quick killing on the market. These latter investors are often on the lookout for a system that will help them beat the odds. While Leland probably had many stable investments (the Windsor being one of them), he had the enthusiasm and curiosity of a true speculator. As such, he was naturally attracted to astrology and pleased for Evangeline to practice under his roof.

Even though a fifth-floor suite was cheaper, Evangeline selected the first floor, no doubt hoping to attract more clients there. Once she was settled, at about 8:00 p.m. on Thursday evening March 16, 1899, Leland asked for a reading, adding, "I want to be your mascot." A few days after the fire, Eva told the *New York World* that,

Mr. Leland had asked me to read his palm. I saw that there was evil in store for him somewhere according to his horoscope and told him so. I told him that I foresaw evil not only for him, but for all New York. In fact, I believed that the next day would be marked by some dire calamity. I told him that the lines in his hand indicated he had but three children. He had four I knew. We both laughed at this, but it was evident that he was worried.

In the later *American Magazine* account given in 1921, Adams reported that,

As I proceeded with his horoscope, I was confronted with evidence of some impending danger, and I said to him, "You have had two disasters, and you are due for a third very soon. The trouble is especially threatening in regard to your family."

(She may have heard or read in the papers that Leland had previously had two other hotels burn down – not an uncommon occurrence.) Evangeline's autobiography fills in more details:

The man was under the worst possible combinations of planets– conditions terrifying in their unfriendliness. I remember telling him that the danger was so imminent that it might overtake him on the morrow. And his reply: "Oh, tomorrow's a holiday. Stocks can't go down!"

Evangeline thought that Leland was impressed by much of the reading, and he even referred some of his guests to her that night.

The next morning, he again showed his interest by coming in to see if everything was comfortable and asked me to write out his astrological indications for the following week. My mind was still so filled with the horror which was hanging over this kindly, hospitable man that I forced myself to consult his chart again. The danger which confronted him was so clearly indicated and so imminent that it seemed as if the man in front of me was being pushed at that very moment into the very depths of disaster.

Evangeline probably did do a reading for Leland the night before the fire, but it is unfortunate that all of the available reports come from her, and are thus neither objective nor written before the fact. She did seem to romanticize her life in later accounts. Adams also says that she was so certain that the next day would be lucky for her, that neither she nor Emma thought the fire would amount to anything. They attempted to save no belongings, simply picking up a few papers and locking the door on their way out.

Adams tells us that her New York success was soon assured because Leland,

In talking to the newspaper reporters that night...told them of my prediction. And in all the papers, the following morning, the story was printed.

This is simply not true. Although there were over a dozen dailies circulating in New York at the time, in none of those remaining can be found Leland's statement regarding Evangeline's prediction of the fire! He was reported to be weak, suffering and apparently completely broken-down, saying to the *Evening Journal*, "I can't say anything for a few days – not until I think this thing over," and only adding that "I pray to God that the death list will not grow." Warren Leland was so distraught at the loss of his wife and daughter in the fire that when he had to identify his twenty-year-old daughter Helen's body at the 51st Street Police Station, the *New York Herald* reported that he raved and tried to throw himself out the window, necessitating restraint and half-hourly injections of morphine. The *Herald* even claimed that Leland, "went insane," and was "utterly unbalanced," continuing that, "It is feared that he cannot survive the shock, and that if he does his mind will be shattered."

This led to the *Tribune* interviewing Dr. Pitkin, the house doctor of the Windsor Hotel on Saturday, March 18:

Some of the papers have said that his [Leland's] mind had failed him and that report I want to brand now as absolutely false... what he has been through would kill some men, and he is feeling the effects of it, but he is as sane as you and I.

Warren Leland, it seems, was too grief-stricken to say anything about Evangeline for the moment; if he did, he might not be regarded as the most reliable witness. Serious papers would not as a matter of course include such a fantastic tale as Evangeline's prediction. While the more sensational *New York World* featured Evangeline's interview, no follow-up with Warren Leland was printed. Leland would die of appendicitis less than three weeks later, and thus be unavailable to either corroborate or deny Adams' story: she could, conceivably, say anything she liked.

While we will never know exactly what Evangeline told her client on the night of March 16, 1899, one thing is certain: Adams had an unerring flair for self-promotion. It was she, herself, who told the reporters about her prediction. If she was stretching the truth a bit, or exaggerating the facts, she was following in the footsteps of a long line of astrologers, occultists, and clairvoyants who did exactly the same thing. The "hits" are repeated again and again; the "misses" soon forgotten, as no one takes the time or trouble to report them to the papers or save them for posterity. It is upon these perhaps slight claims that the reputations of so many prognosticators rest. Adams would go on to secure a mention in London's popular *Modern Astrology* magazine. And finally, on April 30, her predictions for the City of New York would appear in the *New York Journal*, another tabloid.

Evangeline told the story of the famous Windsor fire again and again, and like the proverbial fish tale, it grew. By the time Adams was interviewed for the November 1926 *Pictorial Review*, she'd say, "I predicted the famous Windsor fire almost to the hour." Perhaps even she believed it by then. In the *Woman's Home Companion* of June 1925, she even says,

I had taken refuge in the Hotel Continental at 20th Street and Broadway [after the fire]. Here I was besieged by reporters and consultants. To the former I said nothing except that my work was strictly professional and confidential; that I never made public predictions; and that I could give them no story. But Mr. Leland continued to reiterate his statement that I forecast the disaster – with the result that my reputation was made.

Perhaps Leland had been talking about the forecast – but if so, his report is lost to us. And if Adams had told reporters at the time that she could give no story, she suddenly changed her mind and decided to talk to at least two papers!

In her pursuit of publicity in 1899, Adams seems to have undergone something of an identity crisis. She signed the Windsor register as "Dr. Evangeline S. Adams," no doubt an attempt to capitalize on her education and medical background (though she'd never had any medical training *per se*). *The New York Journal* by-line lists her as "Evangelina S. Adams"; perhaps an effort to appear somewhat ethnic and thus add a dash of romanticism. No matter: like the actress who tries out exotic stage names, only to be unable to part with her own in the end, Evangeline would remain "Miss Evangeline S. Adams," even after her eventual marriage.

The New York Journal was part of the popular press at the time, a tabloid and one of the "yellow journals" typical of the period. It was always on the lookout for sensational stories to feed its readers' craving for outlandish tales. Evangeline Adams' prediction for the City of New York was featured alongside such articles as "American Beauty Seized by the Sultan of Morocco" and "Snake Bite Cured by Serum of Mushrooms." Adams was probably none too pleased by the tenor of the accompanying pieces, but she did, after all, garner the credit, "by Evangelina Adams. Who Foretold the Windsor Hotel Fire." It went on:

Miss Evangelina S. Adams, the fashionable astrologer, became suddenly famous by her remarkable prediction of the Windsor Hotel fire. The ill-fated proprietor, Warren Leland, confirmed the story before his death. He expressed the greatest confidence in Miss Adams and her reading of the stars.

But who wrote this introduction? Once again, it seems like it is Evangeline herself, as no direct quotes from Leland appear, and no reporter's byline is given. The article, though, is fascinating, as Adams is quite explicit in her predictions for the City of New York, which had been newly consolidated on January 1, 1898 at 12:01 a.m.

The Horoscope of Greater New York shows a marvelous future for the city. The zodiacal sign Libra, or the Scales, symbolical of Justice, was rising, with the mighty Jupiter posited therein, when the new consolidated city was born. Libra is ruled by Venus, and Jupiter and Venus are what astrologers term "benefics" – that is, beneficent planets. Jupiter rules wealth, and his influence brings power. Venus rules pleasure and the amenities of life. Their joint influence foretells for Greater New York a long era of progress in population, wealth and the arts.

With much drama, Evangeline went on to predict "a scourge of sickness" for the summer months of 1899. October, November and December she said, would be "marked by many strange and appalling events," such as fires, panics and storms, and even a peculiar disease likely to affect horses and cattle! And, "There will be an alarming increase in the applications for divorce. Robbery, duplicity, and other secret crimes will be frequent."

1901, Adams projected, would be "noted for exposés of municipal fraud...There will be trouble between New York and some of the railroads running out of the city" And, "In 1909 and 1910 there are likely to be popular uprisings. A socialistic unrest will assume greater and more dangerous proportions than ever before."

What a prophecy this is, indeed! The dramatic bravura of the prediction is characteristic of the time, and must certainly have left readers agog. The language is very strong and clear: words like "scourge," "fateful," "appalling," and "evil" imply disaster. But, at the time, many events were perceived as being less controllable than they are today. Epidemics, fires and shipwrecks were common occurrences. It is difficult to conclude much from Evangeline's forecast regarding these disasters: while apparently being specific, events of this type were not uncommon, particularly for such a large city as New York. Unfortunately, these predictions thus seem woefully generalized. But, at times, with her more specific statements, Adams seemed to hit the mark.

Notable is Evangeline's allusion to municipal fraud during 1901; this was the year in which the charismatic William Travers Jerome was elected district attorney, and the respectable Seth Low won the mayoral election. Both had run on a ticket of reform against the Tammany Hall establishment. There was also railroad trouble, as Adams had promised. In a series of rail mergers and raids, Edward H. Harriman of the Union Pacific battled James J. Hill, the Great Northern, and J.P. Morgan for control of the Northern Pacific. This would lead to a market crash in May and would become known as the Panic of 1901. (Hill and Morgan would both later be clients of Adams .)

Evangeline had also forecast a "socialistic unrest" during 1909 and 1910, and it was from November 1909 through February 1910 that the first successful strike at the Triangle Shirtwaist Factory occurred, resulting in the Ladies Garment Worker's Union being recognized as a bargaining agent for the first time.

Unfortunately, parts of Evangeline's forecast were also just plain wrong. She had said that great storms would be frequent from October through December of 1899, when, in fact, there was an extended period of doldrums. Of course, this prediction was published over six months in advance of the event, and by October must have been virtually forgotten.

Perhaps the most important part of the forecast for New York City involved the stock market. Evangeline advised that during October, November and December of 1899,

Great fluctuations in stocks on Wall Street are promised. Great fortunes will be won and lost in a day, and every one whose fortune is small or doubtful should avoid the Street during this period.

She was more accurate concerning this prediction, much more accurate; and this is an area in which accuracy pays off. The "great fluctuations" manifested quite clearly, with the Dow Jones Industrial Average at its high for the year in early September and reaching its low in mid-December. Was it luck? Perhaps Adams had learned Catherine Thompson's predictive techniques well. So well, in fact, that she'd soon be able to exhibit the following testimonial letter, from none other than Jacob Stout, a prominent Wall Street stock broker for over forty years:

You will oblige me by seeing what the stars have for me during the consecutive months of 1900. Your forecasts for the present months were singularly correct.

If not totally reliable or able to be proved, Evangeline's predictions had been accurate in terms of some key city events. Yet even before the New York forecast was written, Adams already had clients and reporters beating a path to her door. After the fire, she and Emma had again changed hotels. This time they found themselves in the Continental, a cheaper hotel further downtown, and not in a particularly desirable or fashionable neighborhood. The two women had been listed among the missing on the day after the Windsor disaster, and many papers reported their new home. Those who had read any published reports or heard the rumors of Evangeline's prediction of the fire could easily find her; apparently they did, for she said that,

Because the story of my prediction to Mr. Leland had been so widely circulated, inside of forty-eight hours I was simply besieged by more clients than I could have gained, under ordinary circumstances, in several years! I was "made" by the Windsor fire. So you see, the stars had not lied to me.

Even if this is an exaggeration – which in all likelihood it is – Evangeline was clearly successful in New York. She had lost her wardrobe and some jewelry in the fire, and Emma had lost an engraved pin, one of her most valuable possessions. But the Windsor Hotel fire had been front page news in most papers for a week: it was a tremendous story. Because Warren Leland had lost his hotel, his wife, his daughter, and later, even his own life, the ladies were riding the crest of celebrity with affluent clients and some of the best-known names in New York social and business life. Evangeline Adams would continue to visit New York regularly for several years, developing her clientele further before settling there permanently.

Evangeline's 1899 forecast had introduced something new: standardization. It would be decades before newspapers began printing the type of horoscope forecasts which are so popular today. But within Evangeline's forecast for all of New York City was a greater specificity, which was based on the time of the year in which people were born:

Persons born about the middle of March, June, September and December of past years will be most affected by the evil conjunction of planets which will take place in December.

Here she considered whether the sun in the birth chart was afflicted by other planets. In addition, she extended her stock market forecast to those born in certain years, considering whether Jupiter, her general significator of wealth, would at that time be afflicted:

Those who were born in any of the following years, 1829, 1835, 1841, 1847, 1853, 1859, 1865, 1871, or 1877, are especially liable to financial reverses, and should adopt a conservative policy in their business if they would avoid disaster.

Adams already did some work by mail for those who didn't have time for personal appointments. The idea of making general forecasts more personal by alluding to particular days or years of birth would continue to be helpful. With this type of information already prepared, an assistant could easily put together a somewhat individualized written report for a nominal fee. When Adams began marketing a regular forecast service, she would think along these lines.

As Dr. Smith had supposedly told her many years before, Evangeline did, indeed, become a great traveller. She crossed the Atlantic to Europe nearly every spring or summer, and travelled extensively in the United States by ship and rail. Her trips were supposedly recreational, but wherever she went she sought out other astrologers, made contacts, and drummed up business. She was always fond of the English, feeling their society to be more ordered and polite. As an extension of her love of celebrity, royalty excited her as well. Although Evangeline Adams was democratic, happily working for clients of all backgrounds and classes, she was quite conscious of her own social status. She always stressed her association with celebrities, successful business people, and European nobility. So it comes as no surprise that she developed a schoolgirl crush on the new King of England, Edward VII.

Evangeline made her first trip to London in the summer of 1902. Along with a friend, she attended the coronation, and found the King extremely handsome (her continued attraction to older men: the king was now overweight, paunchy, and according to many, dissipated). A few days later, Adams was left alone in the city while her friend travelled to Liverpool. She felt a little lonely, but decided to explore, getting on the first bus which arrived and letting it take her where it would. Here we can see how very much Eva loved the excitement and adventure of travel: how many of us would get on a strange bus in an unknown city to no destination in particular? Trusting her intuition, she got off on impulse, only to fall in with a group of expectant bystanders in front of Buckingham Palace. The King was soon to be seen departing for his country home. Luck was with Evangeline as the royal carriage stopped right in front of her. The King looked out and gave her "the sweetest, kindliest, friendliest smile," which she returned wholeheartedly. Her homesickness disappeared, and she forgot all of her "New England prejudices against his alleged unconventional life." She would thereafter think of him as "the kindest man in the world."

Evangeline's affection for the King, which she also called "foolish," was probably similar to what many feel for movie stars today. She was attracted more to his status and the pomp and circumstance which surrounded him than to the actual man himself. But this is the only instance in which she ever expressed her affections, either in her own writing or in interviews. She was thirty-four at the time, and certainly her love life had not been an easy one so far. But we really know nothing at all about it. Save for her few references to early attachments and later marriage, we don't know if she had any other romantic involvements at all. Although she always seemed to have lots of friends and acquaintances, on some level she also remained a very private person. We might speculate that if at age thirty-four her fantasy was for an unattainable man nearly thirty years her senior, her love life probably was not all that lush.

There was a lot going on in London astrologically, notably at this time due to the work of Alan Leo (appropriately named for his astrological sun sign). Leo was an astrologer and keen follower of Theosophy and had founded the magazine *Modern Astrology* in 1895. Through this vehicle, as well as offers for free horoscope interpretations, Leo began to popularize astrology in Great Britain. By the time Evangeline visited London, he had already written and published the textbooks *Astrology for All*, *The Horoscope and How to Read It*, and *Practical Astrology*, which she purchased.

When demand for Leo's free readings became too great, he offered, instead, standardized readings, or what he called "test horoscopes." For a small fee the *Modern Astrology* staff would cast a horoscope and provide various descriptions of the clients' sun sign, moon sign, and other chart factors. These had already been written on individual sheets and mimeographed in quantity. The horoscopes provided a good introduction to astrology for the uninitiated, and were also a relatively simple way for Leo to educate the public while earning some money at the same time. As Evangeline was a subscriber to *Modern Astrology* and always curious about the latest developments, she might have sent away for one of these herself. Within the next decade, there would be imitators of Leo's test horoscopes, both legitimate and bogus, in Britain. As Evangeline herself continued more business by mail, and as she had already standardized some of her work, it would not be too long before she, too, would take Alan Leo's lead and offer the American public an inexpensive written horoscope.

As part of establishing herself in business, Evangeline had her picture taken by a photographer in Boston in 1904. The photo shows her posed with the tools of her trade: on a table sits a globe atop several books; alongside is a small model elephant, considered in the east to be a symbol of good luck. Evangeline stands nearby, holding in one hand a pair of calipers, and with the other pointing to a page in her ephemeris. What looks to us today as an elaborate outfit was rather typical of the time. A loose bodice full of pleats and lace is set off by puffed sleeves with ruffles at the hem. Her box-pleated skirt is form-fitting, and although the ideal figure of the time was considered to be 130 pounds on a five-foot, four-inch frame, Adams, even though reined-in, is shorter and stockier, lacking the popular tightly corseted approach to an hourglass figure. She wears a long and exquisite rope of pearls and rings on both hands. Her dark, wavy hair is a bit haphazardly arranged, with perhaps the hint of a bohemian style.

The photograph is a study in contrasts. It's clear Evangeline was brought up in fashionable society as she seems so conventionally well-bred and well-dressed; but an almost flawless feminine presentation is coupled with a stern countenance and unusual features. It could be argued that without all the lace and finery, Adams looks more like a man. She has a sedate and serious air, and one could say that at the age of thirty-six, with *pince-nez* perched atop her nose, she already looks middle-aged. Her face is almost square, with full cheeks camouflaging any bone structure. Her figure is heavy, and though she had a naturally chunky build, later letters reveal that she also loved rich foods. The nose dominates, round and large, almost bulbous; and in comparison, Evangeline's lips appear very thin and spare. But as usual, her eyes have an arresting gaze: direct and penetrating, they reach out of the picture and appear to size up the viewer with a scientific air, that of the disturbed researcher caught in the middle of some important thought. The photograph is effective; Adams carries an aura of importance, gives a sense that she knows more than we do – a great asset for an astrologer and palmist seeking to market specialized knowledge.

By 1905, Evangeline Adams was firmly established in New York. In the intervening years, she had shuttled back and forth between her old and new homes. The long transition helped her adapt gradually, and she found New York City very liberating. Boston was sedate, literary and patrician, characteristics which Adams herself possessed. It was also much more formal, and Evangeline's angry relatives had continued to provoke her at every turn. New York was big and sprawling, also considered somewhat brash; but it was much more alive and vital. And it was also the place to be if one wanted to branch out in a big way. Certainly, there were many more opportunities for business among the smart set and financial men.

While the Continental Hotel had been alright for temporary purposes, Evangeline did not want to settle there for good. An active person, she "couldn't stand seeing so many women sitting about doing nothing." Carnegie Hall had been completed in 1894, and soon after, living and working studios were added to the large terra-cotta and brick building on Seventh Avenue and West 56th Street. Designed by the same man who had created the Plaza Hotel and the Dakota Apartments, the studios were an immediate hit. Their quiet uptown location adjoining the famous music hall, as well as their large, airy spaces, attracted music teachers, artists, photographers and many other creative careerists. Enrico Caruso made his first American recordings here in 1904, and Charles Dana Gibson and Isadora Duncan were others who rented studios. The hall allowed all its tenants to live and work in the same space, a situation which Evangeline found ideal. Here she enjoyed all the hub-bub about her: "I knew everybody was working and trying to accomplish something in life." She fit in nicely with this eclectic group of artistic types and found the environment stimulating. So much so, that she would stay in the building for the rest of her life.

Adams originally rented two rooms on the fourth floor, with her office in one and personal space in the other. Her advertisement in the 1905 *New York City Directory* (sort of a telephone book before phones were common) lists her simply as a palmist. As the years wore on, however, she would at times call herself an "astrologist and palmist" and sometimes just an "astrologist." In much the same way, she seems to have periodically re-arranged her space, seeing clients in Room 402 for a stretch, and then re-organizing things and interviewing in Room 403. While Carnegie Hall provided a stable home, it would appear that things were anything but static.

In February of 1907, Evangeline's youngest brother William died. William Adams was only forty-three years old, and had been working in the railroad business in Chicago for many years. He left his wife, Stella, thirty-seven, along with two children, Ralph and Gertrude Adams. While Eva's association with all family members was somewhat distant and periodically strained, she seems to have had the closest relationship with William's family. Especially after his death, she wrote to, visited with, and helped out the struggling family, and appears to have been attached to them.

But for the most part, work continued as usual. With her intelligence, good breeding and ineffable sense of what a client wanted and needed, Adams brought respectability to palmistry and astrology. She took a great deal of pride in her work, dressed well, and acted professionally. In this manner she was able to continue to attract and maintain a well-to-do clientele.

Richard Harding Davis, a top war correspondent and novelist, came to see Evangeline in 1907. Not a believer in astrology, he sought, instead, material for his book, *Vera, the Medium*. Here's what he described:

The reception parlor bore but little likeness to a cave of mystery. There were no shaded lights, no stuffed alligator, no Indian draperies, no black cat. On a table, in the center, under a heavy and hideous chandelier with bronze gas jets, was a green velvet cushion. On this nestled an innocent ball of crystal. Beside it lay the knitting needle with which Vera pointed out, in the hand of the visitor, those lines that showed he would be twice married, was of an ambitious temperament, and would make a success upon the stage.

Something in her rapt, distant gaze, in the dignity of her uplifted head, in her air of complete detachment from her surroundings, caused even the most skeptical to question if she might not possess the power she claimed, to feel for a moment the approach of the supernatural.

Later photos of Adams' office still featured a "heavy and hideous chandelier." The crystal ball, however, was either Davis' invention or a decoration: Adams was never said to use one. However, the description of the heroine sounds very like it might be taken from life.

Evangeline had no idea who this handsome and husky fellow was. She did note that his sole purpose appeared to be to make her "mad": "Everything I said he contradicted – until finally I dropped his chart and launched into a passionate defense of my beloved science," as she had done so many times before. Davis was an experienced foreign correspondent, known for his dramatic adventures and masculinity; he probably had no trouble provoking Evangeline.

Davis' novel was a romance about a young, innocent, girl who is duped into fraudulent occult practices at an early age, only to be saved by an interested district attorney. In it, Vera, too, launches into a passionate defense of her practices. This description appears to be taken from life as well:

They saw her drawn to her full height; the color flown from her face, her deep, brooding eyes flashing. She was like one, by some religious fervor, lifted out of herself, exalted. When she spoke her voice was low, tense. It vibrated with tremendous, wondering indignation.

The two later made up as Davis revealed who he was, and thanked her. But Adams would soon be called upon to once again defend her practices, this time before a much tougher adversary: the City of New York.

Chapter 8: *Problems and Publicity*

In the spring of 1910, people all over the world were observing the increasing light of Halley's comet with great anxiety. Since astrologers from the earliest times had regarded comets as predictors of disaster, many were seized with terror. Still, Evangeline Adams doesn't seem to have made any prognostications based on the comet's appearance. Yet, perhaps it was a signal of events to come the following year.

At the time, Section 889, Subdivision 3 of New York's Code of Criminal Procedure characterized "acrobatic performers, circus riders, men who desert their wives, and people who pretend to tell fortunes" as "disorderly persons." As far as circus performers are concerned, Evangeline pointed out that the law is rarely enforced:

In the spring, Madison Square Garden swarms with these "disorderly persons." And even men who desert their wives are allowed to roam freely on the city streets.

Yet every so often, the authorities would invoke this law in an attempt to rid the city of fortune-tellers. Although Adams strove for legitimacy, her type of practices could be called into question. Certainly frauds and fakirs abounded, then as now. Early in 1911, Second Deputy Police Commissioner Flynn ordered an investigation of fortune-tellers and soothsayers in New York City, and many were arrested. Mrs. Isabella Goodwin was one of the police matrons who arranged to have readings in order to collect evidence.

Mrs. Goodwin called on Evangeline Adams in Carnegie Hall, met with a secretary (by this time probably Mrs. Melvin D. Reed, who lived with her husband right around the corner), and arranged for an appointment. In response to her inquiries, she was told that Adams was an astrologer who "never told fortunes" (it sounds like Adams was already careful to give the proper description of her services). Goodwin later returned for a reading. A newspaper reporter from the *New York Herald* related her experience:

Business at Miss Adams' studio in Carnegie Hall is conducted on an impressive scale. The walls are hung with tapestries, and rare Oriental and animal rugs ornament the floor. The thought of getting to the consultation room for less than $10 perishes at the door.

Evangeline ran a professional shop, with beautifully decorated offices, a secretary and appointments. Animal rugs were at the time all the rage, and as usual, Evangeline kept up with the times.

The *New York World* revealed some of Goodwin's testimony:

When my palm was read by Miss Adams, she told me that I had been born under planetary disturbances; otherwise I might have been born of wealthy parents. She said I believed in big philosophies and not in small dogmas. Miss Adams further said that at the present time old men admired me, but that later I would be attractive to younger men. She also said that I had better marry at once as after this year a marriage would be unhappy. She told me, however, that I would have more luck if I remained single. She said that if I had been a man I would have been a promoter. She said she was an expert on stocks.

Goodwin was also told that her hand bore the "mystic cross," the pattern that The Great Cheiro also claimed to possess, which would keep her from harm. This account combines conclusions drawn from both palm reading and astrology; Evangeline had continued to practice both. At times Goodwin mixes these up – planetary disturbances, for example, cannot be read in a palm.

Although one of Adams' readings typically lasted at least a half hour, we have only a short recap. Yet we can see that she addressed the practical issues in which most people were interested: love, money and success.

On Thursday, January 12, 1911, in the late afternoon, Detective Miller arrested Adams. She was charged with a misdemeanor in practicing fortune telling. Of the six alleged fortune tellers arrested in the raid, Evangeline was the most successful and affluent. Newspaper articles focussed on her, and the *World* headline ran:

Society Palmist Seized in a Raid
"Fears No Harm"

Evangeline Adams says she's read the hands of Morgan, Heinze, Dryden, Nobles and leading actresses. She Lives in Luxury in Carnegie Hall Studios.

The *Herald* concurred:

All eyes rested on Miss Evangeline Adams when the six were brought to police headquarters. She had made the journey there in a taxicab, and wore sables and plumes.

As usual, Evangeline had style, despite her naturally undistinguished features. She always strove to make a good impression. Smartly dressed in a gray tailor-made suit with black furs and muffs, she came before Magistrate Murphy in night court, and he requested bail in the amount of $500. Evangeline was unable to comply. Clearly nervous and upset, she asked Murphy what the punishment could be. "Six months imprisonment," was his reply. With that she flushed and began making efforts to telephone friends who might be of assistance. Banks were already closed for the day; a large amount of cash was not so easily found. It looked like she might have to spend the night in jail.

Finally, a friend, Joseph Gwynn, came along with his wife, offering real estate security in lieu of the bail money. The court refused to accept it, but Murphy paroled Adams anyway. She clearly didn't look as if she belonged in jail. The case was scheduled to be heard the following Monday.

"The five other persons arrested sighed wistfully as Miss Adams bowed in the general direction of the lieutenant and moved leisurely out of the room," concluded the *Herald*.

Evangeline had heard of other astrologers and palmists being arrested, but never truly imagined she could be one of them. She had a great deal of pride, believed wholeheartedly in her work, and always treated clients honestly, with respect and sympathy. Yet there was still great opposition to astrology and palmistry in many circles. When a reporter from *The New York World* requested an interview, Adams leapt at the chance to present her side of the story for the record. It was nearly twelve years since the Windsor Hotel fire. The planet Jupiter, the ruler of her horoscope and regarded as a life-long benefactor and friend, had since made one complete circuit around the zodiac. Even though there might be some difficult situations to face, Evangeline felt she was in a "lucky" period, and realized that, as she had twelve years before, she could capitalize on the arrest to gain greater notoriety and attract some publicity. And she did:

Miss Adams said she had expected trouble. "Wonderful conditions surround me astrologically, however, so nothing can hurt me." She exhibited a note from Lady Paget in which the writer said, "Wonderful woman, all you said about the King came too sadly true."

"I was the only astrologist who predicted the death of King Edward. Had it not been for his sudden death, Lady Paget had arranged that I should read his hand."

Evangeline had not actually been the only one to predict the King's difficulties, as he was a public figure with whom many astrologers concerned themselves. A.J. Pearce, an English homeopath and editor of the popular *Zadkiel's Almanac* had advised against the King travelling during 1910. In March, King Edward had caught cold while in Biarritz. The resulting complications led to his death in May.

Edward VII had remained a favorite of Evangeline's, and she had continued to study his horoscope. Minnie Paget was one of the ladies of the court, and through her Adams had hoped to secure a formal introduction. The King's hand had already been read by "The Great Cheiro," and he apparently had an interest in the occult. But Adams tells us in *The Bowl of Heaven* that it was not to be:

Lady Paget, who was a great favorite with King Edward, never came to New York without consulting me; and on one of these occasions, she told me that she had spoken to the King of her visits to me, and that he had not only expressed interest in the science but had commissioned her to invite me to England to discuss astrology with him and to read his horoscope. I promised to make the trip, but I found myself carrying an increasingly heavy load of work, and let the journey to England wait. The next year, Lady Paget came again. This time, she asked me to write out the King's horoscope and send it by her to Buckingham Palace. Again I promised and again I delayed – for my first preliminary calculations convinced me that I could draw no horoscope of this beloved man which would be a fit message to carry to a king.

"If he lives beyond next May" I finally told my visitor, "I'll either come to see him or send him his horoscope."

Death predictions are something many astrologers of the past keenly explored. While extremely difficult to forecast, death occurred more typically at younger ages than it does today: the "dangerous years" indicated astrologically were more easily fatal. But once again, Adams is trumpeting her successful prediction after the fact, and she used this "success" for all it was worth. An astrologer who could accurately predict death must surely know more than most.

Evangeline later received a card from Paget, confirming her forecast of the King's death. She later reproduced Paget's card in the July 1925 *Woman's Home Companion*, which read, "Wonderful woman! You were right about the King." By the time Evangeline's autobiography appeared the following year, this quote had expanded to: "Wonderful woman, all you said regarding the King came too sadly true," paraphrasing the *World* reporter's exaggerated misquote. As in the case of Warren Leland, we still don't really know what Evangeline said to her client in the first place, or what Minnie Paget was actually referring to when she said that Adams had been "right about the King."

Still, testimonials such as Lady Paget's were important to Adams' reputation, particularly in times such as these, when it was called into question. Adams still faced fortune-telling charges, but she had already collected plenty of evidence to suggest her competence and good faith. The walls of her drawing room and studio were covered with signed photographs of prominent men and women, presumably her satisfied clients; and she was never shy of talking about her work and experiences, as we can see from the rest of *The World* interview:

"See here!" said Miss Adams, opening a drawer of her desk and producing a mass of letters. She showed in one the words "Please find $500 enclosed for my month's reading."

We must remember that $500 from a single client would pay a hefty percentage of an astrologers' living expenses today! The interview went on:

"My work is chiefly along big lines. Take the stock market for example. Some of the biggest financiers have come to me, not for daily or weekly fluctuations, but for my astrological knowledge of impending panic and depression or a great rise in values. I have never failed to gauge the stock market correctly in such changes."

Evangeline claimed to have predicted the Panic of 1907, also tough to do. If we can find no confirming documentation, the alleged patronage of J. Pierpont Morgan may be more to the point. Morgan was one of the country's leading bankers, but he also sat on many corporate boards and had interests in railroads, telephone, General Electric and U.S. Steel, then the biggest conglomerate in the country. An extremely pragmatic man, he also had a strong mystical bent, and some thought even a psychic feel for financial trends. Adams said that Morgan visited her several times in his later years and subscribed to her regular monthly service of astrological indications for business, politics and the market. Evangeline felt him to be skeptical at first, but he was soon convinced, even inviting Adams to come to Egypt and join him on his famous yacht, the Corsair. Morgan allegedly wanted her to join a group investigating the occult in the parts of the world where there was archaeological evidence it had originated. Evangeline says she declined the invitation, simply because her own work directly with clients was more fulfilling.

Fritz Heinze, the Montana copper king, never recovered from the Panic of 1907, although he continued investments in many railroad and mining projects. Another big celebrity businessman of the time, his consultation with Evangeline might have resulted from her alleged prediction of the Panic. Adams profited greatly from having Heinze on her roster of prominent clients. Seymour Cromwell, later a three-term president of the New York Stock Exchange, became a client at that time as well, further attesting to her reputation as a market forecaster.

Evangeline was able to cite many other prominent people as patrons. Among British nobility were the Duchess of Manchester and Lady Paget, as well as the Lord Chief Justice Pallas of Ireland. In the United States, the names were just as well known, including former Governor Douglas of Massachusetts, John P. Dryden of Prudential Life, the Broadway producer Daniel Frohman, and Mrs. August Belmont. Famous actors and members of New York society rounded out the list. Adams remembered Lillian Russell as the most "thoughtful, friendly, gracious person" among the stage celebrities she knew. With clients like these, Evangeline was already the top fortune-teller in New York and possibly in the country. Like many professionals, she had relied primarily upon word of mouth and recommendations. Yet beginning at this time, she also regularly took out advertisements in the New York City Directory. The directory was used by thousands of people, and advised that Adams could be consulted on astrology and palmistry at her Carnegie Hall studios, quoting as evidence of her capability her own headline about predicting the Windsor Hotel fire.

Evangeline returned to court for her hearing on January 16, 1911. After detective Isabella Goodwin and Adams had both testified, Magistrate Murphy dismissed the case, perhaps due to lack of evidence or the impression that Adams appeared to be sincere. Evangeline had actually won. In a sense she had been vindicated, and she was able to turn the entire incident to her advantage, gaining the type of sensational publicity to which she otherwise had no access. After all the excitement, she went out to her home in the country to relax and recover.

Evangeline had been renting a house in Darien, Connecticut, about an hour's ride on the train north of New York. While she lived at Carnegie Hall during the week, her weekends were spent in Darien. There she'd relax and entertain. Even though much of Adams' life was dedicated to her work, she also had hobbies.

Some, of course, were related to astrology. She loved to read, and would search for the birth data of her favorite authors, whose horoscopes illuminated their work for her. She looked over the charts of current celebrities and put them in a growing file, studying the events in their lives, their periods of success and failure.

Evangeline continued to keep pets, and usually owned several small dogs; she often kept Pekinese, Yorkshire terriers and the like, and occasionally a cat. She'd cast their horoscope charts in order to help them avoid the dangers she felt were signalled at birth, took them with her when travelling, and treated them with the greatest love and affection. She still rode horseback regularly, and photographs through the years often feature her in a riding habit. (She had named her own horse, a lively animal, after her favorite planet, Jupiter.) Occasionally, Adams visited her relatives in Chicago, but more often she enjoyed longer journeys abroad during the spring and summer. When in New York City, she attended the theater and took leisurely drives in the park with friends.

Although Evangeline felt her horoscope denied any success in speculation or games of chance, she liked to play bridge. In order to compensate for what she perceived were negative horoscope factors, her only rule was to follow her intuition. As this was strong and highly developed, she probably took many more tricks than her horoscope promised! She loved having people around her, and would entertain guests, chatting about the theater, books, psychology and her favorite subjects, astrology, palmistry, spiritualism and the metaphysical.

Adams was particularly fond of collecting antiques, another life-long hobby. She purchased Sandwich glass, Currer & Ives prints, and early American artifacts such as spinning wheels and lanterns. These stayed at her weekend retreat, which represented in its decor her New England side. Her more esoteric side was apparent in her Carnegie Hall studio, which got its exotic flavor from oriental scrolls and curios. Evangeline had included a miniature elephant in her first business portrait in 1896, and had continued to collect them. The elephants, in jade, ebony, ivory and gold, roamed all over her office, on her desk, tables and bookshelves. Adams claimed that many had been gifts from Mary Pickford and Douglas Fairbanks, the King of Siam, and J. Pierpont Morgan, among others. One of the earliest, she said, was given to her by President Grover Cleveland. In Indian legend, elephants support the universe, and the elephant-headed god Ganesha rules good fortune. To Evangeline, the elephant statuettes similarly represented luck and bounty.

Evangeline's middle brother, Charles, died in October of 1913. At fifty-two years of age, he was a single man with no children. He named his sister executrix of his estate, leaving everything to her. The complex family dynamics were evident: Charles left exactly one dollar to his older brother John (John was now fifty-four, firmly established as treasurer of a Chicago coal company, with a wife and two grown children). While Evangeline had certainly never been close to John, either, they were at least on cordial terms. She still continued a warm association with her sister-in-law, Stella (youngest brother William's widow) and her children. In many ways Eva treated her niece Gertrude like her own daughter. While still a teenager, Gertrude came to stay at Carnegie Hall periodically. For one stretch, she worked in the office, learning to cast horoscopes, typing and doing other administrative chores.

Evangeline had another studio portrait taken at the time, a consummately professional piece of work by Arnold Genthe. Genthe was a renowned photographer who'd made his name through documenting Chinatown and the San Francisco earthquake. He subsequently photographed celebrities like Sarah Bernhardt, Theodore Roosevelt and Isadora Duncan in his New York studio. Known for his modern, impressionistic style, his portraits were quite different from the stiff, formal shots of earlier times.

As usual, Evangeline is done up beautifully. Her wavy hair is neatly parted in the center and full at the sides, a single strand of pearls around her neck, with her shoulders draped in a delicate floral-patterned fabric. Evangeline's patrician bearing is also evident.

The shot is softly lit and slightly out of focus; this was Genthe's style, but also flattered the forty-ish subject. Middle age suited Evangeline, and she now appears somehow more attractive than in her youth. Lipstick has probably been added to define her mouth, and powder, perhaps, gives a translucent glow to her complexion (always a Puritan at heart, Adams seems to have avoided cosmetics). Yet the nose, it must be admitted, is much too large for anyone, and the *pince-nez* placed upon it only serve to accentuate its prominence. Evangeline does look the stern school mistress here. Yet, as in all her photographs, her eyes are striking, even behind the spectacles. This time, however, there is a sadness, melancholy and even accusation in the glance. The master photographer has captured something deeper. Evangeline seems to have lived through more than she would like, to have seen more than she wanted to see. Ultimately, amidst all of the trappings necessary to a posed portrait, she appears uncomfortable, and possibly a very lonely woman. If one studies the picture long enough, she looks even on the verge of tears.

A studio portrait of Evangeline circa 1904

Evangeline's advertisement in the 1910 New York City Directory

Windsor Hotel proprietor
Warren F. Leland

Evangeline's crush --
King Edward VII

Arnold Genthe's 1912 portrait of Adams

Part of any prominent astrologers' stock in trade is predicting the future. The sensationalist overtones of doing so are what attract attention, and a correct prediction is viable proof of the astrologer's competency. It is risky, though, to go on the record with an important forecast. If the astrologer proves to have been wrong, it can have a detrimental effect on the reputation. Yet Evangeline was up for the challenge, particularly when she was young. Her 1899 *New York Journal* forecast for New York City, although partly general and partly incorrect, had also at times been startlingly accurate. This was written when she was actively seeking to expand her client base. As the years went on and Adams' practice provided a better living, she didn't need to risk promoting herself in this manner. She never published a forecast quite like the one for New York again. Yet as a highly visible astrologer, she did continue to forecast publicly from time to time. However, even during her lifetime, it would have been impossible to determine exactly how often her forecasts were accurate. Most were given privately, and even the public ones were sometimes open to interpretation, much as the Delphic Oracle was in its day.

President Theodore Roosevelt had left office in early 1909, went on safari to Africa and visited Europe before returning to the United States and a nationwide speaking tour. It soon became clear that he would once again run for the presidency in 1912. Roosevelt was still coasting on the popularity of his earlier terms in office, but Evangeline, in looking over his horoscope, announced he would not be elected. As it turned out, she was right. (At least she said she was, after the fact.)

Adams had continued marketing general forecasts for the coming months and years. Based only on the interrelationship of heavenly bodies for a specified time period, Evangeline needed no personal birth charts, and thus could do the work once and capitalize on her expertise, selling the same forecast to many clients and generating quite a bit of income. In her general indications for 1912, she called attention to a period of three years beginning in July. The planet Saturn would be in Gemini during that time, and as Gemini was considered to rule the United States, there should be some important events. In particular, Adams recalled that every war in which the United States had previously engaged had come about under a similar affliction of the sign of Gemini. She counselled that our diplomatic relations must be carefully handled.

Much did develop on the international scene, with the United States playing an increasingly active role. During 1913 and 1914, Secretary of State William Jennings Bryan negotiated a series of treaties which he hoped would avert the outbreak of World War I, though war in Europe began in the summer of 1914. Although the United States' entry into the war was delayed until 1917, we had for some years been increasingly drawn into the fray. With the sinking of the Lusitania in 1915, President Wilson began to change his neutral stance, causing Jennings Bryan to resign. The U.S. also began interventionist policies in Mexico and Haiti in 1914, eventually sending marines to both. U.S. troops had actually helped depose Mexican President Huerta in 1914. Had Evangeline's forecast pinpointed the beginning of difficulties for the United States, or does our current perspective cause us to consider this forecast inaccurate in light of subsequent events? While her forecast seems accurate, there are always some international policies developing in any three-year period.

In a sales brochure a few years later, Adams congratulated herself on the "careful wording of the forecast" which she said attested to the "discretion of the responsible and enlightened astrologer." She had been careful not to say that the U.S. would actually go to war. Instead, she pointed out the effects of a past cycle of Saturn on United States history, and noted that the cycle would repeat once again from 1912 to 1915, making diplomacy important. The implication was clear, but she had shied away from expressing it specifically. This was in direct contrast to the type of prophecy she had published in 1899. As she had said that "great storms will be frequent," but was met with extended doldrums, it became clear that precision in language might not have been what was called for. If she had forecast "unusual weather conditions," for example, she would have been right on the money either way. Perhaps her changing style and tone were the result of shrewd thinking or retrospective evaluation; possibly they were simply indicative of the times. Although Adams reportedly predicted that King George V's reign would be a "bloody one, replete with war and suffering" (he ascended to the throne in 1910 and would rule throughout the first World War), she would no longer be quite so fatalistic or prophetic as most astrologers, herself included, had been. As we move into the teens, we find Evangeline lightening up her heavy-handed and authoritative style in favor of something more easily assimilated.

American society was becoming more liberal: dire predictions and fatalistic prognostications were no longer either appreciated or understood as they had been in the nineteenth century. New social and humanitarian ideals proliferated, and, particularly in the United States, one was not felt to be necessarily doomed to the horrendous fate he might be born into. The innovative and even bizarre were introduced in the arts, and certain portions of the population flirted with psychoanalysis, communism, free love and birth control. Men and women were not as segregated as they had been only a decade before. By 1910, almost a quarter of all American women were working. The following years featured longer and leaner, high-waisted styles; women's ankles were boldly exposed in the mid-teens, they had thrown off layers of petticoats and corsets, and enjoyed greater freedom and independence. The women's suffrage movement, too, began to pick up momentum.

Certainly, an astrologer had to forecast, but also walked a thin line, as New York City law still forbade "pretending to tell fortunes." While business, weather and political forecasters were immune from prosecution, astrologers had to be more careful. We get an idea of the new twentieth century astrology in a letter to the editor of the *Paris Herald*, which was printed in October of 1911, in response to a query about astrology:

"Constant Herald Reader" desires astrological information. May I say that the greatest living "expert" and authority, perhaps, is Miss Evangeline Adams, Carnegie Hall, New York City. Instances of her absolutely marvelous readings of the past and predictions for the future, merely working out the scientific horoscope by means of the nativity and sex, only, would fill pages of the Herald. The practical benefit of this is in that, while predictions forewarn the subject, threatened disaster may be averted if known in time, for life is not a journey in an environment of cast-iron fate, unalterable and relentless, but a progress in which the intelligence, the sense of moral responsibility, the power of will that seeks cooperation always with the Divine will, determines its cause. While Miss Adams is really a past mistress of scientific astrology, working out a horoscope as a mathematical astronomer would work out a problem in the sidereal universe, she is also a woman of a singular loftiness of spirit and flawless integrity of purpose, with an intense and unfaltering devotion to her profession.

Unfortunately, the writer remained anonymous. It could have been a client, friend or well-wisher; somehow the many superlatives and the effusiveness of praise even suggest that the author was Evangeline herself!

Across the Atlantic in London, Alan Leo, the modern astrologer whose lead Adams had taken in standardizing written horoscopes, was going through a similar transformation in his astrological readings. Leo had already published a number of books on astrology, some of which Evangeline had bought on previous trips to London. Leo and his wife had embraced Theosophy, which gave them a springboard from which to stress the spiritual and universal aspects of astrology. The Theosophical Society was dedicated to exploring unexplained phenomena, and believed that there existed a secret universal doctrine from which all religions derived; astrology fit nicely into their scheme. (Evangeline Adams, though, seems not to have been influenced by Theosophical ideas, carrying on with her more traditional astrological background.)

The public is always eager for forecasts, and Alan Leo's standardized horoscopes included this type of material. Leo was arrested in London in April of 1914, accused of trying to "unlawfully pretend to tell fortunes" in a mail-order horoscope reading. As one of England's most visible astrologers, he had been singled out. Like Evangeline's earlier case, his was dismissed at his court appearance on May 6. The experience was a difficult one, however, and Leo would, as a result, concentrate more and more on psychological and spiritual astrology, rather than forecasting, stressing that "character is destiny."

Back in New York, Evangeline had recently settled into new quarters. She continued to maintain both work and living spaces at the Carnegie Hall Studios, but after eight years in the same suite, had moved up to the tenth floor. The new space was near the top of the building, with much more light and air, and a more spectacular view than before. This move up really did coincide with Adams' increasing prominence. When Police Commissioner Woods' office decided once again to crack down on fortune-tellers, Evangeline was one of the first to be visited. Isabella Goodwin, who had testified against Adams in the 1911 case, was now a detective. This time she did not see Adams, but instead visited a supposed psychic and was startled when the lady blurted out, "I don't like the work you are doing and I am trying to make out what it is." Another woman detective paid $5 to Evangeline for a reading on Wednesday, May 13. *The New York Times* carried a detailed report a few days later:

The evidence against her was obtained by Detective Adele Priess, and the warrant for her arrest was issued by Chief

Magistrate McAdoo. Detective Roos of Headquarters, who made the arrest, said that Miss Adams had an expensive suite of rooms in the Carnegie Hall Building, at Seventh Avenue and 57th Street, and that she was consulted by many women prominent in society. Her reception room was crowded with fashionably dressed women when he interrupted her work, he said. Miss Adams was held under $500 bail for examination next Wednesday.

As before, Adams' arrest resulted only from undercover police efforts and not the complaint of an actual client. Evangeline tells us in *The Bowl of Heaven* that,

The first case brought against me was thrown out of court. The judge stated from the bench, after hearing the opposing witness, that it was obvious I had not broken the law and that I had done nothing which could be construed as fortune-telling. But I wasn't satisfied. I have always tried to visualize just one step at a time in what I am pleased to call my "career." And now, I had but one ambition: to legalize astrology in the state of New York. So when another enemy of the science came to me anonymously, secured a reading which she claimed was "fortune-telling," and hailed me again to court, I went with a willing and determined heart.

This time, I retained the best counsel available, Clark L. Jordan of New York, and told him that I wanted him to earn his money, not by having the case against me thrown out of court, but by having it tried. I wanted to settle this question. And I did.

The above was written in 1926, in retrospect, and Adams as usual puts a positive spin on her experiences. In all likelihood, however, she was upset and nervous, wanting to do anything possible to be out of the jam in which she found herself. In none of the many newspaper write-ups at the time is there any mention that she, herself, asked that the case be tried.

We may, however, gain some insight into what Evangeline was thinking from a fictionalized account of the Adams trial, written by Iris Vorel. Vorel dedicated her 1933 book *Ad Astra* to the "loving memory of my teacher Evangeline Adams," capitalizing on her relationship with Evangeline. As Adams wasn't known to actively teach individual students, Vorel probably worked for her, drawing up astrological charts and gleaning insights from her forecasts and pre-written horoscope interpretations, as well as the occasional personal astrological insight directly from Miss Adams.

Vorel's fictional heroine is a young, beautiful woman astrologer named Mariska Lawlor. But much of the rest of her account is a thinly veiled romance based on Adams' life, which she must have begun writing either before or immediately after Adams' death. Well into the book, Vorel throws aside the mantle of novelist and includes on a facsimile of her own stationery the following statement:

Mariska Lawlor frequently confided to me that she dreaded nothing more than legal proceedings. To be "haled to court" seemed to her a supreme crucible. She thought it best to settle any possible action out of court, even at a monetary sacrifice.

She was stunned by her arrest. Influential clients volunteered to try to have the case quashed. But Mariska felt this was not her personal case, – rather it was astrology as a profession that was placed before the tribunal of society, and the Forces had selected her as a channel. She recognized Karma, and she accepted it.

We cannot know if this account reflects Evangeline's true feelings. But certainly, there was as much publicity in the tabloids and as many clients and friends crowding the courtroom for Evangeline's arraignment as for the fictional Mariska, Iris Vorel no doubt among them.

At Adams' arraignment on May 20, Mrs. Priess testified and Adams submitted an affidavit to the court, recounting her experiences. A clipping from the *Journal American* newspaper morgue describes the event:

Every seat in the West Side Court was taken yesterday afternoon. A large part of the audience was composed of well-dressed women, friends and clients of Miss Adams, but there were also a few of her men well-wishers.

The case was adjourned until May 25. Attorney Clark Jordan then requested another postponement, maintaining he had to learn all about astrology in order to represent his client effectively. It would take some time to study this complex subject. The presiding magistrate, John J. Freschi, agreed, and the hearing was again put off.

Freschi was a young man at the time, not yet forty, and was said to have graduated from New York Law School before the age of twenty. Appointed a magistrate five years earlier, he was by then knowledgeable of the laws and how to interpret them. Later known as an extraordinarily patient man, he was nevertheless severe in sentencing if he felt the crimes justified it.

We have a good record of Adams' trial in New York City's *Criminal Reports*. The trial was heard in a municipal court, and was in no way, as Adams may have later imagined, a testing of New York State law. The trial report contains the magistrate's statement and summary, along with lengthy transcripts of the hearing. It is not a complete transcript: this no longer exists. Freschi first sets out the considerations upon which he will base his judgement:

This case presents two considerations; first, the question of fact in order to determine what actually was stated by the defendant, and secondly, whether such a case comes within the meaning of the words "pretend to tell fortunes" of the statute alleged to have been violated.

The practice of astrology is, in my opinion, but incidental to the whole case and has bearing only on the question of the good faith of the defendant, as I will point out later. The statute provides that persons who pretend to tell fortunes shall be adjudged disorderly persons and punished as prescribed therein.

Detective Adele D. Priess testified for only about five minutes. Many of the statements which she remembered Adams making in reading her horoscope and her palms were not unlike those witnessed in Adams' earlier trial and did seem at least somewhat fatalistic. The magistrate continued:

Assuming that this is a substantial account of what happened, this evidence, if uncontroverted, would entitle the people to a conviction. A prophecy of future events involving a negative or affirmative deception constitutes a violation of law.

But a defendant is innocent until proven guilty, and Freschi extended Evangeline the benefit of the doubt. Priess had claimed that she met with Adams for about thirty-five minutes: in her five minutes of testimony, she must have left out many details. It would also be easy to forget many of the involved statements made in astrological jargon.

Evangeline claimed that the interview lasted more than an hour. Because there was a discrepancy between the two reports, she testified at length on her own behalf. Her counsel helped elicit the following account. Evangeline had first asked for the date, time and place of the supposed client's birth, and drew up her usual horoscope chart wheel.

After I had the chart erected, I told her I got characteristics from the hand. I asked her to sit to the left of my desk, of a small table. I asked her to place her hands on that table, palms down. I glanced over the hand and told her many things about her nails. She should never take antikamnia, nor any coal tar products, because there was a tendency to suffer from poor elimination, and anything that depressed the heart would be bad for her. Then I referred to her third finger. That it being long indicates that she had quite strong impressions, the kind of impressions that the Wall Street men call "hunches," and if she would go by these "hunches" without talking them over with any one that she might be fortunate in speculation. I also said that the left hand indicated the natural tendencies, was supposed to rule until twenty-eight, and the right hand the balance of life, and that as this third finger was longer on the right hand the indications were that the last half of her life should be more fortunate than the earlier half. I pursued my usual method [with her birth chart]. One of the things that I laid a great deal of stress upon was the position of her moon. The moon was in conjunction with the planet Neptune. I asked her what happened to her mother, if there was any strange fatality connected with her mother's life. It took her a long time before she would commit herself. At last she said, "Yes, my mother was shot but didn't die until eight years later."

I spoke of the fact that the planet Uranus during this year would be in conjunction with the sun, which occurs only once in eighty-four years, and that it was also an epoch-making period. That this was the planet that brought about changes, a great deal of development in the character, etc., and that if she were a young girl it might have caused her to have an opportunity to marry. That in this case it might bring some one into her life who would bring some new interest or something of a philosophic or scientific character to her. She then gave me the date of her son's birth. I said emphatically it was a very unusual horoscope.

In his cross-examination, the assistant District Attorney, L. S. Lockhart, concentrates on a few key points. Did Evangeline make fatalistic pronouncements, or did she refer to particular planets, signs or lines on the hand? A distinction is made: it is not illegal to share established information having to do with the hands or horoscope if one is careful to make clear that that is exactly what is being done. A direct prophecy of future events, on the other hand, such as "you will marry," "your son will die," etc. implies occult or mystical knowledge and possibly fraud, and is consequently considered breaking the law. In referring to the detective's testimony, we can see that the court again and again questions Adams on these two points, referring to the policewoman's statement.

Magistrate Freschi: Did you say to Miss Priess in words, substance or effect "Your daughter is very ambitious, she was born when Saturn was rising, she sometimes gets discouraged, but that sign passes over just like a wet blanket?"

Adams: I explained the opposition of Mercury indicated that she would have periods of depression and that it was similar to a wet blanket, but Your Honor, I could not give a reading without mentioning the planets. My contention is if I did it in the case of Isabella Goodwin, when I did not suppose it made any difference whether I did or not, and I knew the Magistrate threw that out of court because I did it, is it logical to suppose that I changed my method and to this client I did not do it? Is that logical?

Lockhart: And in speaking of the daughter's future the prosecutrix claimed that you used this form of language: "Your daughter will marry well, but your older daughter will make a far better marriage than the young one?"

Adams: No, sir, not in so many words.

Lockhart: Do you remember just how you did speak of that?

Adams: No, I really don't.

Lockhart: But you are certain you did not state the daughter will marry well and the older daughter will make a far better marriage – you dispute that you used just that form?

Adams: Yes, absolutely, and my client knew it too.

Lockhart: In speaking of the son, the prosecutrix asserts you said: "Your son will be very successful, he makes friends very easily. He should be careful about his companions as he is apt to be influenced by them. He should guard against dissipation." How did you say that about the son, that he will be successful?

Adams: Not as it is put there. She further states that I said he would be killed. If I had said that why would I have cautioned her as to what he did?

Lockhart: This is the language she claimed you used: "Your son should be very careful as he will die as the result of accident or just like that" (you snapping your fingers). Did you say that in that way?

Adams: No, sir, not that way.

Lockhart: Do you remember what you said about the son?

Adams: I would not like to say now, I am tired. I know certain planets were in certain aspects, which indicated danger of an accidental death and that because of that I advised him not to work where there was high voltage. I did tell her he had ability along electrical lines, but that he ought not to work in high voltage because of this aspect in his horoscope which indicated danger of accidents and even accidental death. I said it just that way.

Evangeline is careful about what she says. She's had several months, after all, in which to prepare with her attorney. Yet at times, she appears to be exasperated by the cross-questioning and re-questioning. Minute detail was never her strong point, and the court forces her again and again to explicitly state what words she used in a reading conducted over six months earlier! She does get to the point of actually saying, "I am tired." At times Evangeline seems more than a little evasive as well. She also keeps consistently to the party line, the "right" answers to the District Attorney's questions.

Lockhart: Do you remember whether or not you said you saw two marriages in her hand?

Adams: I remember that I saw two lines which I pointed out to be indicating the possibility of two marriages.

Lockhart: Those lines are always at a certain portion?

Adams: Right there (indicating).

Lockhart: At the base of the smallest finger of the hand, on the side of the hand?

Adams: Yes.

Lockhart: Then she claims you said, "I should say you are going to meet a man for whom you might form an attachment but I would be very careful about marrying him in case his circumstances should be such that he could not get along without your help?"

Adams: No, I did not say that. That is not my language and my way of getting at it.

Lockhart: Did you say too, "you are going to be more successful and have more magnetism in later life than in earlier life?" Did you say that in that way?

Adams: No, sir, I went into a very careful explanation of hands and fingers.

Lockhart: Well the witness does claim, however, that you did say that that fact was shown by the third finger of the right hand being longer than the third finger of the left hand. Now did you say to her: "There is a new life opening for you?"

Adams: I explained that Herschel is in conjunction with her sun this year, and that that always indicated new vibrations, new conditions, and I went into an explanation of the planet Herschel being with her sun did indicate certain things, but nothing in the way of –

Lockhart: Did you say: "I should say that you were going to have a violent love affair?"

Adams: I don't remember saying it. I explain in the beginning I simply give what is shown by the stars. If I read for a client I always say "This is indicated" and I always explain that no astrologer can conscientiously say that any one thing will happen. Sometimes a lady will say "Will I be married in 1914?" I say, "I don't know whether you will or not I think you have an opportunity to be but whether you will I can't tell. Astrology does not indicate you are going to be hailed to the altar." I am very careful to say what will occur, because I don't know. In fact, I simply say, "This is likely to be, guard against it, if it is bad. If it is good, make the most of it." There is no client that comes to me that does not realize they are simply getting my ideas of what the planet will do or so far as the planet indicates. They draw their own deductions.

Lockhart: You merely read the indications?

Adams: Absolutely, that is all I ever do. I am very careful to do it. I am careful to do it not because I think the law was involved, but because I do not want any responsibility. I do not want to feel that I have anything to do with it. I say I have nothing to do with it, I simply read the signs. An astrologist feels a great deal of responsibility and tries to make it plain. Human nature is very funny.

Here, finally, we can clearly see the complete transformation which Evangeline's forecasting style has undergone. It's been fifteen years since she made the all-encompassing statement that "a scourge of sickness will pass over the country, and deaths will be frequent and terrible." In its place we find instead, "guard against it, if it is bad." Clearly, this played well with Magistrate Freschi, who concluded:

Counsel contends that the defendant did not pretend to foretell any event, that all that occurred was an attempt on her part to explain the positions of the planets and read their indications without any assurance by the defendant that such reading was a prognostication of future events.

There is no claim here that the defendant was garbed in special garments or that there was any air of mysticism about the place; it was a simple apartment with library furniture without signs of any kind in or about the studio, except to indicate that it was the office of the defendant.

Several works on modern astrology as well as very old books on the subject were produced in court... These were used by the defendant while testifying and in the construction of the horoscope in a supposed case. In the reading of the horoscope the defendant went through an absolutely mechanical, mathematical process to get at her conclusions. She claims that astrology never makes a mistake and that if the figures are correct, the information given is correct.

The defendant raises astrology to the dignity of an exact science – one of vibration, and she claims that all the planets represent different forces of the universe.

In addition to the considerations regarding what is or is not fortune-telling, Freschi also took Adams' sincerity into account. Did she appear to be trying to take advantage of a clients' credulity? Here, once again, we can see that Adams' professional demeanor, long years of experience, and personal convictions carried the day:

The sincerity of the defendant's determination upon the opinion of her work from her own perceptions and a study of authorities cannot be questioned. She certainly does seem to have a thorough knowledge of the subject. And in this, she claims no faculty of Foretelling by supernatural or magical means that which is future, or of discovering that which is hidden or obscure; but she does claim that nature is to be interpreted by the influences that surround it.

The statute in question is peculiarly worded. "Pretend to tell fortunes" are to be considered. This law was designed to prohibit persons who make pretense or make believe to tell fortunes. A deception or concealment of the truth is essential in each case. It is really a certain degree of quackery practiced to the detriment of the community, in general, that is made unlawful by this statute.

When the defendant prepared her horoscope of the complainant and got the relative position of the planets at the time of her birth, basing this horoscope on the well-known and fixed science of astronomy, she violated no law. Her explanation of the relative positions of the planets constituted no violation of law. For the palmist to tell that a certain line in the palm of the hand is the "life line" or the "head line" or the "heart line" has never been held, as far as I know, a violation of this law now under consideration. But it has been held to constitute one a disorderly person, within the meaning of this statute, to say that the life of a certain individual will be long or short.

Every fortune-teller is a violator of the law; but every astrologer is not a fortune-teller. I believe that there is a line of distinction between the person who pretends to be able to read the future and tell with positiveness what will or shall happen; and the one who merely reads a sign as indicating what ought to happen but is particular to make it plain that he is not attempting to predict future events. The former is a charlatan, an oppressor and an imposter; the latter is surely not a fortune-teller as he is commonly understood.

Evangeline was jubilant. Most newspapers covered the story, and all quoted her as asserting that astrology was now established as a legal, legitimate science, on a par with law and medicine. This is obviously how she felt, and clearly she could expect no more problems with the law. Yet this wasn't strictly true; Magistrate Freschi never actually declared that astrology was a science.

Let's remember that Freschi, from the beginning, felt the practice of astrology to be incidental to the case. What he evaluated was whether or not Adams had predicted the future in no uncertain terms. To do so, he listened to her testimony and evaluated her character. So Evangeline, herself, had been vindicated, and not palmistry or astrology. Another palmist or astrologer on another occasion might indeed prove to be a fortune-teller.

The law was not changed; and yet a precedent had been set, which would influence how astrologers and palmists would be dealt with in New York City in the future. Not all would automatically be found guilty of fortune-telling; the issue would in the future be addressed on a case by case basis. Even in this sense, it was a landmark case, which is why it attracted so much attention.

On this occasion, Evangeline Adams once again benefitted greatly. Many New York City papers carried coverage of the story (perhaps they were alerted in advance by Adams). The wide press exposure, including a recent photo published in *The New York World*, enhanced Adams' reputation and added to her notoriety.

As with many incidents in Evangeline's life, this one, too, presents us with a number of mysteries. There are many conflicting statements and missing pieces to the story. In all of the newspaper reports, Adams has "said" or "claims to be a descendant of President John Quincy Adams," or is "directly descended from President John Adams." We know she was not. Did she say it? It is not included in the report of the trial, and all the newspapers seem to have taken their similar accounts from the same unknown source. This could likely have been Adams' promotional material. In her sales brochure, "The Law and Astrology," which would soon be printed, Evangeline recaps the case and includes Freschi's positive statements. But she also includes the following:

Miss Evangeline S. Adams is a direct descendant of the famous New England family which gave two Presidents to the United States... When a century ago, John Quincy Adams, as President, was shaping the destinies of the new nation, he little dreamed that a hundred years from that time, a descendant of his would be influencing and moulding the destinies of a wide circle of latter day Americans.

Of course the implication that Evangeline is that descendant is clear – but it is never explicitly stated. She's not really lying, only telling a misleading story. It seems likely that in 1914 she already had a similar brochure, which she was sure to deliver to prominent newspaper reporters as part of the press packet she would have had time to assemble in the months between her arrest and trial.

It also appears very much in keeping with Adams' character to speak in her own defense and attest to her prominent lineage. If she did, indeed, also claim in person to be a "direct descendant" of the presidents, we can excuse her for being in an extremely agitated state. If she truly felt that her very survival was at stake, certainly an affiliation with American heroes could do nothing but help.

Which brings us to another mystery. Magistrate Freschi's report does not include all of Evangeline's testimony. Although there is exhaustive opinion and much repetition, ellipses, indicating that some of Adams' testimony has been omitted, are inserted in a number of places. What is missing? Adams clues us in, again in her autobiography:

I had insisted, in order to bring the demonstration of the science down to the moment, that I be allowed to cast a horoscope and give a reading, then and there, in the presence of the court.

Judge Freschi said this request was reasonable. He did more than that. He himself gave me the dates of a person quite unknown to me; and from the day and hour and place of this unknown person's birth, I told that judge things which he afterward admitted gave him a new insight into the person's mentality and character – a demonstration that was all the more impressive to him, because the "unknown" turned out to be the judge's own son!

There is no record of Evangeline casting Freschi's son's horoscope. Freschi in the Court Report does mention that, "books on the subject were produced in court, used by the defendant while testifying and in a supposed case." This supposed case might have been that of Freschi's son.

In trying the case, the magistrate was obliged to address the police complaint and Detective Priess' experience. The defendant was then allowed to offer her side of the story. This is what the law requires. Yet, in hearing Adams read an unrelated horoscope, he went one step beyond the law. Evangeline interpreting a "supposed case" should have no bearing whatsoever on the matter at hand. As Freschi himself said, "the practice of astrology is but incidental." Maybe the reading helped Adams demonstrate exactly how she handled her client interactions. But Freschi's son's horoscope furnishes no proof of what Adams did or did not say on the afternoon of May 13, and doesn't indicate the good faith of the defendant, either. It does not belong in the permanent record, as it did not belong in the courtroom. This Freschi obviously knew: he left it out. But what of the following odd change of topic at the end of the report?

So it is claimed here in behalf of the defendant that records prove that certain personages of note classed under certain planets in the ascendancy of the time of their birth have come to death in a certain way and that therefore all others born in similar conditions should meet the same fate.

It is a vague, general statement. But in making it, Freschi negates all that he has previously said. In effect, his conclusion is, *Astrology does indeed predict the future, it can even predict death, and Adams has shown it to me.* It has been supposed, and often repeated, that Adams read Freschi's son's horoscope, and said he'd die in a certain manner. And, apparently, that was the manner in which the son had passed away. Only those with personal information about the magistrate who were also present in the courtroom over eighty-five years ago would know the truth, as it has not been captured for the record, and Evangeline, herself, provided no details.

Unfortunately, the story has only been further embellished over time. A cable television movie in the mid-nineties that featured Adams went so far as to say that she predicted the son's drowning, and that this proved correct (the idea of drowning being the latest addition to the tale). Once legends get started, rather than questioning the actual facts, those with an imaginative bent tend to take things even further.

Another question lies in the period of delay between Evangeline's arraignment and her hearing. The attorney Clark Jordan had requested the postponement; gossip and rumors have circulated on this point. It has been suggested that in the intervening months, John Freschi made quite a killing on the stock market. As Evangeline counselled many key financiers, there is the hint that the magistrate was bribed with an insider's tip. Iris Vorel's account also suggests that Adams had "pull" through her influential clients. Perhaps, too, Adams may have offered some free astrological advice on what times were best for Freschi to invest. Or possibly the court date was selected by Adams simply because she felt it was a more auspicious time astrologically for her.

There is nothing available to either prove or disprove these theories. Certainly, John J. Freschi appears to be on Adams' side all along, at times even straining to find her not guilty. He does not ever seem impartial. But we can reach no conclusions from this fact alone. The magistrate might have felt sorry for the obviously educated and cultured woman approaching middle age, may have disagreed with the arrest, or even objected to the fortune-telling law itself.

Freschi continued to have a solid and stable career, notable mainly for the criminal cases he tried. Yet a few odd things surface when one begins to examine his past. While his *New York Times* obituary indicates that he had received his law degree from New York Law, that institution has no record of him on file. Freschi had attended New York University, whose records indicate that while he was part of the class of 1898, he didn't receive a bachelor's of law there until 1915, the year after the trial! Should Freschi have even been sitting on the bench in 1914? Did he prejudice the case in Evangeline's favor? There is really no hard evidence to support these assertions.

The case did have its ramifications. As Adams was not found to be breaking the law, she continued forecasting in much the same way as she had done for the past eighteen years. Her books and interviews thus contain predictions, albeit only periodically. Adams seems ever careful to indicate exactly which planetary combinations lead to her conclusions; this was the way to stay on the proper side of the law. Alan Leo, England's popular astrologer, had quite the opposite experience. Like Evangeline, he had even alluded to death in some of his written reports. He was arrested once again in 1917, found guilty, and fined. As he had already been leaning in this direction, he then determined to do away with forecasting in his work altogether. Feeling it necessary to begin re-writing all of his books and reference material, he began this tremendous task, only to die of a brain hemorrhage a few months later.

Evangeline's trial in December of 1914 also changed her own perceptions. In the *Criminal Reports*, we clearly see that astrology comes out ahead of palmistry. It appeared more scientific, depending as it did on astronomy, its legitimate half-sister. Countless historical authorities could be invoked, going back thousands of years. Textbooks were produced to support statements made. But there was no authoritative text on palmistry save Cheiro's, and he was a showman of such recent vintage that his books were probably of dubious value. While Evangeline had been an avowed astrologist and palmist in earlier years, henceforth she would simply be an astrologist. In fact, she would even go so far as to claim in 1926 in *The Bowl of Heaven* that "I do not read minds or faces or handwriting or palms."

In the years leading up to the United States' entry into World War I, Evangeline had an unusual employee: the infamous Aleister Crowley. Born in 1875, Crowley had been brought up on his father's English country home and would later inherit a fortune from the family brewery business. Although his mother had dubbed him the Great Beast 666 of Revelations, he had spent his youth perfecting pursuits typically preferred by the wealthy, becoming a fine mountain-climber and chess-player. Crowley dressed flamboyantly, had a wicked sense of humor, and was a prolific author, writing and publishing verse and erotica while still at Cambridge. Like Adams, he had come from a strict Christian upbringing, against which he would rebel throughout his life. He soon rejected God, revelled in the notoriety gained from exploring the darker side of sexuality and drugs, and experimented with opium to induce a higher state of mind. Crowley was fascinated by the occult, and joined the Hermetic Order of the Golden Dawn in 1898. This group, as the Theosophical Society had done before it, attempted to present a coherent philosophical belief system, but put the emphasis on magic, divination and visionary experience. Here Crowley learned about the Kaballah, Tarot, alchemy, astrology, numerology and ritual magic. He rose quickly through the ranks of the Dawn, but eventually left the order after W.B. Yeats refused to accept him as his heirarchical equal (Crowley believed Yeats was jealous of his own superior skills as a poet). He subsequently married, and in travelling through Egypt in 1904, found a stela of Horus in the Boulak Museum which was labelled as Exhibit 666. Convinced this was a meaningful coincidence, Crowley was eager to accept what he believed was later dictated by a praeternatural entity: it became *The Book of the Law* and was all that he could ask for and more, taking pot shots at both Jesus and Mohammed, while confirming him as lord of a new epoch.

Crowley formed his own magical group in 1907, and began publishing *The Equinox* magazine a few years later. By 1912 he was the British head of the German erotic and occult group the *Ordo Templi Orientis* (O.T.O.). But the advent of war in Europe in the summer of 1914 changed things. For a short time, in true British aristocratic fashion, Aleister became obsessed with a desire to serve his country. Although now nearly forty, he felt his skills as a sharp-shooter, cryptographer, writer and linguist should be helpful to the war effort, and tried to join up; the English government was not interested. After a painfully long attack of phlebitis, Crowley accepted an invitation to visit New York for a few weeks. Boarding the Lusitania in late October, 1914, he was bound for America and ended up staying for over five years.

Crowley arrived in a country where both British and French war propaganda proliferated, and he was disgusted by what he perceived as their blatant stupidity. A chance meeting led to his employment on the staff of *The Fatherland*, a German propaganda newspaper. Although America's sympathies leaned toward the British Allies, Crowley admired German intelligence, and felt that their propaganda efforts were much more polished. As he tells us in his autobiographical *Confessions*, he determined to come to the aid of his country via the only route now possible. In his articles for *The Fatherland* he would attack England so strongly and broadly as to make the German cause seem absurd. Crowley counted on the American public having more critical ability in literature than they did. Everyone, including the secret service, simply assumed he was on the side of the German cause. Some evidence suggests that Crowley was a British influence agent, but he was also a complex man known for his irony and sarcasm. We also cannot be certain of the accuracy of his account in *The Confessions*, which he admitted he dictated under the influence of heroin.

Due to a lack of funds and a large book deal gone bad, Crowley stayed on in New York. Chronically unable to practice magic at this time, he sought more work as a writer and was able to sell several pieces to *Vanity Fair* magazine. Crowley describes being introduced to Evangeline by the editor of the *New York World*:

He had asked Evangeline Adams to meet me as being a famous astrologer. The meeting led to a lengthy association. She wanted me to write a book on astrology for her. The plan failed through her persistent efforts to cheat me out of the profits, and her obstinate ignorance of the elementary facts of nature combined with an unconquerable antagonism to the principles of applying common sense to the science. I learned a good deal, nevertheless. The work kept me concentrated on the subject.

Their association at first seems patently absurd. Why would such a "good girl" as Evangeline associate herself with the self-styled "bad boy" of magic? The two actually had some good astrological combinations, although both possessed great obstinacy. Aleister Crowley, however, had much to recommend him. Possessed of a brilliant mind, he was an expert occultist and had already studied some astrology. With typical passion, he plunged himself into the study and soon felt able to rather accurately surmise the rising signs and sun signs of new acquaintances. Yet his main value to Adams lay in his writing talent, and they began a book together.

Crowley's editors John Symonds and Kenneth Grant propose that as, "the work was not commissioned by a publisher, and was never published, it is rather difficult to see how Evangeline tried to cheat Crowley "out of the profits" as he had claimed. Their work together does appear to have been very much collaborative. But Crowley has said in his autobiography that due to his financial difficulties, not only his assignments with *Vanity Fair* but also "my work with Evangeline Adams kept me going through the summer." Evangeline was paying him for his work. She probably wanted Crowley to write a "work for hire" in which he would get payment for his writing but no royalties from any subsequent books, and have no rights to reprint work done expressly for her.

It is abundantly clear that Evangeline wanted and needed Aleister Crowley to write for her. During her trial testimony in 1914, she had said that,

I am writing a book on astrology. I am holding it over simply for future information. All the balance of the book is finished. I should have published it last year but I wanted to find more facts to give my colleagues about Neptune.

A 1921 magazine article reported that,

For about ten years Miss Adams has been at work, preparing a comprehensive series of books on astrology with David Seabury, former Professor of Psychology at the Culver Institute, as a collaborator.

Professor Seabury was a man nearly twenty years Adams' junior, who would later bring out several books of his own; we can only guess why their partnership faltered.

Evangeline had forty-plus years of personal experience doing astrology for clients, her notes from teacher Dr. Smith, and the astrological expertise found in her ever-growing library of traditional astrology books. Yet somehow, her book project had never materialized. Adams must have had her own copious notes and an incredible array of birth charts from both public and private sources, but could not, herself, get the project off the ground. If we remember that Dr. Smith had written her promotional brochure before the turn of the century, it's logical to surmise that Evangeline, herself, was not a real writer and needed someone to put her knowledge on paper.

With the help of Crowley, probably from 1915 to 1916, she hoped to finally launch the project.

The book was to be written for an audience unfamiliar with astrology, and included a simple chart-casting method and overviews of the planets, signs and houses. The bulk of the work would be made up of in-depth descriptions of all the planets in signs, houses and inter-aspects, and illustrated with examples from real life.

Crowley, however, complained about what he perceived to be Adams' lack of mastery of both astronomy and astrology, saying that,

She thought the planets were stuck at random in the sky like so many plums in a suet pudding. In thirty years of daily use of the Ephemeris, she had never observed that Neptune takes fifteen years or so to pass through a sign of the Zodiac, and told her clients that Neptune being in such and such a sign at their birth, they must possess various curious powers. When I pointed out that this applied to everyone born in three lustres, she was at first bewildered, then incredulous; and, proof being produced, angry and insulting.

The planet Neptune had been discovered in 1846, over sixty-five years before, but its horoscopic interpretation was still not standardized. Crowley points out the difficulty in interpreting Neptune in the astrological signs, and yet his own astrological manuscript, published in 1974, well after his death, shows that he, himself, did just that. He must have objected to what Evangeline asked him to do and how he was to do it. This was probably typical of their disagreements. They had been helpful to one another, but each had their own ideas and found it difficult to compromise. Yet both benefitted from their association. Crowley earned a living and came away with a greater understanding of astrology, while Evangeline had gotten a solid start on her book.

And, as we shall find, Crowley's "A Treatise on Astrology" contains many sections which are nearly identical to parts of Adams' 1930 book, *Astrology, Your Place Among the Stars*. Nevertheless it remains at times easy to see where each dominated, and what their contributions were. Their extraordinarily different attitudes and backgrounds are apparent, as they often lead to obvious differences in subject and tone.

Although Crowley had written about contemplating the planets and stars as a way to expand consciousness in a 1913 essay, in his *Confessions* he says that his long association with Adams kept him "concentrated on the subject" and that he "learned a good deal." These statements imply that Crowley did not have a thorough understanding of astrology until he began his work with Adams. He did not seem to follow-up on his assertion that he would collect photographs of persons representing each sun sign and rising sign, or any of the other astrological research projects mentioned in his *Confessions*. Crowley did not write much more on astrology after he left the United States to return to Europe in 1919. He included his birth chart in his *Confessions*, but no further astrological discussion. Crowley's last major work, *The Book of Thoth* included a standard astrological table with the modern planets Uranus, Neptune and Pluto added, and a scheme for categorizing the planets' meaning, but nothing more. Nor did he ever continue the joint project on his own, as Adams eventually did.

John Symonds and Kenneth Grant, the editors of both the *Confessions* and *Aleister Crowley: The Complete Astrological Writings*, state in their introduction to the astrology book that the joint work "was to be published under both their names" and that Crowley "was not a dedicated astrologer but a magician who used astrology as one of his weapons." This statement must come from reliable sources, as Symonds had already written a book on Crowley and was also his literary executor. Kenneth Grant had been Crowley's secretary and was a life-long student of his philosophy. The editors go on to say that, "astrology therefore played a minor role" in Crowley's activities. Crowley was also primarily interested in birth chart analyses, rather than the predictive side of astrology that so attracted Evangeline.

The talents which Aleister Crowley brought to the project were a wide range of expertise in the occult, an understanding of metaphysical principles, a literary background, a penetrating intellect, and a great facility for writing. Crowley was certainly the writer, working with Evangeline's basic guidelines and adding his own exposition and conclusions. Her vast astrological background, compared with his own lesser one, makes it likely that the original material was primarily hers. The extensive use of celebrity charts owed much to the English astrologer Alan Leo's reference work, *A Thousand and One Notable Nativities*, but often drew on Evangeline's large collection of birth data as well. In the end, either Adams and Crowley misunderstood one another, or Evangeline changed her mind and decided to publish the work under her own name only, which must have rankled Crowley even more.

Symonds and Grant, after their own voluminous studies of Aleister Crowley's work, say that Evangeline's "mind and style are discernible in the text." Evangeline tries consistently to make astrological chart indications clear in her published works and is generally unbiased and constructive. She seems ever-aware of writing for a larger popular audience. Crowley, on the other hand, is dramatic, often biased, and brutally honest. In discussing the meaning of Uranus in the sign of Taurus in Oscar Wilde's chart, he notes that,

Wilde's work, shallow, insincere, and stolen as it was, yet produced a tremendous, and we are bound to admit, a not altogether desirable effect upon the younger generation, especially among the half-educated.

While the same reference to Uranus in Taurus in Evangeline's book, *Astrology, Your Place Among the Stars* states that, "Wilde's work produced a tremendous effect upon the younger generation, and its permanence in literature seems now assured."

Crowley's work on the rising signs and sun signs that he talked about in his autobiography probably also contributed to Adams' earlier book, *Astrology, Your Place in the Sun*. This also contained passing references to the tarot, which was a specialty of Crowley's but something that Evangeline did not practice. The two finally went their separate ways, never completing their astrology book together. Years later, after both Adams and Crowley were dead, the O.T.O., one of the occult groups that Crowley had long been affiliated with, bought the rights to Adams' first two astrology books.

After their long relationship, Aleister was quite angry with Evangeline. It has been suggested that they had even had a love affair   (if true, a love/hate affair would probably be more appropriate). While Adams politely never spoke of Crowley in public, he wanted to speak out and wrote the essay, "How Horoscopes are Faked" in 1917, which appeared in *The International*, a German avant-garde arts magazine. He begins:

I have always been opposed to the receiving of money for anything which has in any way to do with the occult sciences. Because they are so important and so sacred, one ought to be particularly on one's honour with regard to them. As the Scripture says: "Avoid the appearance of Evil."

Crowley's religious background is evident, and we can see at once how idealistic he was, but he had never, himself, chosen to make a living from astrology as Evangeline had, since he had the Crowley Ale fortunes to support him. Crowley goes on to complain about Adams' claims to scientific accuracy, as she often didn't insist on calculating a chart to the exact degree. They simply have a difference of opinion here, as we have already seen that Evangeline agreed with Dr. Smith that the overall interpretation was more important than spending too much time with the minutiae of the horoscope. Crowley then takes another idealistic stance:

It may be said that a horoscope is a complete map of the life and character of the native. To read one properly would mean at least a week's continuous work.

In business practice, however, only so much time can be allotted to each client for a reading, so it will necessarily be somewhat incomplete. If Evangeline took a full week to interpret each chart, she could never make a living. Aleister also objected to Adams' standardized and mimeographed astrology reports. Due to the holistic nature of astrology, a horoscope should ideally be synthesized by the astrologer personally, since conflicting indications appear in most natal charts. As a purist, Crowley is correct in his objection, since in standardized reports for each sign and planet, conflicting statements can easily occur. And, in addition, Adams did read horoscopes when no birth time was available. For greatest accuracy, one must have the correct time. The birth time, even today, is not always available; in the nineteenth and early twentieth centuries, it was often not recorded. In order to give the eager client something, the working professional must at times make do. As Crowley didn't have an astrology practice of his own, he didn't understand this and felt that Adams simply wanted to take money from whomever would give it.

She has to get the dollars from the people who do not know in the least at what hour of the day or night they were born. She has the impudence to assume it doesn't matter, all the time insisting upon her wonderful scientific accuracy.

Crowley's fundamentalist roots begin to show when he talks about the possibility of blackmail when dealing with such a large segment of a local population:

Women are particularly foolish with astrologers. They tell all their love affairs.... The astrologer becomes mistress of these women, body and soul. Perhaps she does not blackmail them; but she is in a position to do so if she wishes. At the very least, the victims realise their position, and are careful to do anything the astrologer may ask.

Although there has never been any real suggestion that Adams actually manipulated her clients, Iris Vorel did hint that Evangeline could rely on some of her more prominent clients for help or even influence when she needed it.

Crowley continues:

Then again there is the matrimonial agency graft; and the highly profitable business of entremetteuse. (We do not assert that in the particular case we are discussing these things are done, but they could be done. It is immoral to permit the existence of a secret of this kind.)

Aleister Crowley suggests what might possibly happen – he's careful not to say it did occur in Evangeline's case (an *entremetteuse* is a female pimp). Crowley also never questions Evangeline's sincerity of purpose:

There is no need to cast any doubt upon the sincerity of the belief of the woman. She talks astrology day and night. She dreams of it. She sets a horoscope for her vast family of cats and dogs and is scared out of her life when some planet threatens her horoscope.

Crowley did worry, however, that Evangeline baited her clients into more expensive personal consultations by getting them hooked on her cheaper reports, concluding that, "Superstition is so extraordinarily strong that when faith is established, there is no limit to the amount of which the victim can be fleeced."

Aleister Crowley's essay is also valuable in that it probably accurately describes Evangeline's business at the time: personal consultations, mail-order horoscopes, and her monthly forecast indications service. He describes the real result of Adams' brush with the law, characterizing her monthly forecasts as "fortune-telling, pure and simple."

These pages are carefully examined by a lawyer, for we are now getting into the danger zone. The phraseology is very carefully chosen, for nothing must be said which would be indictable as a prediction. Thus, instead of saying, "You will be lucky in speculation during the first week of October," the phrase is "financial conditions seem to be operating favourably during the first week in October."

It is apparent that Evangeline had been frightened and upset by her earlier legal problems. She consequently took many other precautions:

The astrologer is extraordinarily careful about making appointments. One has to have very good introductions. Word quickly goes round as to what the police are doing. For example a few months ago it was rumoured that a red-haired detective had been engaged, and all women with red hair, unless previously known, had to pass the 33rd degree before they reached the centre of the web. There is no doubt in the mind of the astrologer that she is breaking the law. She lives in continual terror of the police. She knows well enough that it was only a fluke that she was not convicted at her previous prosecutions. However, she boasts openly of her "pull" with certain society leaders who can protect her from the

*police. Properly managed, evidence is easy to obtain. Will not Mrs.
Isabella Goodwin look to it?*

There must have still been talk about the policewoman who had
arrested Evangeline in 1911!

There was great economic growth in the United States during the
teens; inflation increased, racial and labor tensions mounted, and
many more women entered the work force. Americans were no
longer as optimistic or self-assured as they had been only a decade
before, and in their disillusion with traditional institutions, many
turned to astrology for guidance. Adams' business expanded
particularly during World War I; the demands from the families of
soldiers were great. She was always eager for more business, simply
adding additional people to her staff as needed.

Mary C. Scheinman, a single woman who had lived in Pittsburgh
and Chicago, was now Evangeline's most important and visible
employee, running the office, scheduling appointments, and hiring
and supervising part-time or temporary workers, many of whom were
out-of-work actresses. Mary had originally answered Adams' ad for a
secretary, but as she was well-read and had a cultured background,
was soon helping her with much more than standard secretarial work.
She accompanied Adams on many of her trips to Europe, and as she
was dedicated to her work, became indispensable. As Mary's father
and grandfather before him had both been rabbis, the spiritual
overtones of astrology probably also appealed to her.

All of Adams' employees learned how to cast charts. Mary had
been taught by Evangeline and she instructed the new workers.
Although astrology was a fascinating study, much of the necessary
chart-casting work was of a dry and clerical nature. With many more
requests for mail-order horoscopes, there was also much typing,
filing and clerical work; sales brochures and rate sheets were also
sent out. Most of this work was done by the secretaries, who
calculated horoscopes and selected the proper descriptions of
planets, signs and aspects from dozens of mimeographed sheets. Of
course errors did creep in. But at the time, Adams was offering a
unique service to the American public, and there was growing
interest.

Evangeline's niece Gertrude no longer helped out at the office.
She was married in April of 1920 to Claude Curry, in their native
Decatur, Illinois. Evangeline had no doubt selected a good
astrological date for this important event.

Evangeline had always enjoyed reading the charts of youngsters: she felt that astrological guidance could help parents to better understand and mold their children in the most positive way possible. She had recently read the chart of a fourteen-year old boy, an Aquarius like herself, who had several horoscope placements similar to her own. She felt he would make an excellent astrologer, but the boy thought the whole thing idiotic, and he hardly believed what she had to say. As he grew up, however, he was curious enough to read more and more astrology, and was finally convinced. Carroll Righter would later become one of the mid-twentieth century's most well-known astrologers, writing several books, publishing a daily forecast column, and acting as a consultant to the elite in Hollywood.

Ella Wheeler Wilcox was another famous friend and client. Wilcox was one of America's favorite poets in the late nineteenth and early twentieth centuries, writing a poem a day for syndicated newspaper distribution across the country, and frequently contributing essays to popular magazines as well. A sensation at thirty-three when a book of her poems was criticized as immoral, Wilcox was extraordinarily drawn to metaphysics, frequently attended seances, and studied Theosophy. While many criticized her work as banal or sentimental, she took it quite seriously, claiming that she comforted millions. Adams, as ever, avoids discussing their relationship, but Ella Wilcox was probably both a friend and regular client. Evangeline used one of Ella's poems as a standard in her mail-order work, and repeated it in *The Bowl of Heaven*. "The Winds of Fate" summed up her attitude about fate and free will:

> *One ship drives east and another drives west*
> *With the self-same winds that blow,*
> > *'Tis the set of the sails*
> > *And not the gales*
> > *Which tell us the way to go.*
>
> *Like the winds of the sea are the ways of fate*
> *As we voyage along through life,*
> > *'Tis the set of the soul*
> > *That decides its goal*
> > *And not the calm or the strife.*

Chapter 11: *Here Comes Mr. Jordan*

In the 1920's, society seemed split between extremes. Although women could now vote, a more conservative period followed World War I, exemplified by the prohibition of alcohol, immigration quotas, and fear of communism. Physics promised that the only reality was the principle of uncertainty. New theories of psychology implied that men were irrational, and the experience of war made people less sure that they could master their own circumstances. The older generation's faith was shaken, but the younger one welcomed the advent of the jazz age, read Fitzgerald and Hemingway, and lived for the moment. Youthful enthusiasm replaced seasoned maturity as the dominant force. The rise of modern science made anything seem possible; in order to compete, philosophy and religion had to supply the excitement and pizazz that youth demanded.

The twenties soon ushered in another period of increased interest in the occult. Spiritualism again reached a peak in popularity, and some newspapers and magazines began regularly printing astrology features and columns (although these were not the same as today's horoscopes, which didn't come along till later). The voices of evangelists and fundamentalists spread the Christian gospel through an emphasis on the supernatural and miraculous, while eastern beliefs again flourished, and Rosicrucianism, Yoga, Theosophy, Christian Science and New Thought spread further. Evangeline Adams also offered answers to many of the questions which troubled these early twentieth century Americans, and she was eager and willing to help.

Adams was as busy as ever with personal consultations and her various written reports and forecasts for the future. Her book project had been quite ambitious and perhaps because of this, had not progressed any further. She continued to collect valuable astrological information, but was not much closer to condensing it into book form than before. She still needed the help of a good writer like Aleister Crowley, but one with a more cooperative attitude.

Early in 1921, a client asked Adams' advice on a business deal. She read his chart, also casting the horoscope of the other gentleman involved. As the story goes, Adams was immediately attracted to this other man's horoscope, and asked to meet him. This was duly arranged, with the man coming down from Boston in order to do so.

But apparently things didn't "click." "Nothing happened right away," she tells us in her autobiography:

But about two months later the young man was leaving the Commodore Hotel to take the Knickerbocker for Boston. The porter was walking on in front with his bags. Suddenly he felt the urge – the young man, not the porter – to again see the lady who had been attracted by his horoscope. He went to the telephone and called her up. It was then twenty minutes to one. She told him that she had an appointment at one o'clock, but that if he'd come right up, she would see him for a few minutes. He gave up his train and came to see the lady. Two years later they were married.

Evangeline Adams was fifty-three at the time. The man was George E. Jordan, Jr., of Cambridge, aged thirty. The story, as usual, is probably apocryphal, or at least exaggerated. "All my life I've known that a man born with that particular pattern of the stars at birth would come into my life some day," Evangeline later told the *New York Mirror*. Despite this romantic pose, Adams was more likely to have been looking for a writer to help with her books, or a businessman to help organize, promote and expand her business, rather than a husband.

Jordan was born in Salem, Massachusetts, not far from Evangeline's hometown of Andover. According to his own biographical account, he had begun his career as an auto mechanic ("mechanical expert" was his phrase), and went on to run a lumber business in his twenties. During World War I he was connected with a Boston manufacturing company which supplied metal containers for food that was sent to the trenches. In another account, he claimed to have founded this firm, and to have also been engaged in the oil brokerage business. His father had imported flax from Ireland and Belgium for many years, and Jordan, Jr. had an interest in this firm as well.

In the *New York Herald* of April 7, 1923, George tells us more about himself:

It developed, as I say, that my horoscope proved I was perfectly fitted for occult work. For twelve years, while in business in New England building up small corporations and organizing manufacturers, I had depended on astrologers, particularly in such matters as selecting office forces and signing important legal papers. Now I know I was destined to be an astrologer. And let me say that I have manipulated from $10,000,000 to $50,000,000 at one time and another, but never have I thrilled to the love of the work as I have to astrology.

While some of these claims may be true, Massachusetts census records from 1920 tell quite a different story. Here we see Jordan, age thirty, living at home with his parents, his father at sixty-two retired. The family, including a sister and elderly aunt, all lived in a rented house in Cambridge – hardly a situation to suit a man who had handled $50 million! George Jordan, Jr., is listed in the census as an independent insurance broker, which may be more to the point. As Jordan was an even better salesman and publicist than Adams, his stories are apt to be just that: stories. Although obviously something of a blowhard, Jordan had clearly been knocking about for most of his adult life without making much of a career at any one thing. Business seems to have attracted him, and he probably had many loose affiliations with a number of firms, working when he needed the money or was lucky enough to make a deal.

George Jordan and Evangeline made quite an odd-looking couple. He was tall and gaunt, with square shoulders, a moustache and glasses; she was short and by now somewhat stout and graying. If she had appeared plain or even homely in youth, she made a more attractive middle-aged woman. Yet Jordan was nearly twenty-five years her junior. While he attempted a matinee-idol look, complete with a brown moustache and slicked-back hair, the result was eerily reminiscent of a young Donald Sutherland playing a Nazi spy. Bags under his eyes and hollow cheeks made him appear older, and his spareness and apparent discomfort and awkwardness gave a spooky and haunted appearance. In a full-length photo, his shoulders seem to hold much tension and are oddly out of balance with his long and lanky frame.

Even so, he appealed to Evangeline, and later in the year opened a walnut-panelled office across the hall from her suite. He supposedly had begun to study astrology in earnest, but in reality he had now become Evangeline's business manager and began to help her expand. Jordan might have had a genuine interest in astrology, but was probably more attracted to the opportunity that Evangeline's unusual business provided.

Adams had another major change in her life at this time. While she had previously rented summer and weekend getaways in Darien, Connecticut and a house she called "The Zodiac" in Hebron, New Hampshire, she now bought an old Quaker Meeting House in Yorktown Heights, Westchester County, New York, near the site of a revolutionary war battle. Not a long drive from midtown Manhattan, it was in the early twenties still considered the country.

Evangeline had continued her passion for antiquing, had already collected many interesting Colonial pieces, and said she enjoyed drawing plans for remodeling old homes. While she was earning a very good income by this time, her only real luxuries were buying antiques and travelling. Her home and property were later valued at about $9,000, which was more than twice the price of a typical middle-class three-bedroom home at the time.

There was, of course, an astrological story relating to the purchase of Adams' new home. She had felt she was under excellent planetary influences for making a purchase, but spent several weeks house hunting, all to no avail. Upon re-examining her horoscope, she thought that passivity, rather than activity, would bring the desired result. In visiting a friend the next weekend, Evangeline happened across the old meeting house, right next door. The history of the building no doubt attracted her, as did the opportunity to convert it to a colonial cottage. Since it hadn't been a home before, there was no water on the property. Choosing an auspicious day for finding water, Adams tells us that she sunk a well and was happily rewarded.

At times referring to the place as a "farm," she hired a couple to keep the grounds, with enough room for livestock. (The fictional Mariska Lawlor, based on Adams, had also bought a "modest farm" in Westchester.) The home was perched on the top of a hill, with its four acres shaded from view by scores of elm trees. The decoration strove to preserve the charm of the original, century-old building, and re-create its time. A lantern owned by Miles Standish adorned the mantelpiece, with the rest of the house lit by candles. Mahogany and maple, old glass and candlesticks filled every corner, with here and there a lucky elephant figurine. The house was featured in a women's magazine publicity spread that made it look like a museum. It was neat and tidy, and Adams lived in her new home every weekend, and frequently hosted her many friends there.

One of Evangeline's more famous clients was tenor Enrico Caruso, a Metropolitan Opera star, who, she said, had never crossed the ocean during the war years without first consulting her. Only forty-seven, Caruso had an attack of pleurisy in December of 1920, which later developed into pneumonia. Evangeline first told the story in the December 1921 issue of the *American Magazine*:

I was called to the telephone three times between five o'clock and seven – seven in the morning mind you! As a rule, I can put off these inopportune demands. But, in this case, the woman who called me was in a state of such desperate anxiety that I couldn't refuse to give her my immediate attention. When she called at five o'clock, she wanted to know whether the sick man was going to die. I looked up the matter and told her that he would not die of that illness. Then I went back to bed; but at six I was called again, only to hear the same question. All I could do was to repeat what I had said before. But at seven she called a third time, and asked me again if he was going to die!

And again I said, "He won't die now. Not from this illness."

"But Miss Adams," she cried, "he is dying! The doctors have given up hope and the priests are administering the final sacrament. He's dying!"

I wanted to say, "Well, if you are so sure he is dying, why do you ask me?" But of course, I realized her state of mind, so I simply repeated, "He won't die now! He will come through this attack."

Caruso did, in fact, recover, and insisted on returning to his native Naples the following summer, where he suffered a relapse.

In July, the same person that had called me up that morning last winter again consulted me about the famous singer. I told her then that I doubted if he would ever sing again and that he was likely to die suddenly at any time. He did die within two weeks.

Adams would re-tell this story many times. It is unfortunate that it is another of her own accounts, with no one else's version available to confirm it. She walks a very thin line. If astrology, as she had been saying in recent years, could not tell a definite outcome, but only trends and influences, how could she possibly predict death? It is a question which we must ask ourselves again and again when reading Adams' subsequent interviews and publicity pieces, as she repeats her past successes with great pride. Her conviction in the power of astrology always stands firm. Yet even when she professes to believe that individuals have the power to shape their future, her anecdotes and experiences consistently point in the opposite direction. Evangeline Adams has read the stars, which indicated a particular outcome. The stars are invariably right (even if Adams admits to misinterpreting them), with individual clients either benefitting in following her advice, or losing from not doing so. Yet in none of the tales do we ever find a client influencing the outcome.

With the arrival of George E. Jordan, Jr. and his modern business methods, Adams became a commodity. As such, her identity is that of seer, and all publicity material must stress this fact. She is no longer a wise and thoughtful woman, but someone who possesses secret and occult knowledge. She now has a public identity, an image, which must be consistently maintained in order that the public be made to respond in the most favorable manner possible. Jordan would continue to market and exploit this image over the succeeding decade. A later article in the October, 1930 *Fortune* seemed to sum him up most accurately:

Mr. Jordan, a large, suave gentleman given to checked suits and diamond tie pins, is perhaps fifteen years younger than his wife. He is a promoter of parts. And although his name is never mentioned in connection with Adams' astrology, there are those who think that his wife's bureau is his biggest promotion to date.

The 1921 *American Magazine* feature is a case in point. It is the first in what would become a lengthy series of publicity pieces on Adams, telling her life story as a long string of successes in astrology. These pieces, as one astute reporter would observe, were "as alike as one griddle cake to another." They served a purpose: to promote Adams' services to a wider audience.

The 1921 piece begins with the great Caruso account and is done in an interview format with Adams. She tells of her regular services, and, stressing confidentiality, names no names (except Caruso, whose family, she explicitly states, has given permission for her to do so). Her clients are the great and near-great of society, as well as regular folks. They are big stock market operators, heads of corporations, bankers, railroad presidents, physicians, lawyers, politicians, statesmen, clergymen, bishops and even Catholic priests.

Businessmen want to know how the market will fare, but Adams stresses that even though she's called every big market break recently, it's impossible to predict daily fluctuations. Parents consult her regarding their children, and even when they should be born! Race horse owners have charts cast for their colts, and pet lovers for their dogs and cats. Questions of love, money and health are the most common ones Evangeline answers, and although she stresses that "forewarned is forearmed," the article concludes with another fatalistic portrait – that of Warren Leland and his helpless role in the disastrous Windsor Hotel fire.

This is a choice piece, which was read by quite a large audience. It says everything Jordan could dream of, and more. Quite possibly he supervised the writing himself. It must have generated much new business, both personal consultations as well as mail order work. From this point on the real Evangeline fades into the background; we must wonder how she felt about it. She had always been immersed in her astrology and doesn't ever seem to have been choosy about what was written about her – as long as it was published. She seems to have trusted Jordan completely, giving him free rein to handle business and promotion as he saw fit. If this meant overlooking or avoiding explicit factual details, it was just more of what Evangeline was already comfortable with.

For the first time in history, most people in the United States were living in cities. Mail could now be delivered across the country by air, and radios began appearing in homes. Movies and mass circulation magazines proliferated, and along with baseball, football and other sports, created a popular national culture. Mass marketing and advertising techniques advanced rapidly and underwent a revolution as they began utilizing psychology to sell. Many businesses used principles long ago established by quack doctors across the country: tell 'em anything, as long as it sells. The popular culture was becoming more and more a part of the American scene and George E. Jordan, Jr., hopped on the bandwagon with enthusiasm. In order to appeal to a wider audience, Jordan simplified Adams' story, making it easily palatable and accessible. Evangeline became less and less human, complex and real, and was soon a commodity for sale, dramatized to a super-human level. The private person became a public persona. An idealized self was marketed, an angle found. The angle is astrology and only astrology – palmistry is no longer referred to at all.

This process grew out of Adams' innate qualities. She always tended to exaggerate a bit, to tell her stories in the kindest light possible. She enjoyed publicity and part of her always craved attention. But Jordan stressed the legends rather than reality, the outer trappings rather than the real person. We hear only about the death of Caruso, the connection with the Adams clan, J.P. Morgan's patronage and the prediction of the Windsor Hotel fire. They are fantastic tales which at once delight and pique our interest. Are they true? Can they be verified? No one has ever sought the answers to these questions, although many seem to have strong opinions without looking into the matter at all.

Astrological periodicals are still churning out repetitions of the same old myths: Evangeline Adams made astrology legal in New York State, and advised J. Pierpont Morgan. Did she advise Morgan? We have only her word on this; there exists no other corroborating evidence. A 1992 astrology newsletter repeated that "J.P. Morgan gave her credit for predicting Black Friday and the crash of 1929 and testified in court on her behalf." This was repeated verbatim from a 1985 piece, with added flourishes. No one had paused long enough to consider that her client, Morgan, Sr., had died in 1913, much too soon to have done either of the above. So-called reporters often seem to quote directly from the same account, repeating and further exaggerating for interest, without assessing the source or supporting documentation. Did Evangeline ever say she was directly descended from the American presidents? Not in so many words; she always skirted the issue (in a *Boston Herald* feature from December 5, 1930, she says, "It horrified the descendants of John Adams to have one of their number dabbling in heathenism.") Promotional profiles are repeated years later as writers return to the E. Adams file in their newspaper morgue, pulling old clips and repeating the same tales over and over again.

Who writes history? We hope that historians do, those who are trained to consider carefully and sift through many varying accounts to arrive at a safe approximation of the truth. But often, in reality, those who speak up and speak out write history. Their voices, opinions and attitudes are recorded in books, newspapers and magazine articles. If they speak long enough and loud enough, their voices begin to predominate over the vast array of conflicting accounts.

Jordan, Jr., knew this. He knew he had the ability to manipulate public perception for his own ends. Society was starved for something to believe in, something to shake them up with evangelistic fervor. Jordan would make them come running to spend their money on his new god, astrology. If Adams was high priestess of the art, believing fervently in the helpful objectivity of astrology, Jordan believed even more firmly in its ability to attract the masses and generate income. The public at large no longer needed simple bread and circuses; Americans were for the most part well fed and well entertained. They craved something which touched their core in the most primitive and basic way; something which, like sex and money, fed a seemingly insatiable urge. Jordan had felt it, and he knew. Only the lure of the occult could also impact so powerfully on our instinctive desires. He was one of the first Americans to exploit astrology on a large scale, but he would certainly not be the last. And perhaps he didn't realize that along with astrology, he would be exploiting his own wife. Perhaps not.

Evangeline, for her own part, was blissfully ignorant that there should be any distinction made between the real woman and the public persona. For the moment at least, she continued on in much the way she had done before, unaware that her association with Jordan would do anything more than help greater numbers of people learn about the efficacy of astrology. She trusted him, and had a certain childlike faith and naiveté that astrology was good for everyone, that educating the masses about astrology would be a universally good thing. Never mind that great minds of the past had struggled with its philosophical implications for millennia, frequently coming to different conclusions. Never mind that astrology was a tremendous study that she well knew took months and years to even begin to understand properly. She would change things; she would bring people a greater awareness of what astrology was all about. If this had never been accomplished in over 2,000 years, Evangeline Adams had enough of an ego to presume that she was the one pedagogue capable of doing so.

Possibly because of increased publicity, the New York City Police Department soon targeted Adams in yet another sting operation. Policewoman Helen B. Osnato visited Adams for a reading and later returned for an arrest. Evangeline was arraigned on January 24, 1923, and once more released on $500 bail. This time, as opposed to her previous arrests, she had George E. Jordan, Jr., standing by to help. The charges were soon dropped, due to the previous court precedent set in 1914. Yet Evangeline had by now come to rely on Jordan. If we look back to Iris Vorel's fictionalized account of Adams' life, we can gain some insight. The fictional astrologer Mariska Lawlor's eventual husband and protector is also named George. Vorel says: "George was a friend and counselor who guided her through life's ways and byways of which she was ignorant."

The fictional George advises his astrologer on fees, advertising, planning and legal affairs, very much like his real-life counterpart. Vorel added that,

Marriage did not present itself as an escape from harassing economic perplexities, but a greater mission did it hold for her – spiritual companionship and mating on an exalted plane.

For someone as idealistic as Evangeline, this was an attractive prospect. Over time, the relationship with George, on her part at least, seems to have developed into love. Of course, there is no way to accurately assess exactly what the relationship meant to either one of them. Adams' staff felt that she was sincere in her affection for George E. Jordan, Jr. She had turned down marriage in the past, and, at the age of fifty-three, had apparently not yet had another serious relationship. Many of her staff, however, could not understand why she chose this particular man; they disliked Jordan and could not see the attraction. They felt that Jordan had simply been in the right place at the right time to play on Adams' affections, that he had inveigled his way into her life, had ulterior motives, took advantage of her generosity, and may have been unfaithful to her. In time, it also appeared that he had a drinking problem.

This opinion of George Jordan was unusually consistent. Adams' family was also upset by the relationship. Possibly the age difference gave them reservations. Evangeline's niece, Gertrude, after all, was only a year younger than her new "Uncle George." But they appear to have also heartily disliked the man. Evangeline had managed reconciliations with her family, and her affection for her niece, Gertrude, was unreserved. Yet, with her new affiliation, another rift developed.

Why would Adams welcome marriage at this time of her life? She had been an independent woman for over thirty years and was highly regarded and extraordinarily successful in her field. She had friends, hobbies, and interests, and lived a full and vital life. Yet, apparently, she still dreamed of a closer bond.

Certainly she did want some emotional support. It was evident that she had been extremely distressed by her first two arrests, and her difficulty in raising bail in 1911 had left her shaken. Her increasing years made her more vulnerable. If she had any doubts about finalizing her relationship with Jordan, her arrest in 1923 proved that he would do the things she couldn't do.

She also sought a business partner, someone to be there when she couldn't be. This Jordan had already become, and he professed to a great interest in what fascinated her the most: astrology. Jordan was a Gemini, the astrological sign most associated with writers and writing – he might be the successor to Aleister Crowley and get Adams' book projects off the ground. Adams was dedicated to her work, and to form a partnership with someone willing to expend time and effort towards achieving the same goals must have been irresistible. She was flattered by his perception of her as a leader in the field, wooed by his ability to gain publicity, and hoped they could make a successful match. A marriage would seal their business partnership in a more formal way than any contract could.

If anything, Evangeline Adams was idealistic. Even though she had heard about many relationship problems through her counseling work, she still had a romantic side. She always dressed in a feminine manner, preferring frills, lace and scarves. Her compassion and idealism helped her see only the good side of her prospective mate: how he expanded her business, increased her income, and helped her personally on a day-to-day basis. If he drank or was disliked, he became an even more sympathetic figure in her eyes.

Evangeline's horoscope was difficult for relationships; that had been reiterated to her by many years' experience. Saturn was a strong influence, but she hoped it would improve her situation over time. While a nineteenth century astrologer would have cautioned Adams to avoid marriage completely, the new views which she propounded, that promised that individuals could counter their destiny, had apparently influenced her personally as well.

Iris Vorel might once again provide a window onto Evangeline's thoughts and feelings. Mariska Lawlor's teacher had taught her that in astrology,

All adverse aspects could be mitigated by those who had learned to consciously apply the cosmic laws. "By knowing, we can prevent, and frequently circumvent evil." Mariska recalled this bit of his philosophy. Perhaps hers was just such a case. In mutual devotion to the stars – united in the interest of astrology – they might be able to transform their present friendship into a temple of true spiritual mating. Nothing could destroy their love, once they had found each other on a pinnacle so lofty that ordinary adversities could not touch it. Perhaps she could achieve the miracle and draw George up to her level of consciousness.

Evangeline knew that, despite what any of the newspaper articles had said, she and her George, like Mariska and the fictional George, had some very difficult planetary combinations between their two horoscopes. She must have believed she could overcome them; her own teacher, Dr. J. Heber Smith, who had pointed out such astrological liabilities in her earlier relationships, would never have approved.

We shouldn't overlook the lure of sex, either. If George Jordan's appearance and physique were not appealing to the women on Adams' staff, he was still a young man. Age differences hadn't mattered to Evangeline in her youth, and they certainly didn't inhibit her now. Like most career women of her day, she had probably chosen to delay marriage until after she was past child-bearing age. She was now at a point where she need not fear pregnancy (birth control, although available by that time, was still considered shocking in most circles).

Whatever the reason or explanation, the marriage went ahead as planned, accompanied, of course, by a wave of promotion and publicity. Evangeline's lucky planet, Jupiter, in its twelve-year cycle around the zodiac, had once more returned to the place it had occupied when she had gotten so much publicity for the Windsor Hotel Fire in 1899 and her first arrest in 1911. It promised to be an auspicious time. Keeping the public's perceptions in mind, Adams claimed to be fifty and Jordan forty-two on their marriage license; in reality, she was fifty-five and he thirty-two. They were married quietly on a Thursday afternoon at the Little Church Around the Corner. While Evangeline had not kept up with her Christian roots, church records nevertheless indicate that she still considered herself a Congregationalist. Jordan, as befitting his age and present occupation, was Unitarian.

The *New York Herald* of April 7, 1923 announced that the marriage would,

... result in a merger of their interests, which will just about give them a monopoly. Their horoscopes have said right along that they should marry late in life. They intend to sail for Europe, and after a short trip will go to England to negotiate for the opening of a branch office there. If that scheme is successful they will be the only international firm in the astrology business.

Although the English deal fell through, promotion continued. After a two-month honeymoon, the couple returned to New York. Jordan could well have been the one to arrange for reporters to meet them upon landing. Their marriage was already old news. Evangeline concentrated, instead, on looking ahead and made some unusual predictions for the near and more distant future of the United States. The following is from a *Brooklyn Eagle* article dated June 14, 1923:

Arriving Astrologist Sees New World War Due in 1942

There's no hope for prohibition this year. The stars are against it. Evangeline Adams arrived today on the White Star liner Homeric from Cherbourg and Sharpton.... "The planets turn men's minds to the wet trail" she said. This condition will last till the end of the year.

"Jupiter has been retrograde for the last three months. When it turns in the opposite direction, the market will do what it hasn't been doing – go bullish."

"From 1942 to 1944, the United States will be involved in another civil war. Uranus will be in the sign of Gemini – where it stationed in the Revolutionary and Civil wars. The war will start in America and spread until it becomes the greatest war the world has ever known."

Certainly Adams was incorrect for the moment regarding prohibition – it continued till 1933. And her market forecast this time was wrong. The summer of 1923 suffered a brief slump, with some analysts seeing the period as a mini-bear market. As in her New York City forecast, Evangeline used a horoscope of the United States based on its "birthday" of July 4, 1776. While the time she used has been hotly debated among astrologers and historians since, it produced a chart with a Gemini ascendant, or Gemini rising, hence her mention of Gemini. But Adams' forecast for a war in 1942, nearly twenty years away, if not accurate in its details, is nevertheless chilling to consider in retrospect.

Chapter 12: Big Business

Under George Jordan's guidance, Evangeline's astrology business grew by leaps and bounds over the next several years. Adams garnered a profile in *The Biographical Cyclopaedia of American Women*, which appeared in 1924. Columbia Pictures announced that it would film "The Life of Evangeline Adams," and was negotiating with May Robson to play the lead. Adams' office space had tripled by 1926, so that she now held almost half of the tenth floor of the Carnegie Hall Studios tower – a tremendous amount of space. Jordan maintained a suite of his own on the ninth floor, still segregating himself from direct involvement in the day-to-day operations.

The mail order business, in particular, increased rapidly as a result of promotion and publicity. Various accounts cite increasing numbers of assistants and secretaries – from "more than a dozen" to forty-four. Most were part time and many were temporary, and the number varied with the work load. The employee pool consisted of stenographers, secretaries, writers and mathematicians, with the bulk of them being women. Most, if not all, learned how to cast horoscopes and must have learned at least something about astrology.

With Jordan came "big business methods, steel files and systems" according to an article in *Outlook* magazine. Public relations coverage was done on a wide scale, with many newspaper and magazine write-ups. Work on Adams' big astrology book had been halted in favor of her autobiography, which would serve as their biggest promotional vehicle to date. Everything was done in an organized and business-like fashion.

While the office waiting area still boasted signed photos and endorsements from famous clients, tier upon tier of filing cabinets soon lined the walls, containing the birth data of thousands of people across the country. Near the entrance was a receptionist's desk, where appointments were made by phone or in person. Visitors could easily find brochures on "The Law and Astrology" (featuring testimonials and a summary of the 1914 trial), copies of old interviews, and the stock mimeographed biography of Miss Adams. A huge anteroom contained the desks of many assistants, with much natural light from the broad tenth floor windows facing West 56th Street . At the back, where she could supervise it all, was Mary

Scheinman's desk. Beyond this lay Miss Adams' office, and she was formal enough to always be called "Miss Adams" by all of her employees, including Mary. Adams' room had an exotic flavor, with oriental rugs and ornately carved Jacobean furniture. Evangeline's many elephant figurines remained a presence and shared the space with a large Buddhist statue and other Asian artworks. Not much attention had been paid to the decoration over the years, and the office was more functional than attractive. Yet it still somehow bore an air of Victorian New England. Bookcases lined the back wall, and included many of Adams' rare astrology volumes and a *Who's Who* for finding celebrity birthdays. There was one chair for the client, slightly smaller than Miss Adams', across from a desk. An overstuffed sofa lay by the window; heavy draperies on the remaining walls gave a somber look. The brass chandelier that had been criticized by the novelist Richard Harding Davis twenty years before was still in evidence. The ceilings were quite high and enormous windows made the office airy and spacious.

Adams had doubled her prices since 1915, with the charge for a personal interview now $20 for a half hour. There was no over-lapping of appointments: a secretary would sound a buzzer to indicate when the proper time had elapsed. Adams would see up to ten people a day, but in later years, in order to conserve her strength and spend more time on her books and other promotions, she cut back to twenty-five a week. Yet from personal readings, alone, Evangeline could, therefore, make from $500 to $1000 a week, at a time when the median American income was around $2000 a year. She did, of course, have mail-order income as well, but added expenses with all of the employees. Her rent was comparatively low, with the office, considered a "posh" address, only $2,400 for the entire year. Appointments were much in demand and had to be booked at least several weeks in advance. When one was cancelled, there was always someone else eager to fill the void. Evangeline had early on made it a rule not to break appointments herself and felt this contributed to her success.

Those with less cash, or who lived in other parts of the country, could always send away for written work by mail. A natal horoscope delineation sold for $10 and contained about twenty-five pages. It was said to "assist in further understanding the inborn aptitudes manifesting themselves, and latent possibilities." Some of the report was boiler-plate about astrology and how to use it, but most was made up of the mimeographed sheets addressing personal horoscope placements and included a short personal forecast for the future. The message was consistent: the stars impel, they do not compel. Don't be afraid of astrology, it can help you. Forewarned is forearmed. You can shape your own future if you dare.

The planetary report for one year was the most popular, particularly for businessmen,

Serving as a daily guide in business, health, domestic and social matters, pointing out the most auspicious periods for asking favors, for inaugurating new ventures, planning social functions, as well as when to travel, when to make new friends, when to avoid misunderstandings, when it will be necessary to give more than usual attention to health, and also when it would be well to utilize your time for routine work alone.

This was based on current transits of the planets, calculated only from the date and year, and as such, was applicable to all. Selling for $25, it was a big moneymaker, as the work had only to be done once, and then copied. Clients would subscribe and were sent the forecasts on a monthly basis.

The personal planetary indications also sold for $25; rather than addressing the world at large, these concentrated on what the individual should expect for the next five years. In George E. Jordan's illimitable flowery prose, it was said to address the current horoscope by,

Outlining the big swings of life by which all successful men and women set their sails to the fullest capacity, and with willingness, supreme confidence and self-control through intelligent non-resistance guide themselves and their ambition through the path of life.

Evangeline Adams was by now middle-aged, with salt and pepper hair and a stocky build. Her square jaw was now even more so, and her face was furrowed. She had continued wearing spectacles, and preferred sensible shoes. Her fashionableness had given way to piquant eccentricity. Soft-spoken, she nevertheless possessed a clear voice, and had retained her Boston dialect. Adams had never had a bubbly or charming personality and was still reserved and formal, almost somewhat dour in manner. She didn't smile easily, and most photos show an almost grim visage. But she was kind, sincere, *nice*. People liked her, and she was well thought of. Prominent astrologer Ellen McCaffery, writing a few years after Adams' death, said she had met,

...many hundreds of Evangeline Adams' clients, and more than 90% still speak with gratitude and admiration. Whether through her

astrological expertise or simply her experience of life, she had the ability to help many through their problems of life.

Iris Vorel concurred, saying that those who knew Evangeline could "write volumes about her benevolence and sympathy." Estimates of Adams' annual income place it at about $50,000, which would have made her wealthy at that time, though Adams did not live extravagantly. Her house was not ostentatious or large, and money was spent primarily on travel or antiques, there being time for little else, considering the press of her business obligations.

Evangeline reserved her mornings for meeting with the staff, planning the day and attending to correspondence: and there was an enormous amount of correspondence. Requests for new orders were accompanied by follow-up notes, cards of thanks, and letters outlining exactly how Evangeline's forecasts had come to pass. One magazine article a few years before had supposedly drawn 11,700 letters in a few days. Against her own advice and better judgement, Adams typically ate lunch on the run. The afternoons were left for consultations, regularly scheduled in advance. The horoscope chart was pulled for repeat clients, or quickly drawn up by assistants.

After the client was ushered into Adams' office, Evangeline first studied the chart, then entered into discussion regarding current problems and concerns. She had said in her autobiography that,

The horoscope shows the balance of forces at work in my client's life. Often it shows a lack of coordination between the mental and spiritual, and I believe it to be my task, with the light of astrology, to assist him so far as possible to regulate his powers and so bring balance or harmony into his life. I strive to be governed by honesty and charity, but I do not burden my client with my considerations of general truth and balance. I deal with his situation. If he comes with shoulders bent under the burden of life, I am usually able by studying his stars to help him to distribute the weight so it may be carried without loss of equilibrium.

While Evangeline strove to be impartial and objective, she felt more and more the need to "comfort and uphold" her clients as they struggled to follow the patterns indicated by their horoscopes, and often referred to clients as her "astrological children." She felt she could see the difficulties which lay before and behind them, and tried, compassionately but realistically, to help them achieve balance. This, she felt, would inspire health, confidence and courage as it was based on the divine law as revealed by the horoscope. Adams did not ordinarily trouble her clients with these philosophical thoughts, however. She was practical and addressed immediate problems. In understanding that all things must come to an end, that bothersome situations would clear up in time, she helped many to avoid becoming discouraged.

Adams received more personal visits from women, but said that her clientele was evenly balanced between the sexes. Men had a tendency to either write or telephone, and sometimes even sent their wives for the information they needed, as the playwright Eugene O'Neill did.

Evangeline claimed in an April, 1927 *Brooklyn Eagle* interview, that, "I work 18 hours a day and have done so for over a quarter century." While this is surely an exaggeration (giving her less than six hours a day to eat, sleep and do anything else!), she was truly a workaholic. She continued,

There is no game, no diversion, I could engage in that would be half so fascinating as my own profession. I see the whole world pass by me in microcosm. What could I possibly do which would be half so absorbing? The heartaches of the world as well as the hopes and strivings come to me for help.

Throughout the years, Evangeline had refused to give specific information on particular stocks, or to predict the daily fluctuations of the market. She felt this was impossible, and relied, instead, on examining the larger swings, at times forecasting the direction the cycles would be heading. The most important thing she considered was whether the individual horoscope promised luck from speculation (Evangeline thought her own did not, so she could not benefit from her own advice).

Adams continued to enjoy consulting on marriage, profession and birth, even advocating Caesarian births to insure more favorable signs for the newborn. She felt that parents had a responsibility to help their children develop in the manner their horoscopes indicated and to avoid imposing their own ambitions on their offspring. In the most delicate way possible, she even supported birth control. The following is from *The Bowl of Heaven*:

I am concentrating my efforts at present toward helping fathers and mothers to bring out the possibilities of the youngsters they already have – and postponing until a more receptive future a consideration of the babies they know not of.

(It must be remembered that even though birth control was moving into the mainstream, thoughts of this kind were still radical in the twenties; Margaret Sanger's clinic was raided by New York City police as late as 1929.)

One of the most gratifying tasks Adams enjoyed was her work over several years for an adoption agency. She would read the babies' horoscopes and advise on the best type of home for them, occasionally comparing them with the charts of prospective parents.

Although skeptics continued to doubt, Adams' work spread across the country. The *Outlook* article concluded that:

She is a powerful influence, maligned by some as a sucker-grabber, faker, and racketeer, but to many she is faith and hope – Evangeline Adams of Carnegie Hall.

Evangeline's supporters seemed to now greatly outweigh the few opposed. Claiming to have over 100,000 clients in her thirty years of experience, Adams felt that she, herself, was constantly learning from them. Their lives and experiences illuminated their horoscopes for her. But Evangeline also continued to learn about life. She felt she learned most from the men and women who "see life's problems in the raw," those who had crossed the line, so to speak. In this category she placed blackmailers and robbers, as well as women with many lovers: she felt they helped her to understand particular problems and thus allowed her to better help her more conventional clients. She also concluded that "there are very few people in the world so far gone that astrology cannot help them to come at least part of the way back." But she was also chagrinned to learn that a woman who had kept a "questionable resort" had for many years used her planetary indications in order to avoid trouble with the police!

Adams did find, as time went by, an increasing diversity of women's interests. While formerly interested primarily in the home, love and marriage, in the 1920's women asked more questions about business, travel, stardom, and even the horoscopes of their pets. Of course, relationships were a key issue for many.

Evangeline often counseled delaying marriage for couples she felt were mismatched. In the *Woman's Home Companion* of June, 1925, she described her advice:

My usual method, when I find a girl and a man rushing to their doom, is to suggest delay. If I ask either of them to take my word that the attraction is temporary and physical, they invariably feel that what I say might be true of the average couple, but that they are exceptions and that nothing could make them less interested in each other. But in many cases, they have the faith in the science to say: "Oh well, if by waiting a while we are going to be much happier, we'll be on the safe side and do so." They often come back to me, after waiting beyond the limit of the first physical attraction, and tell me they found that they were so completely out of harmony that they broke the engagement.

Some of Adams' clients were legendary and included prominent men and women from innumerable professions. Evangeline had always remained popular with people in the entertainment field, and she served countless legitimate stage and movie actors. Although she was always careful of confidences, she often got permission to make specific mention of some of the stars she counseled. Certainly, many of these people craved publicity and were only too glad to endorse the astrologer's work. When some died, Adams apparently felt free to use their names, as in the case of J.P. Morgan. Metropolitan Opera singer Lillian Nordica, still remembered as one of the great Wagnerian sopranos, was one of her early New York clients. Other famous singers included Geraldine Farrar and Riccordo Martin, also of the Met; and Manhattan and Chicago Opera Company soprano Mary Garden. The famous actress Mrs. Leslie Carter was one of Adams' first New York clients. Stage actresses Laurette Taylor, Ina Claire and Eva Le Gallienne were friends and probably clients. Actor Richard Mansfield had not only his own horoscope, but those of his wife and son read, too. Dramatist August Thomas is forgotten today, but was then well-known for the Broadway shows *The Witching Hour* and *Harvest Moon*. Evangeline's relationship with him was possibly reciprocal, as Thomas had for some years been a press agent for the thought-reader Washington Irving Bishop. Even Charlie Chaplin and screenwriter Anita Loos were said to have consulted Adams. It was reported that Mary Pickford changed travel plans when Evangeline warned against a plane trip. Producer Charles Wagner rounded out the list. Other creative clients included English travel and adventure novelist Talbot Mundy; author and literary agent Elizabeth Marbury; Ray Long, editor of *Cosmopolitan* magazine; and Lord Northcliffe, founder of the *British Daily Mail* and *Daily Mirror*.

Those on the "social register" had both more money and time to spare, and these, too, made up a large portion of Adams' clientele. Mrs. Oliver Harriman, Mrs. August Belmont, Lady Paget, Gloria Morgan Vanderbilt and her sister Thelma were all said to have consulted Evangeline.

There were many prominent businessmen and politicians represented in Adams' client files as well. John W. Weeks was a Massachusetts Congressman, one-time U.S. Senator, and later Secretary of War under President Harding. As his Boston brokerage house was one of the largest and most respected in the country, he may have sought financial advice and was an early client. Although Adams didn't reveal their names, the head of the New York institutions for the insane also consulted her, as did a director of the Horse Show Association. Another one of her famed businessmen clients was James J. Hill, president and chairman of the Great Northern Railroad. His actions, along with those of Edward Harriman and J.P. Morgan, had precipitated the panic of May 9, 1901. Evangeline also mentions the charts of social acquaintanceships who were probably not her clients. These include Cardinal Gibbons, Reggie Vanderbilt, and William Jennings Bryan.

Adams often reiterated that it was against her principles to predict the results of elections or prize fights. Perhaps she felt that she would encourage gambling or influence the outcomes if she did so. There were a number of notable exceptions to this supposed rule, however. *The New York Telegram* reported that in June of 1923, Evangeline had stated that President Warren G. Harding was "under particularly good planetary influences, with consequent benefit to the nation." Unfortunately, Harding died suddenly of a heart attack in August! (Nevertheless, Adams still claimed in the *Woman's Home Companion* of June, 1925, that Harding's horoscope, "clearly indicated his elevation to high office as well as his early death.") Evangeline thought she did better regarding Calvin Coolidge's chances in 1924, saying that his election to the presidency "was astrologically, as well as politically a foregone conclusion. He was under the very best of conditions." That year, people seemed to be even more interested in the New York Governor's race, with many assuming that young Colonel Theodore Roosevelt, Jr., would win against incumbent Al Smith. Evangeline felt there was no contest because "Mr. Roosevelt was under the very worst of conditions that will afflict his horoscope for twenty-one years." She was right, though she may not have publicly made these last two forecasts; they appeared afterwards in her autobiography. In 1928, Evangeline had also forecast that New York State Governor Al Smith would win in his presidential bid against Herbert Hoover; as luck would have it, he didn't.

There were many more predictions, which may or may not have been public, but which became part of promotional efforts after the fact. Adams was said to have predicted within a few days the Tokyo earthquake of 1923, which killed 150,000, and she claimed to have announced in advance the success of Lindbergh's 1927 transatlantic flight, based on a chart for his take-off time. She "knew" the outcome of the 1927 championship bout between Gene Tunney and Jack

Dempsey, but it would have been in poor sporting form to reveal it beforehand. Some predictions were on a lesser scale. When Adams found George Jordan to be in an accidental period, she advised caution. Even so, upon opening a bottle of champagne (during prohibition, no less!), the cork blew out with such force that it smashed his glasses. Evangeline was also said to have predicted the sex of a calf born to Jessie, a cow on her Westchester farm.

We must also consider the problematic predictions of death. If astrology, as Evangeline had testified in court, only indicated tendencies, and we have free will, how could any astrologer forecast death?

Yet Evangeline reports in *The Bowl of Heaven* that she predicted many deaths. She told a businessman client that, "Either the scheme would die or someone essential to it would die." The essential party turned out to be one-time State Senator J.J. Frawley. (Adams had earlier claimed that Frawley would die suddenly while away from home, which she says also proved to be the case.) To a woman client seeking divorce, she advised reconciliation, because: "The stars indicated as clearly as the dawn indicates the coming day that the husband would not live anyway beyond the following July."

This, too, supposedly came to pass. An early client was actor Joseph Jefferson, famed for his interpretation of Rip van Winkle. Adams said that, "It was my sad duty to foresee the great man's death, and to know in advance that it would happen within thirty days of the time it actually took place."

And Evangeline reportedly also forecast the death of Rudolph Valentino in 1926.

We must remember that these later claims always contain two things: embellishment with time, and promotional value. Evangeline, in print, may thus make claim to greater accuracy than she possessed; and we don't actually know what she did 'say in the original client consultations. Using orthodox astrology, she could easily have forecast a period problematic to health: subsequent death would prove her correct. This seems to be the case in her "prediction" of the death of Tammany Hall leader Charles F. Murphy. An employee of Murphy's was a regular client and often asked about his boss. In 1924, Evangeline, (from her own autobiographical account), told him that "I see conditions unfriendly to the stomach." When the client called two days later, she informed him that, "It's all over now, he's either dead or alright." He was dead, of acute indigestion. But what had she actually said? The credibility of these accounts always remains at least somewhat questionable, simply because they are found in a promotional vehicle, her autobiography, and after the fact. Finally, we must also remember that we hear only the "hits" and not the "misses." Evangeline never tells us when she was wrong – her reports are consistently biased in her favor.

And what of *New York Mirror* writer Philip Payne, who died in his failed attempt to fly to Rome in the plane *Old Glory*? Adams tells us about this consultation in her later book, *Astrology, Your Place in the Sun*. Payne had asked her about the probable success of this venture. The horoscope for take-off, she says, clearly indicated "the long delays before starting off, the unexpected happenings and the ultimate disaster which overtook him." But, if this were the case, why hadn't he followed Adams' advice?

If we think back to Evangeline's 1914 trial, we should again consider the testimony of detective Adele D. Priess. She had stated that Adams told her, "Your son should be very careful for he will die as the result of an accident or die very suddenly just like that," as Evangeline snapped her fingers. This Adams had vehemently denied in court in order to avoid conviction. Yet she so often discusses death in print that it seems probable that she may have put this dire forecast in just that way, in which case she should have been found guilty of fortune-telling.

The practice of Adams' astrology appears at least somewhat at odds with her stated theory of free will. Indeed, the concepts of fate and free will are intrinsic to astrology itself, which posits that there are celestial forces which impact on our lives. The influence of these forces has been variously interpreted throughout the centuries. The Chaldeans thought they could be overcome through magical means, while the Roman Stoics believed that God created an immutable future. Christianity has always been uneasy with astral determinism, as its tenets are based on a deity who can intervene in human affairs. Christianity also needed to support free will, since its followers see themselves as responsible for their own actions.

Astrologers are known for predicting the future, and this is what people expect from them, even today. Many, in fact, feel that the proof of astrology lies in its ability to determine definite outcomes, much as science is purported to do. (Early twenty-first century astrologers typically shy away from traditional forecasting techniques, but at the same time, newspaper and magazine horoscope columns are more popular than ever.)

Although astrological forecasting is often extraordinarily complex, most astrologers practice it, whether they admit to doing so or not. As soon as one describes an influence for a particular period of time in the future, it is a form of prediction. This might be qualified by saying the outcome is God's will or dependent on one's own strength of character. Astrologically speaking, fate and free will are not diametrically opposed, but part of a larger whole. Evangeline Adams, as many astrologers before and since, benefitted from discussing the idea of fate, while at the same time reassuring the public that they had control over their own lives.

Not long after their marriage, George Jordan began to book Evangeline on speaking engagements, which also increased her visibility and reputation. One of the first was held on Sunday, January 2, 1927, at St. Marks Church on East 10th Street in Manhattan. The church was filled to capacity, and the religious and mystical atmosphere was further emphasized by the burning of incense and chanting voices of a minister, deacon, and cantor (the latter likely her friend, Rabbi Charles Fleischer). Although others shared the podium, Adams was the featured speaker. According to a newspaper clipping from Evangeline's niece Gertrude's scrapbook, Evangeline first contrasted the charts of Napoleon and Mussolini. The latter had come to power in 1922, and his authoritarian practices were already apparent. Adams cautioned that "unless he exercises undue wisdom, Mussolini may go down to defeat in two years." He must have found some of that "undue wisdom," since history tells us that he remained in power for over twenty years. Yet Adams followed up with some more accurate predictions, in particular reiterating her forecast for World War II:

Miss Adams said the signs point to a war from three different angles, for religious, racial and political reasons, in 1942, 1943 and 1944. The same sign was in the ascendant when the U.S. entered the War of Independence and again in the Civil War.

Finally, Evangeline left her audience with a forecast for the next few years:

"Beginning with 1927," Miss Adams continued, "with the influences more pronounced in 1928 and 1929, Uranus will be more unfortunate to Jupiter, which rules money matters on a material plane, than in 1921. In 1907 this aspect operated with the result that the United States had a terrific financial panic. It behooves everyone to be extremely cautious in investment and money matters, and be prepared for this threatening configuration of planets."

These are again examples of Adams' use of simple historic cycles. Uranus takes approximately eighty-four years to complete one circuit of the zodiac. In 1776 we had the Revolutionary War;

eighty-four years later, or about 1860, the Civil War began.
Astrological cycles suggested that eighty-four years later, 1944,
would mark another period of war for the U.S. Uranus was also
involved in Evangeline's financial prediction. It had formed a
stressful aspect to the U.S. chart in 1907, creating financial problems
(the "Panic of 1907"). One-quarter of a cycle later, approximately
twenty-one years or about 1928, these conditions should return.

In order to avoid the possibility of arrest, Adams is quite careful
to point towards the particular indications from the horoscope of the
United States which help her form her judgement. She was only
interpreting the signs. And, although this was a public event with
press coverage, the New York City police department kept away
from the scene, and no fortune-telling charges were filed.

What was an Adams reading actually like? There exist a few
first-hand accounts which give us a better idea of how she operated.
Adams, herself, tells us in *The Bowl of Heaven* that she influenced
Tallulah Bankhead's career. The actress had at this time been in New
York for several years, but had not landed any great roles or made a
big splash yet.

*"Tallulah," I said to her one day in the summer of 1922, "you
are under particularly good conditions right now for traveling and
for success abroad."*

*"Oh!" she exclaimed. "I am, am I? I'll see Charles Cochran and
tell him he must give me something in London."*

*The great London manager, who happened to be in New York at
the moment, promised to let her know how things stood when he
returned to England. A fortnight later, he cabled that he had nothing
just then. Tallulah cabled right back saying she was determined to
act in London. He replied: "Do not come at present." But Tallulah
was not to be denied. "Go to hell," she cabled. "I am coming
anyway." Inside of a month she was the great success of Sir Gerald
Du Maurier's production of The Dancers.*

This play itself was a tremendous success, and within the next
eight years, Tallulah starred in fifteen London productions.
Bankhead tell us in her autobiography just how much Adams had to
do with this momentous decision: "Miss Adams told me my future
lay across the water. I was about to be paged from afar. In dismissing
me she said: "Go if you have to swim."

The same story from Bankhead's biographer, Lee Israel, is given
a more dramatic spin.

Tallulah had met the English impresario Charles Cochran at a New York party. She had been recommended by friends as well as a good review, and he asked her to audition for him. Impressed, Cochran returned to England, and soon cabled her regarding "a possible engagement" with Sir Gerald Du Maurier, then the best stage director and manager in London. Cochran told her they were,

"...quite excited about you, and I think there is but little doubt that if you care to take the risk of coming over you will be engaged."

Tallulah and Estelle [Winwood, another actress] frequently journeyed uptown to Riverside Drive to consult the famous seer Evangeline Adams, a dour Scotswoman who predicted the future using a combination horoscope, cards, and the Bible, which she opened randomly and pricked with a pin. During such visits, they would invariably giggle nervously, especially when the mystic dealt the fearsome snake card to Estelle.

Upon receiving Cochran's letter, however, Tallulah went to see Miss Adams alone. There would be no giggling this time; the decision was serious business. Evangeline Adams opened the Bible and selected, at random, a section from 2 Kings which refers to Jezebel, the notorious wife of Ahab, King of Israel. She remained mute at the significance of the passage.

Tallulah returned to the Hotel Webster, where she and Estelle were now living, and told the older actress about what had happened. Estelle said with trepidation, "You realize, don't you, my dear, that Jezebel was thrown to the dogs?"

Tallulah, who had obviously given the matter some thought, replied, "Yes, I know. But before she was thrown to the dogs, she rode with kings and queens." The decision was made.

Tallulah was devastated when, in a matter of days, she received from Charles Cochran another cable telling her not to come. Consorting again with Estelle, she had the solution. She would go anyway, pretending that she had never received the second cable. They would not have the nerve to send her home after she had crossed the ocean just to do the part.

Although this story offers direct corroboration of Adams' influence, we are left with some discrepancies. Evangeline gives all the credit to astrology, but Lee Israel speaks of other divination techniques. As Israel is incorrect in referring to Adams as living on Riverside Drive and being Scottish, we have cause to doubt her details. She may be mixing Evangeline up with another reader, or perhaps she embellished for effect. Adams was never known to use tarot cards. Bankhead, in her autobiography, had only discussed

Adams' use of astrology. But the technique of getting direct messages from the Bible that Lee Israel mentions was one commonly used by the theologian Austin Phelps, father of Evangeline's Sunday school teacher Elizabeth Stuart Phelps. Since it was also used by Iris Vorel's fictional astrologer Mariska, we can wonder if Adams might have used this method herself. When we read some of the other statements about Adams' consultations, it seems that there might have been more than simple astrology going on.

Arthur Hopkins was a successful theatrical producer of the time. He first came to see Adams in the early teens, after he had begun producing plays in New York. In his autobiography, *Letters to a Lonely Boy* from 1937, he told of his earlier experience with Evangeline Adams.

The one professional clairvoyant whom I have known was Evangeline Adams, the astrologist. While she based her findings and predictions on hastily drawn charts, I have always believed that she was a seer in the true sense and could have accomplished startling results with tea leaves, a crystal ball or any other medium of concentration.

I first went to her out of curiosity and was ignorantly skeptical. I had produced only two or three plays at the time and was practically unknown. Taking no chances, however, and thinking to make it more difficult for her, I wrote for an appointment under an assumed name. I was determined in advance to answer no questions.

I went to her studio, and, as I sat across the table from her, was impressed by her strong, wise, honest, New England face. Here was no trace of charlatanism. I gave her my birth date and the hour as nearly as I could.

She made some quick markings on a chart, consulted what looked like key books, made additional markings and in a moment I heard the salient parts of my past, together with a description of my characteristics being so accurately summed up as to startle me. She asked no questions. I volunteered no information. Then she said:

"You are in some artistic activity that has to do with others. I should say it was the theater and that you are a producer. You haven't done much yet but your work is new and different. Yes – that's it. I should say that you are Arthur Hopkins."

That may be listed as one of the major surprises of my life. She told me many things, then and later, and I do not remember her being wrong. I did not always follow her. There was once when she advised me to be inactive for what seemed an interminable period.

She assured me that during that time nothing would succeed, no matter what merit it had. I protested that I could not just step out of the way until the storm had passed. Perhaps the storm was to be part of my experience too, a part I had no right to avoid.

She was right. The storm came and lasted a long time. Somehow I think I was right, too, to battle it.

There was a time when I was considering going to Hollywood. There were two offers, both more than generous as to money, but both rather indefinite as to what freedom of expression I might have. I went to Miss Adams, thinking that she might determine in which studio I would encounter the more sympathetic attitude.

She asked me the name of the man I was dealing with in the larger company. I gave it to her. She found his birth date in Who's Who in America and had scarcely finished her speedy chart outline when she recoiled as though she had been struck. "Oh!" she said. "This man is about to go through a dreadful time. He's going to lose everything he's got, including his present position. You can't look to him."

The man of whom she spoke was at the time worth millions. He was vice president in charge of production of one of the largest picture companies. He had been one of the founders. No position could seem more secure, no fortune more safe, but all that she predicted came true...

The second picture offer was disposed of more speedily. Who's Who imparted another birth date.

"You can't bank on him," she said. "He'll not be there six months."

He wasn't. The fledgling producer never did make it to Hollywood, concentrating his efforts, instead, on the Broadway stage. Hopkins' story does have the ring of truth to it, even if it was written well after the fact. His big productions, such as Shakespearean plays with John Barrymore and designer Robert Edmund Jones, were popular in the late teens and early 1920's, and he was "practically unknown" when he visited Adams; the account *was* written about twenty years after the events described. Yet Hopkins does offer some curious details. He begins by referring to Evangeline as "clairvoyant": she might have been. While she always claimed that her powers were purely the result of "scientific" astrological expertise, many have felt that there was something more. Her intuition, through years of work with horoscopes and clients, had been developed to a high degree. So much so, that it seems to have gone even further, with a psychic attunement perhaps contributing to her readings.

How did Adams know her client's real name, without being told? If we are to believe this statement, then we must conclude that Adams was indeed a true sensitive, or psychic. But even the most gifted of psychics are rarely known to produce much more than initials or a first name. We must also remember that Hopkins is writing in retrospect. If Adams surprised him with accurately knowing his vocation, couldn't he have embellished more details, even in his own mind, over the next twenty years? Adams was also an avid theater-goer, and could possibly have known who her client actually was. Once again we can only speculate.

Evangeline's advice is direct, concise, and to the point. She appears to be quite decisive, and, as she so often said herself, is honest about upcoming planetary influences, whether she felt them to be favorable or not. While astrology concentrates on cycles and timing, Adams comes to a real conclusion when she offers such advice as "He's going to lose everything" and "He'll not be there six months." Most astrologers, especially without proper times of birth, would have only stated that both men should beware of the possibility of business or financial reversals for a particular period of time. These predictions go way beyond what Evangeline stated in court; if these statements are not exaggerations, Adams is literally breaking the law here, as she's predicted specific outcomes in no uncertain terms. If true, they entitle the People to a conviction! Hopkins, however, is completely convinced of Adams' accuracy; he has a bias. Unless he made exact notes immediately after the interview, his statements are drawn from memory, which is subject to even more distortion due to his strong bias in Adams' favor.

Our best record of Evangeline Adams' work comes from the late educator and mythologist, Joseph Campbell. On Tuesday, November 10, 1925, at the age of twenty-one, Campbell visited Adams, and immediately wrote of his experience in his journal. This rules out the kind of creative remembering that probably contributed to Arthur Hopkins' report. Campbell apparently had a general reading, but also asked Adams about a current relationship. His journal notes are preserved in *A Fire in the Mind*, Stephen and Robin Larsen's biography of Campbell. Campbell wrote,

She told me my ruling planet was Venus – that I was either an Episcopalian or a Roman Catholic – that I loved beauty and art – that I'd make a good actor, journalist or playwright – that I'd have to cast about, probably till 1927, before finding my life work – that I

should not worry about my vocation, but try to get the most out of the present. Rosalie, she said, is far more practical than I – and she would judge a man's success in terms of his ability to support a happy family. She will probably not continue at law, and if she does continue she will probably take it very literally. She and I are tremendously attracted to each other physically because her planet Venus & my Mars are almost coincident – but our other inclinations are in totally different directions. If we were to marry we should after the third year be unhappy, for the physical attraction would have waned, & we should have left almost nothing in common. We are at crossroads, going two different ways – it would be suicide for either to turn aside into the way of the other. Rosalie's will is a great deal stronger than mine & I would probably be the one to forfeit individuality and full expression for the 2+2=4 of life, of being a practical husband. She told me that I am tending away from family traditions – that I am inclined toward mysticism – that I could have been a priest, but that I would have been uncomfortable under orthodox restrictions.

Adams is typically honest and authoritative in her astrological assessment of Campbell's relationship, evaluating it in a definitive manner and advising him against marriage, as she had so often done with many other clients. Evangeline is presented in this account as being within the letter of the law in her interpretations. Joseph Campbell consistently reports the use of such safe words as "probably," "inclinations," "should" and "tending," rather than absolutes. His interview was also at a later date than Arthur Hopkins', and he was a much younger man. The differences in Adams' style could have been part of her development over the years, as her trouble with the law had left her cautious.

Campbell's biographers agree that Adams' descriptions of Campbell and his girlfriend, as well as her forecast for subsequent events, "prove them true." Campbell returned to Adams a few years later, presumably getting a better verdict on his relationship with his future wife, Jean. And, in 1934, when he was offered a faculty position at Sarah Lawrence College in Bronxville, he remembered that Adams had told him in 1927 that this period in his life would be one of consolidating his impulses and beginning to find his own path. He accepted the position and remained with the college for nearly forty years.

According to Campbell, Adams seems to have practiced straight astrology. She did, however, describe the relationship in terms of colors and vibrations:

Rosalie, she said, has a very strong will, and a much more primitive constitution than I, with a vibration around the reds as com-pared with mine, which was about a thousand times faster & around the orchids.

Although it seems at first glance to hint at a reading of auras, Campbell's girlfriend had not been present, so her aura could not be read. It may well be that Evangeline, instead, utilized the idea of color as one way of translating the meaning of the horoscope to her client.

In her later book, *Astrology for Everyone*, Adams relates color to the signs of the zodiac:

The heavens are like a great glass dome divided, as the horoscope chart is divided, into twelve segments representing the twelve signs of the Zodiac. Each of these segments is of a different astrological color; and all are continuously moving, passing and repassing, shedding rays of varying strength and color and power.

And, indeed, for each sign she offers several ruling colors. Astrological signs had traditionally been associated with colors, but possibly Adams' use of this concept arose from Dr. J. Heber Smith, who in a more intellectual vein for an 1895 article on astrology in the radical journal *The Arena*, stated that,

These bodies of ours are fashioned from elemental harmonies equally evocable and vanishing, under the operation of light-rays that to the opening perceptions of the reverent student of nature appear not only colors but musical chords.

In other words, the astrologer can understand his work through the idea of color.

Adams also advised the famous playwright Eugene O'Neill on business. In March of 1927, O'Neill and his wife Agnes had moved to Bermuda. As Agnes' father was dying in April, she returned to Connecticut to visit him. While in New York City, she did some business errands for Eugene. According to Louis Sheaffer's biography of O'Neill,

Agnes also, at Eugene's request, called on Evangeline Adams, the astrologist, whom Bobby [Broadway designer Robert Edmund] Jones had recommended as remarkably prescient. Miss Adams, predicting a "bad financial slump for next year for the U.S." advised the playwright "to liquidate & get all overhead expenses cut down," but she also forecast that his economic situation would "pick up about October." Her final word was that he should "close" with the Theater Guild as soon as possible.

This little excerpt shows Adams reiterating her financial forecast for the U.S. in a personal interview; in the following year, 1928, it was to prove incorrect. We can also begin to see her chain of referrals, as Robert Edmund Jones had worked for many years with Arthur Hopkins and also recommended Evangeline to O'Neill. This account is also likely to be accurately recorded, as Agnes wrote her husband shortly after the reading. It seems as if O'Neill took Evangeline's advice seriously. The Theater Guild had been considering productions of O'Neill's plays *Marco Millions* and *Strange Interlude*, but would not make a commitment to *Strange Interlude* until they saw a cut script. O'Neill subsequently pushed for the producers to accept his work and visited New York himself in mid-May, when the Guild placed both plays under option.

Though he had earned only about $3,000 in royalties for his published plays each year during 1924 and '25, in 1926 O'Neill's income jumped to $7,000. Adams' forecast may have been, at least, partially correct, as O'Neill's income increased even more, to $12,000 in the year 1927.

These few personal accounts are in some ways consistent. Adams mainly used astrology; she no longer seemed to practice palmistry. Her clients were impressed with their readings and put faith in her judgement: Evangeline inspired confidence.

George E. Jordan, Jr. - Evangeline's husband

Evangeline on the steps of her Westchester, NY home

Evangeline's Office at Carnegie Hall

Adams in the early 1920's

Evangeline in 1930

The Jordan lot at the West Plainsfield, CT cemetery - where Adams is supposed to be buried.

Chapter 13: *Onward and Upward*

Adams had studied and been exposed to many systems of thought. From her Congregationalist background she had learned morality, discipline and faith; from Unitarianism, tolerance. The ways of Vedanta pointed toward the value of self-sufficiency and strength, as well as an understanding of cycles of experience. Spiritualism stressed the immortality of the soul. While Evangeline subscribed to none of these traditions completely, she took a little from each belief system. For Adams, astrology superseded all worldly religions. Being based on universal principles, or larger forces, it transcended them all. Astrology encompassed the whole cosmos, not any one creed. It thus represented for her the Ultimate Truth. The horoscope indicated tendencies, rather than deeds. One could either be constructive or destructive. It is up to all of us to develop our virtues and avoid negative tendencies. As Adams said, "The moment is ours – to do with it, not always what we will, but what we *should.*"

One of the main reasons for Evangeline's success was her great faith. She understood herself, and lived by her philosophy of life. Her mentor, Dr. J. Heber Smith, her own experiences and those of her clients, had convinced her of the infallibility of astral influences. While she would at times admit to making mistakes in interpretation, she believed that astrology was a divine science, that it was here to help us throughout life. She fully believed in the unfailing accuracy of astrology, and likened the horoscope chart to a map, with herself a guide for those journeying through life.

There were always certain inescapables that each person had to work with, indicated by the birth chart. These Adams saw as natural laws. When one understood them, he or she would be in a better position to deal with them in a constructive manner, but always within the imposed limitations: "Man should not strive too hard to be the master." Free will could be exercised only within the scope of the larger laws governing us. This was Adams' theory of intelligent non-resistance, which had been impressed upon her as a girl. The Universal Will knew best. In all her experience, Evangeline found that it was not to be outwitted; one might as well understand that at the outset.

For Adams, this was no sentence of doom, but a message of hope. In understanding the forces of God and Nature which govern us, we have a better chance of being happy and leading balanced lives. Astrology, by indicating the possible pitfalls, as well as periods of difficulty and success in life, could help us see our lives more objectively and have a better idea of the path we were on. "Evil results from allowing selfish desire to push on regardless of the rights and happiness of others." We must be aware that all of our actions are significant:

Everything is symmetrical. What is given out comes back. No one escapes the divine will. This is astrology's teaching.

The gambler, she felt, would always lose in the end, as he tries to get something for nothing.

Rather than implying passivity, Adams recommended responsibility. Astrology helps those who help themselves! Evangeline preached self-sufficiency, not dependence. She had no patience for those who sat at home waiting for good luck to find them. She felt that the will of the Infinite Power, stronger and wiser than our own, demanded that we work with the tide, rather than fight against it. Some times would be productive, while there must also be periods that suggested patience and fortitude. The key lay in becoming aware of and cooperating with the larger cycles of nature.

Although Evangeline had been exposed to a wide array of occult practices, she ultimately concentrated her energies on helping others to better understand themselves through astrology. She did, however, believe that all honest attempts to find God's truth were valid: "The veil is a thin one. No one can say with certainty how it can best be pierced." She earnestly supported all seekers, no matter how they chose to search.

Adams felt that all of us could raise ourselves to a level, even in the midst of disaster, where we could transmute difficult astrological influences into something grander and be able to learn from all of our experiences in life. Astrology could warn us sufficiently in advance for us to alter our paths, or accept those things out of our own control.

We can never be absolutely sure if Evangeline really believed all that she preached. Mary Scheinman, Adams' office manager, had a more ironic attitude, saying that "The bad things always happen, and the good things sometimes do." Many of Adams' more famous predictions make us wonder if the unavoidables take precedence over what any one individual can do to shape the stream of human events. It is a question that has troubled the faithful since the beginning of time. How powerful or absolute is God's will? How much freedom do we really have? Modern Americans wanted to believe that they were masters of their fates. Adams' stance seems particularly well-suited to her time and place: the twentieth century public would not buy astrology if it seemed too fatalistic.

Evangeline concluded her autobiography with personal reflections on her own life:

I am persuaded by my own mature happiness that my life has been what the stars decreed that it should be – a life of service to others. There is no limitation to the realm of astrology, but man's knowledge of that realm has definite boundaries. And it is my ambition, my one absorbing purpose, to push those boundaries into the infinite until they approach as near as it is possible for humanity to come to God.

The autobiography, *The Bowl of Heaven*, so often referred to in these pages, is a delight. Released in November of 1926, it was an immediate success, going through eight printings over the next four years, and being republished as late as 1970. George E. Jordan, Jr., cannot be deemed a total villain: without his influence, the book would have remained only a dream. It had been Evangeline's fondest wish to reach a wider audience, and she had finally been able to do so.

The book is narrated by Evangeline, who tells the story of her life. She is charm and delicacy itself, and she retains a Victorian sense of decorum and substance which had all but disappeared years earlier. *The Bowl* is a true Adams product: it relates her experiences and tells stories of people she's known. Complete with humor and irony, its fantastic tales of astrological prediction and celebrity experience are very appealing.

Jordan made sure that the book was reviewed and began a massive publicity effort. Certainly with Evangeline already a prominent figure, this was not difficult. *The New York Herald-Tribune* said:

The book is in no sense biography. It is a compendium of "cases" in which the horoscopical forecasts made by Miss Adams for this and that famous person were fulfilled in whole or in part by subsequent events. There is no record of failure; on the contrary, Miss Adams' belief in the infallibility of the stars is repeatedly stressed. Her faith in astrology is complete; her book is therefore utterly sincere. And because of the combination of author, subject and persons talked about, it is unquestionably interesting.

The New York Times suggested that, "Most readers will find many surprises, and the cynical no little amusement in her accounts of her clients." While the *Saturday Review of Literature* perceptively saw that, "Anyone who reads her well-written and interesting book will admit that producing this work alone has gone a long way toward justifying her choice of profession."

The book is extremely well-written. But, we may ask, who actually did write it? Evangeline herself had not been able to accomplish the task before. The book repeats stories previously told many times, summarizing and dramatizing the many press clippings Adams had collected. Yet, it is much more than that, as a consistent voice speaks throughout the work. Jordan probably oversaw the project; but if we consider his credited writing, he was decidedly not capable of the tone and style found in this book. Aleister Crowley, working ten years before, had probably never heard of this project. We can only speculate.

The teen-aged Joseph L. Mankiewicz had been on Adams' staff as a writer. Later to make a big mark in Hollywood for writing and directing such great films as *All About Eve*, *A Letter to Three Wives* and *The Barefoot Contessa*, Joe had entered Columbia University at age fifteen and worked for Adams before he graduated in 1928. Later known for his wit, class and satire, he might well have contributed some of the sparkling prose found in *The Bowl of Heaven*. He's said,

I've written about a lot of women – most of the time not as truthfully or perceptively as I would have liked to, for various reasons.

Maybe Adams was one of the first. Mankiewicz was an Aquarius like Evangeline, so she must have felt him a kind of kindred spirit astrologically. If we wonder why this unusual credit was never included on the famous screenwriter and director's resume, Mankiewicz, himself has also said that, "I don't think I've ever told the truth or confided in anyone the way external people do," and, "You haven't got the information to write a book about my life. Nobody ever will, except me. I can promise you!" A sixteen-year-old boy would not object to signing work-for-hire or confidentiality agreements as Aleister Crowley had.

Mary Scheinman had added much in the way of editing, but her role could have been even larger. As Evangeline also typically had other ghost writers on staff, we may never know exactly who deserves the most credit for this "autobiography."

Excerpts from the book were serialized in such popular national magazines as *Colliers*, *Woman's Home Companion*, and *Pictorial Review*. More interviews were conducted. The world-at-large would finally really know what Evangeline Adams and astrology were all about.

Or would they? Certainly, astrology was clarified. But Evangeline herself was further obscured. *The Bowl of Heaven* was written as a promotional piece. As such, it is free of bold confessions, dicey personal anecdotes, or any hint of sex. Today we are used to the juicy "tell all" biography. But Evangeline Adams was writing at a different time, and she was writing as a professional. Her readers, therefore, only get those facts which are either entertaining, or which support Adams' role as an astrological authority. The only flaw in this book as an autobiography is a lack of insight into its subject as a human being.

All the stories are consistent, relating one Adams success after another. She rubs elbows with the rich and famous, she runs a successful business, her predictions are, without exception, right on target. Another omission is any reference to Adams as a feminist pioneer: in most ways, she wasn't. Although she was independent, stood up for herself, broke social rules and accomplished many things that were uncommon for a woman of her day, the only cause Evangeline publicly espoused was astrology. While she might have gone beyond what most people thought was a *human being's* place, she remained within society's broad outlines of what was proper for a woman. Adams was always a lady who devoted herself to helping others, and this was not only an accepted realm, but also a glorified one as far as the Christian gospel was concerned. Her life was one of duty and self-sacrifice. Her careers – that of a teacher early in life, later as social worker (or astrological counselor), and finally writer, were all in socially accepted spheres for women. Her personal aspirations were simply to help others gain more understanding of the world in which they lived.

The typical criticism aimed at Adams was that she made a lot of money. Hints of duping the public and charging inflated fees were common. While it might be all right for a woman at the time to enter a helping profession, it was not as acceptable for her to make a good living from it. Perhaps the objection was that she earned through astrology; but though her fees were high, Adams was always a thoroughgoing business professional.

The Bowl of Heaven does present Evangeline as a kind, proud lady. Perhaps this was necessary in order that the public accept her. There must be no stain on her reputation. Astrology was weird enough in itself; a spoonful of sugar was probably thought necessary for the medicine to go down. The country had only recently witnessed the famous Scopes "monkey trial" in which Darwin's theory of evolution was pitted against the Bible's creation story. There was still a large segment of the population that regarded practices like astrology – however scientific they were alleged to be – as essentially evil. It is a testament to Evangeline's dedication, caution and professionalism that she was able to go as far as she did. Adams had set out to make the public "astrology conscious" and, incredibly, she had succeeded.

Given her unconventional vocation, the appearance of conventionality was necessary. Her marriage to a much younger man was chancy. As marriage licenses are part of the public record in New York State, both Adams and Jordan were aware that their near twenty-five-year age difference made a sensational story. They thus changed their ages for the record. While the ten-year difference they claimed was still substantial, it was, at least, not shocking.

Even though *The Bowl of Heaven* tells a pretty story, it is wholly acceptable because it is not only fascinating but extremely well done. Yet we may well wonder at statements such as the following:

People ask me why I don't give my forecasts to the newspapers. Public predictions which receive nationwide newspaper publicity savor too much of advertising. I see no objection to advertising – it is a great power – but I have never used it. And now, goodness knows, I don't need it. What I need – what the stars must help me find – are more hours of the day and night.

This statement is simply not true! Evangeline had advertised in the *New York City Directory* for many years, and certainly she frequently made public predictions. If she no longer placed advertisements *per se*, *The Bowl of Heaven* and her public relations efforts – interviews and book excerpts – were in effect doing the very same thing. It is intriguing that such an erroneous statement could get into print. Yet we must understand that advertising in the twenties often had very little truth to it. Ironically, Adams was once again stressing her honesty and professionalism by denouncing advertising. (Doctors and lawyers, for example, are still tacitly expected to be servants of the public good: advertising somehow cheapens the product.)

Although Evangeline had often forecast for the papers before, we do find fewer public predictions in the succeeding years. Making predictions in print was risky; one could be wrong. With a reputation to maintain, Evangeline could no longer afford to be wrong.

The release of *The Bowl of Heaven* in 1926 was a joyful event, but there was another that year as well. A few months earlier, Adams' niece Gertrude had given birth to her third child and first girl and had named her Evangeline Adams Curry. Here was another indication that the Adams legacy would live on.

Gertrude was much attached to her famous aunt and kept all of her press clippings and photos in a scrapbook. She also held onto her letters as well. These are all that remain of Evangeline's personal correspondence. But most of these, as usual, leave us frustrated and wanting more. Since Mary Scheinman usually travelled with Adams as secretary and companion, many of the letters were dictated and typed for the whole office. Addressed to "Everybody," instructions for duplication and distribution to her friends and relatives are often included.

We can glean a few personal facts from Evangeline's letters if we read between the lines. In the spring of 1927, she made her usual excursion to Europe, this time visiting England and France. Travel was, as usual, by ocean liner (flying had not yet become part of the tourist scene). Evangeline travelled on great liners like the Mauritania, Berengaria and Leviathan. Crossing the ocean via this leisurely method of travel was pleasant, a vacation in itself. The journey took a minimum of five days, and promised socializing, fine dining and entertainment galore. It was the proper way to go. Unlike the cruise lines of today, cabins were large and the beds comfortable. And, certainly a plus during the years of prohibition, drinks were practically free. We can easily imagine Evangeline enjoying a well-earned vacation on board, but unable to completely let go of work. Mary, with a portable typewriter, was regularly put to work with correspondence.

Evangeline's letters of June 25 and July 1, 1927 are typical in many respects. Although she usually refers to "we," the only other person mentioned is Mary Scheinman. George E. Jordan, Jr., is obviously absent. Perhaps he felt it necessary to oversee the office during the spring months. But, only four years after their marriage, the honeymoon was obviously over. It is poignant to consider that, now with a husband of her own, Adams is nevertheless still taking a vacation with a paid companion. This might be an indication that the Jordans' marriage had become (or had originally been) purely a business association.

Adams loved London, often commenting on the dignity and order of the people, "I only wish we would copy them in more ways than one." Her interests are unusually consistent. She tells of seeking out an antique door-knocker and attending the Presentation of New Standards by the King. As in earlier life, she again had a special thrill when the new Prince of Wales passed in his motor car – within two feet – and nodded to her. "The secret service man said we were the two luckiest Americans in London at that moment, and it could not have been planned."

Visits to museums, churches and libraries, on city bus tours and on day trips fill the letters, along with details on the weather, visits with friends and astrologers, and dining out. At fifty-nine, Adams seems active, yet speaks of catching a cold and having to retire early at times. In speaking of their visit to St. Paul's Cathedral, which necessitated a climb of over 400 steps, she says, "I must be better or I could not have stood it." Clearly, she had recently had a significant illness.

Evangeline had always been attracted to pomp and circumstance and was thrilled to be introduced to Lord Delaware, who gave the ladies a seat in the House of Lords to witness a political discussion. Later, Adams and Mary were invited by a few of the Members of Parliament to listen to debates from their own private gallery. Evangeline was stimulated by the discussion and gratified to learn that even some of these important politicians had heard of her. She planned on visiting the world-famous Greenwich Observatory (since the seventeenth century the center for planetary almanacs), and then went on to Paris.

Back at home, work continued as usual. The staff was gearing up for publication of Evangeline's second book, *Astrology, Your Place in the Sun*. This book was actually about astrology. Even so, it was still not the project Evangeline had originally envisioned, which was to be a more sophisticated and comprehensive textbook. *Your Place in the Sun* only introduced the reader to astrology: it was designed for the general public and, as such, was no doubt another Jordan product. (Some of Aleister Crowley's writing probably went into it as well.) The book outlined the twelve signs of the zodiac and described the planets in some detail. It also included a table of ascendants, so that readers might find their rising signs, as well as simple instructions for casting a horoscope, and descriptions of the twelve houses of the birth chart. (These last three encompassed only a small portion of the final work.) *Astrology, Your Place in the Sun* addresses the simple sun-signs that are familiar from newspaper forecasts. The book was accessible to the average reader, and it did teach something to those with no access to specialized astrology texts.

Astrology, too, sold quite well, going through four printings in less than four months. Dodd, Mead & Co. was again the publisher, with reviewers once more enthusiastic. The *Boston Transcript* wrote that, "Certainly the book will be welcome to thousands of those who are interested, and just as surely, Miss Adams was just the one to write it."

Chapter 14: *Boom and Bust*

Although Evangeline Adams made fewer public forecasts as time went on, when she had an important prediction based on long-term cycles, such as her forecast for U.S. involvement in a war from 1942 to 1944, she made the most of it, repeating it often whenever the opportunity arose. Her warning for a financial panic beginning in 1927, "with influences more pronounced in 1928 and 1929" was one of these (she had even mentioned it to Agnes O'Neill as part of her husband's reading). Yet even though it was repeated in many interviews, as the time approached the prediction appeared to be all wrong.

The twenties represented a period of general prosperity, and stock prices had continued to climb steadily since 1924. In a prosperous period, this was no cause for concern. By late 1927, stock prices began to rise more rapidly, and many more people became involved in market speculation. Brokers made it easy for anyone to buy: all that was needed was ten percent down, and the rest could be borrowed.

The upsurge in the market helped Evangeline, as many more people began subscribing to her monthly planetary indications, hoping for some greater insight into future trends. But her forecasts only addressed the big swings and curves of the market; she never gave definite information on specific stocks, and never attempted to make day-to-day predictions of the market's course. Adams put the greatest emphasis on each individual's own horoscope. Was it a chart that promised luck in speculation? If not, she advised against unwise investments. If the chart was fortunate for speculation, however, she was able to suggest good times for investing. Even with the most propitious horoscope, one could, at times, be under difficult planetary influences. Or, conversely, in a tough market, an individual in an auspicious astrological period should still do well.

Despite the increased workload, Evangeline took her usual springtime excursion to Europe in April of 1928. This trip, however, also involved business. A number of businessmen in Berlin had hired her to do some work for them, giving her the opportunity to combine work with pleasure. As usual, Mary accompanied her, and they sent letters back home, reporting on the sights they had seen and the things they had done. Evangeline loved her first visit to Berlin and remarked once more that,

I wish our officials, clerks, etc. could take a lesson from the people abroad. Such politeness, such consideration and friendly feeling you never get in the U.S.A., so far as I know, and certainly not in the East. We have much to learn.

She also enjoyed the food, so much so that she commented, "I have had no trouble with my digestion, but fear I have put on weight." The ladies took a side trip to Paris, to be fitted for dresses and gowns.

Evangeline had also taken one of her little dogs, a new puppy, along on the trip. "The little dog was such a comfort on the voyage, and everybody is already in love with her." She was very attached to "Sunaqua," as they shared the same birthday, with the sun in Aquarius. Clearly she appreciated the emotional warmth this little animal provided. (Evangeline felt that Neptunian people like herself, with a hunger for love and sympathy, needed to feel that something or someone depended upon them for affection and comfort.)

Upon her return to New York, Adams dictated another letter to "Everybody," reporting that,

Everything went well with Mr. Jordan at the helm, and everybody was glad to have me at the old stand once more. There were reporters and photographers to meet us, and I got plenty of publicity in the papers.

Even in her letters, Evangeline puts a positive spin on things. But a personal, handwritten note to Gertrude hinted at some of the problems in her marriage: "What made you think Uncle George would not want to see you all?" (She more commonly referred to her husband as "Mr. Jordan" in all correspondence.) Later, to explain her continuing to travel alone, she offers that, "It is almost impossible to leave so many girls without a Captain." As George Jordan concentrated exclusively on the business, it is apparent that he was not the personal helpmate Evangeline had hoped for, as we see from the following excerpt:

Had no trouble at the customs, as my beloved Bob [an employee] arranged everything. It was so wonderful to feel that I had somebody waiting for me who could take all the responsibility and a heart so full of loving attention.

Adams was extremely generous to her niece and her family and bought them all presents while abroad. She seems to have doted on her namesake great-niece, bringing her back a winter outfit, a parasol and a doll from Berlin.

The stock market did continue upward throughout 1928, with only two breaks in the constantly rising prices. Adams' forecast for a financial panic was still incorrect. Volume was incredible, with a new record set for numbers of stocks traded. Although in the midst of apparent prosperity, Adams stuck to her earlier direful forecast and continued to caution investors. Notably, she had this to say in the September, 1928, issue of a well-known magazine:

It therefore behooves the officers of financial institutions and captains of industry to display great wisdom if we hope to avert disaster. Even the individual should make a special effort to live within his means and try to co-operate with the conditions about him.

This came out in the midst of a period of easy money. But Adams had by this time developed quite a reputation on Wall Street and some investors heeded her advice. Her experience with such big names as Seymour Cromwell, president of the stock exchange, broker Jacob Stout, investment banker J.P. Morgan, industrialists Thomas Lawson, Fritz Heinze, Charles Schwab, and James J. Hill, promised sagacity. Many interviews, as well as her autobiography, boasted that she had correctly forecast all recent financial panics.

Although Evangeline based her 1928-1929 forecast on purely astrological indicators, there were some signs to the perceptive that all was not as it should be. While the market continued to surge, both organized labor and farmers were experiencing hard times. Wealth had been concentrated in the hands of a few, with farm income, in particular, declining throughout the decade. But, for the moment at least, most investors perceived that stock market prices would continue to soar, promising an easy return.

Evangeline continued to add more subscribers to her forecast newsletter and individuals who were interested in personal consultations as well. Yet, with her strength declining somewhat, she had by now limited interviews to only twenty-five a week, or five a day: approximately two and a half hours of consulting each day. She tried to spend more time on her current book project, the one originally begun with Aleister Crowley, which would address more serious astrology. This kept her busy.

But at the age of sixty, her health was not that robust. She suffered from rheumatism, gout, high blood pressure, and poor elimination. Her ankles and fingers had swollen, and her neck was now too thick to wear some of her nicer pieces of jewelry. She gave two necklaces bought on an earlier trip to Florence to Mary Scheinman. Evangeline seemed to enjoy eating and often over-indulged, especially when on vacation. In recent years, she had found less time for horseback riding, and the press of business was stressful. Living and working in adjacent spaces during the week was convenient, for when she was feeling weak at times, she would dictate her morning correspondence from bed. By now she had a car and driver to take her to and from her Westchester home on the weekends.

In January of 1929, Evangeline took a trip to the western U.S. for relaxation and pleasure, as well as to seek some treatment for her ills. While in New Mexico, she saw a "drugless and bloodless" doctor renowned for his electric treatments. She visited the Grand Canyon and Hopi Indians, saw some buffalo, travelled to San Francisco, and then took a cruise to Los Angeles, Panama, and San Jose.

As usual, Adams travelled with a secretary. But as her letters from this time are addressed only to Gertrude, they are at least a bit more personal. On January 7, 1929 she begins with, "I am in love with Rodger – a darling white-haired terrier – brought from England by the Bensons, and who is a champion many times." This is an unusual show of affection, but she always found it easy to love animals and was increasingly enthusiastic about them.

Evangeline found New Mexico arid and barren, but was delighted with San Francisco. On January 24, she made special arrangements to visit the University of California's Mount Hamilton Observatory in order to avoid the crowds she expected. Adams felt it was so cold she "almost perished," but was able to see Jupiter, Venus, Mars and the stars in Orion's belt through the huge, fourteen-and-a-half-ton telescope. It was close to her birthday, and she was excited that Venus was in the same degree of Pisces as in her own birth chart. The moon was also in Leo, and this placement was the same in her horoscope as well. Most astrologers concentrate on their books and ephemerides, rather than observing the night sky directly. We can see that Evangeline was one of them, as her description implies a special event:

It was a great experience and I shall never forget the impression it made. The glorious full moon, what a beautiful sight, and how marvelous to watch the sky change.

For Adams, seeing the night sky was more meaningful then for most, as she believed completely in celestial power.

Meanwhile, the financial world had continued to move forward. Gordon Thomas and Max Morgan-Witts, in their comprehensive book *The Day the Bubble Burst*, describe some of Adams' activities at this crucial point in American history.

In her forecast for February 15, 1929, she had said that a "violent upswing" was indicated by the end of the month. This may have been boosted by Hoover's upcoming presidential inaugural in March.

Sure enough, although the Dow Jones Industrial Average had declined about forty points between the first and the fifteenth, it regained all it had lost by the end of the month.

Thomas and Morgan-Witts continue:

Evangeline's fame rocketed in May when she predicted that month's market breaks with uncanny accuracy. The tabloids hailed her as "the wonder of Wall Street" and "the stock market's seer."

Later in the year, at a much more crucial point in time, Adams again reached the masses:

Late in the afternoon on Labor Day [September 2, 1929] a reporter from AJZ, NBC's New York flagship station, telephoned astrologist Evangeline Adams for an offbeat view of the stock market in the coming months. She briskly replied that "the Dow Jones could climb to Heaven."

Her prediction, broadcast on the evening news, cheered tens of thousands of motorists whose cars, newly equipped with radios, crawled along roads clogged for miles around New York with homeward-bound holiday traffic... And, although no one could possibly know it at the time, another record was set on this Tuesday, September 3. The Great Bull Market had reached its high point.

The rest of the month would see prices ease. And, on Wednesday October 23 and Thursday the 24th, prices plummeted, creating near panic on the New York Stock Exchange. "Black Thursday" had virtually everyone selling, and the ticker tapes running close to two hours behind. But for all the losses, the day closed on a high note, with many people feeling that fear alone had created the panic. Stock prices were still well above what they had been the year before.

Thomas and Morgan-Witts talk about the impact of the changing market on Evangeline's business:

Late Thursday evening [October 24, 1929], astrologer Evangeline Adams abandoned private consultations in favor of mass sessions in the waiting room of her studio over Carnegie Hall. It was the only way she could cope with the long line of clients waiting to hear her next prediction for the market.

Twenty-four hours before, whether by canny deduction or some more extraordinary force, Evangeline had foreseen the Crash with amazing accuracy, even pinpointing the pre-noon period as its peak.

The hundreds of people flocking to Evangeline's studio were mostly small investors; men and women now overcommitted to depreciated securities They had met the calls for margin throughout this Thursday. What they wanted to know from Evangeline was whether or for how long the decline would go on – whether they should continue to commit the capital and collateral they still had in order to hold their stocks in the expectation of a rise.

Evangeline knew they wished to be told that, in spite of its tremendous pummeling, the market would recover...

For all her clients, Evangeline had an answer. Having divined that the conjunction and interrelation of certain planets were creating "spheres of influence over susceptible groups, who in turn will continue to influence the market," Evangeline saw good times ahead. Friday and Saturday would witness a substantial swing upward. She would go no further; perhaps, like any good forecaster, she wanted to see the way the wind blew.

Indeed, Friday showed modest increases, and renewed public confidence. But, since Evangeline had for so many years pointedly avoided forecasting on a day-to-day basis, how was she able to do so now?

Her faith was with the larger cycles of nature; these, she believed, would manifest, no matter what. The broader strokes were more reliable; the shorter the forecast period, the more difficult it was to predict with accuracy. Evangeline's teacher Catherine Thompson had published daily and monthly market forecasts in her astrological journal *The Sphinx* thirty years earlier. In doing so she had used the daily transits of the moon, which change from hour to hour. Friday the 25th found the moon moving into Leo with positive aspects to other planets: this was a hopeful sign. Although the moon would square off against Mars on Saturday afternoon, which could cause problems, by the end of the day it would favorably apply to Jupiter – an excellent, if not one of the best of influences.

If Evangeline was, in fact, using the moon as an indicator, she would have also seen that Monday the 28th promised changeable and perhaps confusing conditions. By that time, there was some renewed optimism, as big banking interests stabilized the market by buying up orders which had been placed over the weekend. But constant trading continued unabated, with the largest daily drop in prices seen in the history of the exchange. Tuesday, October 29, found the moon squaring Saturn by mid-afternoon: not a good sign.

And indeed, this was Black Tuesday, complete with total panic, prices cascading ever downwards, and thousands of people crowding onto Wall Street. The crash had struck. Evangeline's forecast for a "terrific financial panic," which she had first made public at St. Mark's church nearly three years earlier, had finally, just at the very end of the period she had specified, come all too true.

Yet, as she had found during the Great War, times of national difficulty were generally busy times for astrologers. Evangeline was pressed for more and more appointments. Her health, however, prevented her from doing all she would have liked. And there were problems at home. Although George Jordan's efforts had been rewarded with success as far as the business was concerned, perhaps the pressure had become too much for him. His father, now seventy-eight and frail, had just had surgery to remove eleven ounces of gall stones. Evangeline wrote to Gertrude on December 19, enclosing a check:

Mr. Jordan is quite ill with his old trouble, largely due to worry over his father's terrible illness... the additional worry about that, as well as his own condition, has just about floored him.

One wonders if she is alluding to his tendency to drink. Gertrude's husband Claude was also on hard times. As usual, Aunt Evangeline was able to offer sound advice:

Get cash for the car. It does seem as though people in all situations of life try to have more than they can afford and are either naturally dishonest or forced into being so.

Her experience with clients over the past few months had led her to again observe more of the complicated side of human behavior than she would have liked. Evangeline ended her letter to Gertrude with the somewhat depressing observation that "according to the planets, there will be little Xmas spirit in the air" this year. And here, for the first time, we can see a little more of the real woman at last, as she signs it "with much love, as always, Aunt Eva." In a postscript, she mentions that she will be sending Gertrude a subscription to an optimistic metaphysical magazine, *More Light.* Must keep the spirits up!

Adams soon granted an interview to the *New York Telegram*, which appeared on February 4, 1930:

Beware of Market, for Hostile Uranus
Is in Control, Noted Astrologer Warns

Neither Ursa Major nor Ursa Minor, the great and lesser bears of the sky, nor Taurus, the bull of the Zodiac, governs the stock market from the standpoint of astrology. At the moment Uranus is in control, according to Evangeline Adams, most famous of the astrologers who cater to Wall Street, and Uranus is unfriendly and chaotic.

"It is a traders' market," the stars tell this gray-haired, soft-spoken New Englander, who has advised some of the leading speculators of modern times. "Nothing is certain. The market will go lower than it went at the time of the crash, but probably there will not be another crash."

"Both the bulls and the bears may suffer in trading. According to the stars, the trader should buy and sell and sell and buy according to the exigencies of the day. Those who wish to avoid serious loss will keep up with every fluctuation of the market. It is no time to invest for profit. Uranus bodes no good for the man who hopes to recoup in Wall Street."

During the October market crash Miss Adams had the most trying time of her career, she said, for all day and all night frenzied speculators sought her advice.

Adams here is quite accurate in her stock market predictions. There were many fluctuations in the market during 1930. The Dow Jones Industrial Average had dropped from 381 to 199 during 1929. In 1930, it began at 244, and climbed to 294 in April. But it would drop precipitously during June, twenty-three percent in a three-week period. Although there was something of a summer rally, by October the Dow slipped below the lowest 1929 level, to bottom out at 158 in December. As she had promised, the market had, in fact, gone lower than at the time of the crash, but there had not been another crash. The country simply began to drift into depression.

Evangeline reported that ordinarily, most clients were primarily interested in love. After the crash, they most commonly asked questions about money and finance.

Chapter 15: *Superstar*

By 1930, Evangeline Adams was at the height of her popularity. Often referred to as America's most famous astrologer, at the age of sixty-two, she had accomplished all she had set out to do. With a tremendous list of satisfied clients nationwide and abroad, she earned an excellent living. Adams had truly made America "astrology conscious." Syndicated daily horoscopes were being published in newspapers across the country, with horoscopes of celebrities' newborns appearing in Sunday papers. Due primarily to Adams' efforts, the revival of astrology was at least ten years old and still gaining momentum.

With the publication date of Evangeline's next book approaching, George E. Jordan, Jr., switched into high gear. He no longer needed to create a persona for Evangeline; it was easy to simply recycle earlier stories to keep the Adams legends alive. Jordan spent much time on the four phones that now graced his desk. Excerpts from *The Bowl of Heaven* soon appeared in issues of the *Woman's Home Companion* and the *Boston Herald*. Jordan and his ghost writers put together articles derived from previous books, to be syndicated to newspapers across the country and published under Evangeline's name. A profile of Adams appeared in the "Personalities" section of *The Review of Reviews*, and in *Fortune* magazine. Jordan booked his wife on lecture tours. And finally, he landed Evangeline a contract to appear for three months on the radio.

Radio! It was the most exciting thing to happen to modern man since the invention of the telephone. Coming into homes throughout America, it united the country and connected the still many disparate elements of the popular culture. While the airwaves were originally considered sacred to the public interest, in no time at all commercial advertisers realized the "reach" they could afford. Jordan had eagerly concurred, realizing how much more money could be made through fifteen minutes of airtime a few times a week. Adams gloried in the attention and opportunity to teach countless thousands about astrology; but her health had not improved. In the midst of all the hullabaloo, she travelled to Florida in April for some warm air and sunshine. Alone, as usual, she stopped at Palm Beach ("too artificial and the people are too bored"), then stayed in a Miami oceanfront hotel, spending her mornings on the beach. Perhaps sensing her mortality at age sixty-two, she had become much more open and emotional, saying in a letter of April 6, "That blessed 'Lover' – how I wish I had him here with me! Hug him for me." While she could openly show affection for her pets, her relationship with her husband, now forty, seems almost strained, and certainly not warm. What more needs to be said about a woman who called her dog Lover and her husband Mr. Jordan?

In Florida, Adams kept busy with friends and clients, as usual. She had also begun to wax nostalgic, remembering her favorite teacher, who had died over thirty years before:

Dr. Smith (Heber) was right when he told me that if I landed in the Sahara Desert, things would begin to move and I would gather the whole world around me. I am as busy as a bushel of monkeys, but do nothing for pleasure – all for the science.

Mrs. Hall, a local reporter who had previously interviewed Adams, now wanted to put her on the air in Florida, but Evangeline's current contract limited her appearances. Europe was a possibility that Hall pushed as well, with Adams deferring to her husband's judgement: "If Mr. Jordan thinks best, I may do so."

The association with Mrs. Hall's paper had proved to be a beneficial one:

I never felt so much at home with any group of people. The editor said he cashed in a lot of money on account of his horoscope which I sent him just before the hurricane, and told him to increase his insurance, which he did, and all the staff knew about me. A lot of people here admit I told them the boom would be over just when it happened, but they were so hypnotized by the success they were having, they could not believe I was correct. It has made my reputation down here very secure.

She was beginning to feel better in this warm and happy place. Receiving an invitation to visit a local observatory, she gushed, "The skies down here are very blue and the stars look so bright and joyful."

She concluded her letter warmly but cautiously: "Good bye, good friends, and please pardon this typewritten copy of my letter, as I must conserve my strength. Yours for more of it."

Some sad news came on April 16: Evangeline's elderly Uncle Edward had died. He was the last of the family remaining in Andover, and her final link with the past; but Evangeline had not much time to mourn. Almost as soon as she returned to New York City, she was on the air. She began broadcasting her show, "Your Stars" over the ABC network, every Monday and Wednesday evening. From 7:30 to 7:45, she'd tell anecdotes of her celebrity clients, repeat her previously successful predictions, and advise about tomorrow. Her clear voice and sure and steady speech were natural for radio work.

Forhan's toothpaste sponsored the show, in what seems like an unusual joining of interests. Yet everyone must brush their teeth, and astrology had the potential of universal appeal. Forhan's included coupons with their toothpaste, and if one collected enough of them and sent them to Evangeline's office, a free, personalized mini-reading would be returned via post. This increased the duties of Adams' assistants. But Evangeline was well paid for the radio work, and the free horoscope was a merchandising gimmick. After three months on the air, (a typical network 1/3 season), Evangeline had reportedly received 150,000 requests. Many of those who enjoyed their free sample would no doubt become regular customers in time. Soon, Evangeline was broadcasting from CBS radio in New York City three times a week. The fifteen-minute syndicated show reached some forty-four stations across the country.

Announcer David Ross would introduce Evangeline; he was followed by the lush chords of Victor Herbert's "Ah! Sweet Mystery of Life!" Reporter Allene Talmey visited the show and shared her impressions in *Outlook* magazine:

To hundreds of thousands, Evangeline Adams is not just another rhythmic name. She is faith and hope, a telegram from the future. Through this dignified astrologian, astrology has become respectable, a subject the children may hear. No longer is it a hidden superstition for the unholy rich and the unhealthy poor. By her suction it has seeped into the middle classes who have reduced this oldest of sciences from the romantic idiosyncrasy of the few to a commodity that one gets by sending in an advertiser's coupon for a free Adams horoscope.

These horoscopes are tossed throughout the land to innumerable housewives, mechanics, manicurists, waitresses, salesmen, clerks – that whole run of humanity who cannot wait for their milk and honey until they reach the promised land. Although they cannot name the officers of the Hoover Cabinet, they know the Zodiac now, the twelve houses of the heavens, the nine planets. They know Leo the Lion, and Cancer the Crab, all by listening on the radio to the sleepy-time voice of Evangeline Adams.

That voice rarely admits that black is black. A shimmering haze hangs over the specific. She tells anecdotes of her success with the great. She describes the fortunes of the next twenty-four hours, describes them so carefully that no matter what happens, she predicted it. She warns and guides, and gently removes responsibility from shoulders, not unlike a butler with a sable wrap. The multitude listens, with many obeying the advice sent out over the air by a wise old lady on the timberline of sixty. As she sits in front of the microphone, nervous, playing with her papers, she might be telling in her Yankee twang the story of the Three Bears, Aries, Pisces and Taurus, who came home one night to find golden-haired Virgo in the smallest bed of all.

Around the speaker at the microphone lounge seven or eight musicians whose faces show a boredom profound and pitiable. When all is over, Miss Adams, adoring the entire performance, hugs David Ross, her announcer, gathers up her platoon of visitors, picks up her dozen little accessories, and exits in a burst of light and gaiety and delightful flattery.

Aside from the great success of her radio show, 1930 was a banner year for Evangeline. Some reports from the time place Adams' fee for personal consultations at $50 per half hour, an extraordinarily high rate ($50 at the time would purchase a three-piece bedroom set, and is a rate that some astrologers might charge today, after so many years of inflation). This fee reflects the fact that Evangeline could command the price, as well as her steady withdrawal from consulting work. She was giving fewer and fewer personal interviews, while the staff was doing more and more mail order work.

In May, *Astrology, Your Place Among the Stars* was finally published. This is almost the book Adams had waited so long to write. While not the complete textbook she had always dreamed of creating, it did contain real astrology, and discussed many individual horoscopes. The book describes the influence of each of the planets and the sun and moon in the signs of the zodiac. As Pluto had been discovered only a few months before, it, of course, was not included. That left seven planets, the sun and moon, along with twelve signs, making for 108 combinations. Each was addressed in some depth.

This is clearly Evangeline's own work, which of course Aleister Crowley had elaborated on many years earlier. For each planet and sign, Adams cites examples from many celebrity horoscopes. She also goes into much detail, at times discussing other chart factors and how they would impact the planet at hand. As usual, she is quite authoritative, and we could say even opinionated at times. Yet she was drawing on over forty years of experience with astrology; she obviously knew what she was talking about.

George E. Jordan, Jr., probably wrote the introductions to each planet. Compared with the rest of the book's bare-bones informative style, his sections are overwritten, saccharine, and at times meaningless, throwing in whatever information he had on hand, as the following example illustrates:

Selene, or Diana, or Luna, is the twin sister of the sun. She is complete woman, in all phases, untouched by male caresses.

The Moon in her increase is the child, innocent and receptive, smiling above the sunset; nightly we see her grow, nearer and nearer to her triumph over darkness, queen of heaven!

Gaze upon her splendour, gaze not only with your eyes but with your heart; follow her in dreams with such strength that dream becomes reality. For the moon is in heaven what the sea is upon earth; and what that is, only they know who truly love the sea.

Your Place Among the Stars also drew on the Adams files for standardized forecast information. Including descriptions of times the sun would be variously aspected by Jupiter, Saturn and Uranus, it allowed readers to come up with their own individualized forecasts. This is much the same material that had been written many years earlier and was regularly being used for the mail order work.

Some, but not all, of the pieces that Adams worked on with Aleister Crowley also appear. Many are virtually identical to those later published under Crowley's name, though they had been trimmed of Crowley's personal opinions and mordant comments.

The book concludes with a few short pieces: "Diseases of Neptune" and "The Problem of Death." The first is a result of Adams' tutelage in medical astrology under Dr. Smith and Dr. Adams. The latter gives us some philosophical food for thought regarding the difficulty of predicting death astrologically. But, as usual, Evangeline equivocates and concludes with "forewarned is forearmed."

Finally, a collection of 100 horoscopes forms the appendix. Most of these seem to be taken directly from the English astrologer Alan Leo's collection, *1001 Notable Nativities*, published twenty years earlier. Often used as examples throughout the text, they include well-known modern and historical figures, grouped according to profession. This was something new for the American public. Evangeline had such a wide audience that *Astrology, Your Place Among the Stars* reached many more people than any serious astrology book had ever done before. Now readers would know more than mere sun signs and could actually begin to read horoscopes.

Adams was also reaching more people through her lectures. An Aquarian herself, she was one of the first astrologers to herald the coming Age of Aquarius. Perhaps egotistically, she had always been a big fan of Aquarians, feeling they produced many of the world's most inventive people. The Aquarian Age, she said, would be a "humanitarian age, where each man is his own saviour." An interest in mechanical things, as well as the resolution of many social problems and the advancement of the human race were promised for this long period, which we were soon to enter, and which would last approximately two thousand years. Carl Payne Tobey, later an important research astrologer, wrote a bit on one of Evangeline's lectures in his 1972 book, *Astrology of Inner Space*. He had attended her lecture at the age of twenty-eight.

I first heard of the Age of Aquarius in 1930 when it was the title of a talk Evangeline Adams gave. Most of the advancements she promised for the Aquarian Age, such as travel in space, have already occurred.

In April of 1931, Evangeline wrote to Gertrude, sending copies of some new astrology booklets they had produced. These thirty-five-page booklets were written for each sign of the zodiac and were designed to be mass-marketed to the general public. Filled with drawings, charts, pictures and the ubiquitous celebrity profiles, they were available across the country at Woolworth's (the proliferation of chain stores in the twenties was aiding her business as well). Much, again, was derivative of *The Bowl of Heaven* and other earlier work.

Adams had also had a head and shoulders *bas-relief* of herself sculpted, which she sent Gertrude as a gift, feeling that it needed explanation: "The *bas-relief* is of myself." Now she was immortalized in stone! This is an extraordinary example of exactly how well Adams thought of herself. As much as our relatives would enjoy seeing photographs, how many of us would actually send a sculpture of ourselves to a loved one?

George Jordan, meanwhile, had his hands full. Little by little, he had taken over the management of Evangeline's business. With much more work now done by the staff, Jordan took on a supervisory role. Mary Scheinman, once so effectively in charge, had already been tapering off towards retirement herself, working part-time, which left a void.

Unfortunately, while Jordan had proven himself as a promoter and salesman, he was not the best manager. He did not seem to have the rapport with the staff that his wife had always enjoyed. Not ever a popular personality, long-time employees resented his new role. Whether or not they were aware of his drinking, it, too, could have added to the problems. And as Evangeline had gotten older and approached infirmity, George tried unsuccessfully to raise his favor with some of the more important clients. As a result, he alienated some of them.

The radio show was still going strong: in July of 1930, Evangeline's contract was renewed for a year, and Jordan reported receiving an average of 4,000 letters daily, an incredible number. In fact, *Radio Round-Ups* reported that Evangeline received the most fan mail of any program in 1931 and said that she "took the country by storm." Astrologers were still hard to find and their fees were generally high for most people, particularly in these hard times. Many worker's wages had dropped nearly fifty percent already. A free reading from America's foremost astrologer provided some hope to the many thousands across the U.S. who listened to "Your Stars." When the world faced difficulties, astrologers often did well.

The great flood of letters and boxtops received was also a direct testament to the popularity of the show. Adams was no longer just a cult figure and off-beat personality. She had become a powerful force, in the unique position of influencing public opinion on a large scale.

Radio broadcasting had been legitimately established only a few short years earlier. In the tradition of freedom of speech, censorship of any kind was forbidden on the air, but all stations were required to be licensed by the United States government. The Federal Radio Commission was created to oversee this burgeoning industry. Most licenses were reviewed without question, the FRC maintaining a predominantly *laissez-faire* policy.

As radio allowed for universal access to information, the airwaves were originally intended to be used solely for the benefit of the American public. But once businesses realized that radio could be a wonderful instrument for advertising and marketing, they began sponsoring shows. Many people objected to advertising on the air, as advertisers were already commonly known for their brashness and lack of scruples. They might degrade the quality of programming by necessitating mass appeal. Others found ads offensive: it was simply not in the public's interest to be bombarded with commercial announcements on a regular basis. Yet sponsorship addressed a real need in radio, by answering the question of station funding; advertisers were soon viewed by many as saving radio by underwriting quality programming, thus allowing the medium to progress.

Coast-to-coast network broadcasting had begun as early as 1926, making it even more lucrative for sponsors to support nationwide programming. Soon the industry had been completely transformed, with the airwaves virtually belonging to the advertising agencies who were producing and packaging shows by the early 1930's.

While the Federal Radio Commission viewed most advertisers favorably, complaints from listeners caused them to begin to hold license renewal hearings in 1928. Unscrupulous advertisers might manipulate and sway the public through overexposure on radio. Because freedom of speech is guaranteed by the Constitution, there was seemingly nothing the agency could do to counter private influence on the airwaves. Any legal document limiting anyone's message would be a direct violation of freedom of speech. But these were the years when Catholics and other conservatives were heavily lobbying the motion picture industry to develop a code of moral conduct for film. By 1930, they had gotten most of the industry to accept a production code, even though it was not actually enforced.

Radio seemed to have more independence; but as the FRC granted licenses to all broadcasters, it was still in a position to call the shots. Each station would be expected to censor itself according to established guidelines. Although adherence to the code was voluntary, the FRC could easily revoke or cancel licenses if it felt a station was in violation of the code. The FRC was able to effectively impose censorship even though technically no threat had been posed to the freedom of speech all Americans enjoyed. In this manner Dr. Brinkley, an enormously popular radio personality, lost his station's license by 1930. The FRC felt he had duped the public by supplying quack remedies.

Most sponsors, network officials, directors and writers were extremely sensitive about censoring themselves. Radio, after all, came right into the family living room. It was broadcast without prior knowledge, or review, of content. It would do no one, particularly the sponsor, any good to offend listeners or provoke disagreements. Advertisers were discreet, limiting sponsor announcements, and usually not mentioning specific prices. Early radio content was extremely tame.

NBC's Blue Network, for example, agreed upon a Radio Industry Production Code in 1932, and published its own guidelines several years later. These were characteristic of most stations in the early years. Sexual innuendo was to be avoided at all costs, with explicitness strictly prohibited (an early radio appearance by Mae West resulted in such controversy that she remained off the air for over thirty years). Political controversy was also to be avoided, and even comedic references to the President, Congress, the Supreme Court or political leaders were to be sedulously avoided (only comedian Will Rogers seemed able to sneak past these restrictions).

Offensive allusions to physical afflictions, unpleasant odors or bodily functions were not permitted. References to laxatives, in particular, were to be strictly avoided (perhaps as they so blatantly invoked the previous three taboos in one fell swoop). It almost went without saying that profanity would not be broadcast. Regional sensitivities needed to be kept in mind. Race was not to be mentioned (an odd stroke for a medium that was popularized to great extent by the fame of *Amos 'n Andy*). And finally, there should be no references to God or religion.

Radio itself had already become amazingly popular, and allowed nationwide reach through syndication. Evangeline Adams became an enormously popular radio star; *the* most popular in 1931, if we are to judge from her fan mail. Her most dramatic letters were read over the air, along with her astrological judgements and suggestions. By far the greater number of these were from adults, with adult problems in relationships or with health concerns. Some had moral dilemmas and crises of conscience. Evangeline always insisted on the infallibility of the stars. She gave specific examples from celebrity charts, and often referred to important public figures who had been her clients, showing how they proved astrological influence or how they had used astrology productively to enhance their lives. (Her interpretation of the Lindbergh baby's horoscope – that he'd be "a flier like his father" – proved to be another dud: the boy was kidnapped and murdered in mid-1932.) Adams often did run close to the boundaries of the guidelines where references to sexuality, political figures and even mention of diseases were concerned. And, as Evangeline presented it, astrology *was* a religion.

Perhaps Adams' popularity was also due in part to the fact that she presented something more exciting and controversial than other radio fare. Soon she had many imitators: a numerology series had originated in Chicago; and Bost Toothpaste, a competitor of Forhan's, offered a success specialist who sent Success Charts by mail. A nail polish sponsored a palmist, and R.J. Reynolds offered verse and advice to women. The Voice of Experience, answering human relations problems, was soon receiving even more letters than Adams had. A woman called simply "Dolores," who had previously done a mentalist act on the vaudeville circuit, began twice daily broadcasts over a public service station and was soon receiving an unprecedented number of letters for cheap mail-order horoscopes. These developments so disturbed some of the public that on May 7, 1931, the Federal Radio Commission issued this press release:

Upon frequent occasions there has been brought to the attention of the Commission complaints against radio stations broadcasting fortune-telling, lotteries, games of chance, gift enterprises, or similar schemes offering prizes dependent in whole or in part on chance. On that subject the Commission has to say:

There exists a doubt that such broadcasts are in the public interest. Complaints from a substantial number of listeners against any broadcasting station presenting such programs will result in the station's application for renewal of license being set for a hearing.

In 1931, many businesses went belly-up as the depression deepened, yet radio advertisers had found a seemingly inexhaustible supply of business. Adams sold countless tubes of toothpaste for Forhan's; their business boomed while others foundered. George E. Jordan, Jr., could soon boast that their mail order business had greatly expanded. Evangeline was weekly converting thousands to astrology, and everyone was deliriously happy with the arrangement. Although bread lines would not begin to form for a few years, Evangeline was still rather well off compared to many. Yet on Friday July 17, 1931, when her lucrative contract expired, Adams delivered her final broadcast. She had been on the air for only a little over a year. As *Harper's* magazine observed shortly thereafter,

The Federal Radio Commission, though in this instance it long denied itself the power of censorship, now frowns so efficiently upon the broadcasting of horoscopes that several profitable contracts have been cancelled by large stations.

In the first skittish days of radio, it was not difficult to arrange for such a cancellation.

The FRC particularly objected to personal questions being answered, although some personalities on the air who exercised the proper decorum and had the right credentials were not challenged. The sale of forecasts was taboo, but Evangeline got around this prohibition with her free promotional offer. "Fortune-telling," however, was prohibited. Many astrologers would argue that they were not fortune-telling *per se*, as Evangeline had effectively done in a New York City Court; but when they forecast the future, most authorities still agreed this was illegitimate. Conservative religious groups had only to write in numbers to the FRC and Forhan's, threatening boycott and adverse publicity. Iris Vorel's fictionalized version of Adams, Mariska Lawlor, frequently received anonymous tirades of abuse after her radio broadcasts, including threats of having her business methods investigated and her show cancelled.

Certainly, astrology had always teetered on the brink of acceptability. It was easy for detractors to say it drew its popularity and strength from negative occult forces or played on the gullibility and superstitions of the people. One could easily write off "Dolores" as a charlatan; but Adams was too popular, too accepted, too much of an established authority to dismiss lightly. Her championing of astrology as a science that could be proven made matters even more complicated. Through radio, she was reaching hundreds of thousands more than she could hope to reach with her books. To more conservative members of society, Adams had, in fact, become dangerous. Pressure was brought to bear. Evangeline Adams was off the air, permanently.

So, too, were the many imitators, the other astrologers, numerologists and palmists of the early airwaves. In fact, although no laws were ever passed to keep them from broadcasting, occult and metaphysical practitioners were effectively prevented from doing so for the next fifty years. While astrologers like to say there was a "blackout" on their topic on the airwaves, the editor of the *New York Astrologer* had this to say in 1935, after studying the matter:

If Astrology is kept educational, if prediction as to personal matters is eschewed, if it is kept dignified and if no money is involved, there is no prohibition against Astrology on the air.

Chapter 16: *Fading Light*

Although her ocean journeys were typically planned well in advance, Evangeline quite abruptly decided to sail in late August of 1931. She had been invited to speak at the first International Congress of Astrology in Berlin and would also seek some cures for her increasing ills.

Accompanied by Lover, her dog, and her employees Franklin and Metta Garth, Eva enjoyed the rest which the crossing provided. For perhaps the first time in her life, she found she knew no one else on board. As usual, she indulged in the fine cuisine, enjoyed the beer, and participated in shipboard activities. She slept long hours, getting up only by lunchtime, and wrote her friends back home that "my rheumatism is better and I feel better each day."

Upon landing, the party made its way to Wiesbaden, which Evangeline found "the oldest and most depressing place I have been in." Although she stayed at a resort noted for its healing baths, things continued in a somber vein, as she found the "coffee vile, food did not seem to nourish me. I did lose flesh and I did sleep about fifteen hours a day." But the mud baths, under the supervision of a noted specialist, were wonderful. Adams felt great after her first fifteen-minute bath, but the aura of the city continued to trouble her. She found the Germans were "terrified of Communists" and concluded her latest letter with, "I want to get away as soon as practical. Things are terrible in London, I hear they fear revolution." And in an abrupt reverse of past sentiments, she added, "We better be thankful we live in America."

Evangeline enjoyed travelling with Franklin and Metta, as they managed everything splendidly for her. But as they visited Cologne, she again compared the United States unfavorably: "You get a feeling of grandeur without the graft of our country. We can copy plenty and be much better off for so doing."

The beautiful scenery of the Rhine revived her spirits, as she anticipated the thermal springs, her next treatment. These were supposed to help with her rheumatism and gout. As usual, she appreciated the company of Lover, saying he was "the greatest comfort and a wonderful traveller."

By the time she went on to the four-day Astrology Congress in Berlin, she was improved both in mind and body. Only one other American was represented and Evangeline was impressed by how seriously astrology was taken in Germany. She was also much more comfortable in Berlin, a city she had enjoyed wholeheartedly on an earlier visit:

You get a feeling of confidence and security everywhere. There is no fear of being cheated or having anything stolen. What a pity our country has lost all sense of integrity. I must go to the doctor for my treatment. I would prefer to be at Yorktown, only would not get the cure I need.

Now sixty-three, it was clear that she was spending much more time seeking relief from her ailments than socializing. But work, as usual, was still the center of her attention.

Before the year was out, another book was published under Evangeline's name: *Astrology for Everyone*. This, more than any of its predecessors, was a George E. Jordan product. The book was once again aimed at a popular audience, this time in such a simple style as to remind one of a book for young people. As usual, chapters were serialized in the *Woman's Home Companion*, and appear to have been written expressly for that purpose.

Astrology for Everyone describes each sign of the zodiac, but breaks them down further into decanates, or three sections of ten degrees, for each sign. Once more we have descriptions of the planets as well. As Jordan had no real astrological knowledge of his own, and was lost without the original input of truly creative people like Adams and Crowley, he did what he was best at doing: recycling, repackaging and marketing. Similar material had already appeared in Adams' earlier books. Stories were repeated from *The Bowl of Heaven* and other sources. *Astrology for Everyone* was well-done, well-written and professionally produced, but there was nothing new besides the decanate concept. Accessible as it was to such a wide audience, however, the book sold well.

Although the public enjoyed the book, others in the astrological community were unhappy. Some were envious of Adams' unprecedented success and resented her wide public acclaim. Any astrologer who knew the basics could have written *Astrology for Everyone*. Astrology is a complex subject, and many also felt the art degraded by any attempt to popularize it through simple sun signs. One such was Sydney K. Bennett, another prominent astrologer who had capitalized on Evangeline's success by recently securing a studio for himself at Carnegie Hall.

Evangeline had joined the Astrologer's Guild the year before and supported them with a hefty donation. With the publication of *Astrology for Everyone*, Bennett was incensed. At the next Guild meeting, he rose, roundly criticized the book, and claimed that

Adams had misinformed the public by promoting sun sign astrology. Bennett went on to demand her removal from the Guild. The membership had only to remind him that he was doing the same thing in his column for the *New York Daily News* in order to settle the matter.

On December 31, 1931, the public was shocked by accusations of adultery levelled at George E. Jordan, Jr., now forty-two. He had till now remained a shadowy figure, only known as the husband and business manager of Evangeline Adams. He had believed completely in the power of publicity, and now it had turned against him. Many New York City papers, both sensational as well as legitimate, carried features on the scandal that was brewing. The Russian dancer and impresario Leo Chenko was charging Jordan with alienating his wife's affections, to the tune of $250,000. Chenko had filed the suit in Supreme Court earlier in the month, stating that Jordan was responsible for "harboring and debauching" his wife Muriel, and using "arts and wiles" to lure her away from her home and three-year old daughter for over six months. Edgar A. Martin, Jordan's attorney, subsequently made a motion for a bill of particulars, in which he demanded to know what acts were committed, their time and place, and the circumstances of the alleged wooing of Mrs. Chenko, also known on the stage as Alexa Alsey. Mr. Martin claimed that Jordan had only a slight acquaintance with Muriel and would not settle out of court: "Mr. Chenko has started something he'll have to finish. The case will be tried."

Attorney David A. Cahill, counsel for Chenko, opposed the motion, saying the details would be revealed at the trial.

Reached for comment, Evangeline said only that, "This is pure blackmail. My husband and I are happier together than we have ever been."

The story is a complicated one, with various details by no means certain. Although the Chenkos had been a successful dancing team, they had lately been unable to secure bookings. Muriel, at thirty, still with a splendid physique, found temporary work as a model for various artists, some of whom happened to have studios in Carnegie Hall. As the *New York Mirror* revealed,

So, what unusual happenstance that Miss Adams' espoused, in his casual visits around the studios, entered the workrooms where the statuesque Muriel was posing? Or that he evinced a sympathetic interest in the young couple whose plight was unemployment? Or, that he forestalled their eviction by paying overdue rent and lending them small sums of money? Jordan's lawyers see no cause for doubt in his fraternal interest.

Frederick Lewis Collins, described variously as a mathematician, secretary and ghostwriter in Adams' employ, subsequently hired Muriel as an astrological calculation clerk. In November, Chenko had begun an alienation suit against Collins, asking for $500,000 in damages and claiming Collins had caused his wife "to remain away from home often." Yet it must have soon become painfully obvious that Frederick Collins was in no position to come up with $500,000, or anything near that sum.

At that point, Evangeline began receiving mysterious telephone calls. Supposed newspaper reporters showed up at her home and office with threats, according to Jordan's attorney: "If you don't settle this suit against Collins, damaging stories about you and your business will be printed!" Evangeline should pay on Collins' behalf! The Jordans had secured a near-monopoly in popular astrology, which had overcome the skepticism still prevalent about the profession. Bad press could hurt them deeply.

Yet Adams was incensed, and refused to capitulate. She fired Collins on November 21, and Chenko's $500,000 suit soon lapsed. By December, he had filed the $250,000 suit against her husband, and Evangeline observed that, "Evidently he has come down."

Attorney Martin added,

We all know about it, have talked it over among ourselves and are content that Chenko will not collect. Miss Adams understands and does not mind the suit.

Whatever she did or did not understand, the show had to go on. In her *New York Mirror* interview, Evangeline said,

This tragic circumstance will make no difference in the trust I place in my husband. If anything, it will draw us closer together. I am sure that justice will be done.

When all was said and done, we must wonder about what had actually occurred. A good reputation was essential to business, and, since the cancellation of the radio show, it was imperative to retain a good reputation. (Adams and Jordan had been extra-careful in the past, as evidenced by the fact that not one of the gossipy features even made mention of the more than twenty year age difference between Jordan and his wife.) Economically, the country was sinking into depression. Without the free advertising radio provided, business had already fallen off. Negative publicity over the matter was kept up for several months. This was due partially to the unfortunate occurrence of yet another law suit.

On January 8, 1932, the Magnetik Manufacturing Company, located just a few blocks away from Adams' Carnegie Hall studios, alleged that Evangeline had pirated their ten-cent astrological chart blanks, claiming she sold them to her clients at a dollar a copy. The charts had been patented the previous February and featured a calendar indicating favorable days at a glance. It was claimed that Adams had used them in August. Magnetik asked that Adams be kept from circulating the chart further and that she pay $25,000 in damages for ruining their sales.

Jordan made light of this allegation as well, claiming they had discontinued use of the Magnetik chart. "It's not really a chart, but just a listing. They are misinformed if they think they can copyright it."

Although Adams stuck to her guns on the legal issues, and was, in print at least, nonplussed, she had always had a tendency to worry. Still disappointed over the loss of her radio show, and with her health at a low point, she almost immediately escaped back to Germany, heading again to the healthful baths. Her high blood pressure, enlarged knuckles and gout provided her with an immediate excuse for the trip, but stress and fatigue probably played a larger part. She rarely, if ever, travelled in winter. When she returned several weeks later, her condition had remained unchanged, though she wrote to Gertrude on January 29, 1932 that a client had given her a "native cure" which had miraculously made her joints "almost smooth once more – showing that the doctors do not know what they are talking about." Enclosing a less-than-idyllic typewritten forecast for the coming year, Evangeline added that Gertrude should,

... not let anything in this work worry you realizing that nothing indicated in astrology MUST happen, provided you know what is likely to, and then work against it.

Eva encouraged Gertrude to try to save a little each month, as the family was not yet back on its feet financially and still needed help:

In a day or two I shall write you again, sending you a check, and I feel things are beginning to pick up, so you need not fear our not being able to send it to you right along.

The law suits seem to have disappeared. Maybe, like the fictional Mariska Lawlor, Evangeline "thought it best to settle any possible action out of court." After such a flurry of publicity, there was no further mention of either in print; but they took their toll. Evangeline's reputation had been bruised, and with it, astrology's ever-precarious reputation as well. Through Adams' efforts it had become fashionable, even acceptable. Now she was no longer strong enough to continue to fight adverse publicity. Despite her recent optimism, business did continue to decline steadily. As the year wore on, employees were let go. Although her name remained alive through her books, Evangeline, herself, was also fading slowly away.

The ever-resourceful Mr. Jordan had in the meantime come up with yet another book project. *The Evangeline Adams Guide to 1933* would be easy to put together from the general indications for 1933 that had already been written for clients. But, as fewer people were willing to pay a premium for this information, it would be designed for the general public, and sold in book form at a reasonable price.

As Evangeline always concentrated on her public persona, it has been difficult to ascertain exactly what the real woman was all about. Even in personal correspondence she was often guarded, stressing the up-beat while avoiding discussions of problems. As she got older she had become more open. Eva's last letter to Gertrude is more honest, sincere, and real than any we have seen before. It is as if, at the very end of her life, she set aside some of the inhibitions she had in the past. Writing on Thursday, November 3, 1932, Evangeline shows all of her true strength of character. She is generous and caring, has no tolerance for dishonesty or insincerity and is forceful when the occasion demands it. Her strong moral fiber and Congregationalist roots reveal themselves in the sound advice she has for her niece. And, sadly, the Depression had finally caught up with Adams. She had sent Gertrude her used fur coat for the winter, but noted that,

Everyone must cut down to the very limit until these terrible times are over, and then we will have acquired a habit which will make it much easier to save. I hope Claude [Gertrude's husband] will come out of his difficulty and that it will be a good lesson to him. He must not only avoid evil, but the appearances of evil.

Interestingly, Adams echoes Aleister Crowley's criticism of herself in her Bible reference. She goes on,

If you find that he [Claude] is spending one penny on anyone but his family after he gets back in business and making money, that will be the finish and I shall do everything to help you get free of him. One either travels straight or is crooked and that is all there is about it. We are hoping that after the election business will start to come back and that until Claude is making money, we can help you out more, but I can just tell you that it is very hard sledding and unless we do more business we shall have to put up the car, and that

I do not consider would be wise on account of my health. Next spring
perhaps we shall find a cheaper car and a cheaper chauffeur.
  With love to all, as always, Evangeline.

Adams' health had been failing for several years; she suffered
from high blood pressure brought on by arteriosclerosis. Yet she had
still continued to work, as the deepening depression brought many
people seeking advice and guidance. This contributed to her
emotional strain: she couldn't completely rest or relax. She had felt
well enough to attend a performance of the Broadway show *The Late
Christopher Bean* on Friday night, November 4, 1932. (The play, set
outside of Boston, was about the impossibility of putting a price on
things of intangible value.) On Saturday, after taking a hot bath,
Evangeline suddenly felt faint and lost consciousness. Her doctor
diagnosed the condition as a mild stroke and ordered complete rest.

Adams knew she was dying. At some point over the next few
days, she wrote a short note requesting simple services at The
Church of the Transfiguration, where she and George Jordan had
been married less than ten years before. On Thursday afternoon,
November 10, Evangeline suffered a second, more massive stroke.
Her doctor pronounced her dead of a cerebral hemorrhage at 4:00
p.m. George Jordan claimed to have been at her bedside at the time,
and immediately released a press statement: Evangeline had been
under "extreme strain" for months, and had foreseen, "a period of
adverse aspects and conditions over which she had to use the most
extreme diplomacy to avoid the result which she hoped to avoid."

While he implied that she had predicted her own death, there is
no evidence to indicate that she had done so astrologically. It often
does not take the talents of a seer to realize one is nearing the end.
Jordan claimed her prediction came only a few days before, after the
initial stroke. While later rumors would suggest that she had politely
declined a twenty-one-night lecture tour that autumn after foretelling
her own demise, friends reported that in the spring, Eva had said she
had no important planetary aspects coming up that fall. Even so, the
Brooklyn Eagle a few days later published a feature entitled, "Did
Auto-Suggestion Kill Astrologer Who Forecast Own Death?" The
verdict was mixed: a psychic research expert claimed it possible,
and a psychologist nixed the idea. An Episcopal Bishop who was
also an astrologer opined how, "the astrologer feels no fear of death"
as it is a rebirth into another world.

All of the local papers carried detailed obituaries, and, in typical
Adams fashion, there were many inconsistencies and errors printed.
Some said her age was fifty-nine, some sixty, and one seventy-two

(she was actually sixty-four). Many reported that Evangeline was descended from John Adams or John Quincy Adams. Some papers repeated her continued belief in "another war in 1942." Some implied she had been an eccentric, others stressed her faith and wise counsel. All, however, acknowledged that she had lived a fantastic life and had become a force to be reckoned with.

The body of Evangeline S. Adams lay in state on Sunday November 13 at her Carnegie Hall studio from 12:00 to 7:00 p.m. Many clients, friends, fans and well-wishers visited. Thousands of telegrams of condolence had been received.

Episcopal funeral services were led by Reverend Dr. Randolph Ray at the Church of the Transfiguration. Although Adams had never been a member of the church, she and Ray had been friends for over a quarter of a century. The services had originally been scheduled elsewhere, until one of the secretaries found the note in which Adams, sentimental to the last, had requested the Church of the Transfiguration, where she'd been married. Nearly 300 were present, with the church full. Most were women, but there were people from all walks of life: laborers, professional and business people alongside the well-to-do. The coffin was covered with a blanket of tea roses and greens. Among many others, there were three floral tributes in the shape of stars.

The organist opened the service by playing Adams' radio theme song, Victor Herbert's "Ah! Sweet Mystery of Life!" Dr. Ray pronounced the sentences for the dead, read the psalm and the lesson, followed by Metropolitan Opera tenor Rafael Diaz singing "There is no Death." Dr. Ray then spoke of Adams' great love and compassion for her fellow man:

She showed an affectionate understanding of life and was interested in life in all its fullness. That magical word charity, which has lost something of its meaning today, she had an intuitive understanding of it. She was, indeed, a wise, kindly woman, whose belief in the eternal spirit was steadfast. So we come with a spirit of joy today because we know that is the spirit in the larger sphere which she carries on.

Frank Gilmore of Actors Equity Association spoke on behalf of the theatrical profession, which she had always supported. Rabbi Charles Fleischer, Evangeline's long-time friend from her Boston days, read her favorite poem, Sir Edwin Arnold's "After Death in Arabia":

He who died at Azan sends this to comfort all his friends:

Like a hawk my soul has passed.
Love the inmate, not the room –
The weaver, not the garb – the plume
Of the falcon, not the bars
Which kept him from those splendid stars.

The organist played the Herbert melody once again, and Evangeline's body was taken to Woodlawn Cemetery in the Bronx for burial.

Evangeline had drawn up a will in June of 1927. In it, she left $2,000 to her niece Gertrude, and $1,000 to each of Gertrude's three children. She gave gifts of $100 each to her brother John and his two children, and $100 as well to Gertrude's brother, her nephew Ralph. George E. Jordan, Jr., received the bulk of the estate: the house in Yorktown Heights, the New York studios, the rights to Adams' books, the astrology business, all furnishings and other property. Although Jordan had been the most important person in Adams' life, work had been the most important thing. Evangeline accordingly left bequests to each of the faithful assistants who had worked hand in hand with her over the years. Emma Brush, who had been present at the Windsor Hotel fire, Mrs. M.D. Reed, who witnessed the early trials, and Mary C. Scheinman, who had so effectively managed the burgeoning business, all received $1,000 apiece for their years of dedicated service.

While these figures seem modest today, they were princely sums in the early depression years. For $1,000 you could buy a grand piano *and* a mink coat. $100 would fully furnish a dining room and a bedroom. The remainder of Adams' estate, including the value of the book copyrights, was estimated at about $60,000. This would be equivalent to almost two million today. George E. Jordan, Jr., was now a wealthy man.

Not one to waste time where business was concerned, Jordan immediately set out on his duties as executor of the will. The internment had taken place on Monday, and by Wednesday, all the legal papers were completed and signed. Within the next few weeks, George did a massive mailing in hopes of keeping the business afloat:

In Memorium
Special Christmas 1932
Membership Offer of the Planetary Indications
For 5 years: $10

A desperate measure, indeed, as one year's indications had formerly sold for the same price.

Jordan had put the final touches on *The Evangeline Adams Guide to 1933*, which came out in January to generally good notices. *The Saturday Review of Literature* kindly said,

It seems to me a sincere and intelligent book, often naive, but engagingly so. In the long run the astrologers have probably had as high a percentage of correctness as the Investors' Services and the Technocrats.

Many purchased the book, as it supposedly represented Adams' last word on astrology. It had, in fact, been just another potboiler put together by Jordan, and was quickly forgotten.

Without Evangeline, George E. Jordan, Jr., was no astrologer. No matter how he tried to capitalize on Adams' name (the business was now called "The Evangeline Adams Studios"), no matter how much he advertised as an astrologer and her principal student, he could not keep the business going without his wife. Mary Scheinman stayed long enough to help wrap things up. Employees were let go, and Jordan did not renew the lease on the six large studio spaces in Carnegie Hall which the company had occupied for the past seven years. He did keep Evangeline's original studio and work space for another six months and his own office until May of 1935. But things were not going well.

A year after Evangeline's death, Jordan wrote a memorial for his wife for *The National Astrological Journal.* Perhaps he still grieved over the loss of Evangeline, but there is no trace of sentiment in his overblown prose:

I shall leave to others the province of fixing the precise place which Evangeline Adams occupies in the procession of great astrologers whose names glorify the annals of history. It suffices for me to add my humble wreath to the memory of one whom I knew so intimately as her husband and co-worker in the vineyard of service to mankind.

Those who have read her autobiography, "The Bowl of Heaven," will recall the fascinating story of her adoption of astrology as her life's work. With typical courage and determination, she accepted the martyr's "crown of thorns," endured privation and humiliation, yes, even ostracism, in order to pursue what she believed to be the cause of humanity – through the science of the stars, the ancient and honorable science of astrology.

The *Brooklyn Eagle's* obituary said of Evangeline Adams that "Eugene O'Neill, it was learned today, is working on a new play about her."

Perhaps her former client had been intrigued with Adams' story. Many of O'Neill's works dealt with the search for God and religion. He had used numerology to choose race horses and had also had his palm read. In his notes, he evidenced an interest in esoteric wisdom in play ideas relating to "man and his soul," Taoism and Gnosticism. In 1927, the year after Adams' autobiography appeared, O'Neill had noted an idea for a play about an astronomer "whose scientific convictions of the unity of creation, rhythm and beauty of all leads him into astrology." From 1931 to 1934 he had been at work on a cycle of plays about an American family over the course of a century. The first of these would be called "The Calms of Capricorn" and the last, set in 1932, was called "The Life of Bessie Bowen." Bessie was a businesswoman tycoon who eventually became the head of a huge manufacturing company.

However these ideas might suggest an interest in the life and work of Evangeline Adams, no play about her was ever completed. And Columbia Pictures never went ahead with its plans for the film of her life that had been announced in 1924.

We might wonder what became of those who had so importantly influenced Adams' life. Evangeline's Sunday School teacher, the feminist Elizabeth Stuart Phelps, had married a much younger man at the age of forty-four. The marriage appears to have been something of a disappointment. Phelps continued to write until her death from heart failure in 1911. But she no longer wrote about independent women and never received quite the acclaim that her earlier work had garnered.

Evangeline's teacher, Boston astrologer Catherine Thompson, had advised her cousin, Francis T. Owen, astrologically, and as a result he made a great success as a coffee broker, and subsequently turned over $100,000 in commodities notes to her. Upon his death in 1922, his family claimed he was not in sound mind when he made the notes. Thompson contested the action, and her belief in astrology was used against her, even though she retained Clark L. Jordan, the attorney who had so effectively represented Adams in 1914. The jury agreed instead that Mrs. Thompson was a woman of such dominating personality that she obtained mental control over Owen, making him "the best meal ticket for his cousin the world ever saw."

Thompson remained in Boston, and the schism between she and Adams was never mended. In 1933, she wrote to the new editor of Alan Leo's *Modern Astrology* magazine, suggesting that Adams had actually been nine years older than she claimed. Down on her luck, Thompson had been living in a hotel. By Christmas she owed several months' rent and was notified that she must vacate the premises by January 1. She suffered a stroke shortly thereafter and was taken to the Pauper's Ward of the Peter Bent Brigham Hospital, where she died, unable to speak to her friends, although she had tried to communicate something. As requested in her will, she was dressed in her best white satin evening gown and cremated, the ashes being scattered into the Charles River from the Longfellow Bridge.

"The Great Cheiro" nearly died from a bout of double pneumonia in 1920, but was nursed back to health by a woman named Mena Dixon Hartland, who reportedly had the smallest hands of any woman Cheiro had ever known. He fell in love and soon married her. The palmist continued to write on metaphysical and occult topics, and claimed to have predicted the deaths of Queen Victoria and Lord Kitchener. Appropriately enough for a man who loved drama, he finally became a Hollywood screenwriter and died in 1936 at the age of seventy.

After presiding over Evangeline's 1914 fortune-telling trial, John J. Freschi served as the chairman of Manhattan's draft boards during World War I and was elected judge in 1931. In his thirty-four years on the bench, he had presided over some sixty notable trials, gained a reputation for great patience, and was known for meting out severe sentences when the occasion demanded it. His appendix burst while in his chambers on a July afternoon in 1944, and he died soon thereafter.

Although Freschi had claimed in 1914 that Evangeline Adams had "violated no law" and "had raised astrology to the dignity of an exact science," the 1999 New York City penal code still holds it a misdemeanor if someone "holds himself out as being able, by claimed or pretended use of occult powers, to answer questions or give advice on personal matters."

Aleister Crowley wrote feverishly for the rest of his life, primarily on magic. After being expelled from Italy in 1923, he travelled to Tunisia, France and then Germany, finally returning to England for his last fifteen years. Fighting poor health, financial trouble and perhaps even drug addiction, he died in a boarding house in Hastings in 1947.

George E. Jordan, Jr., was living in Epping, New Hampshire in July of 1958 when he had Evangeline's remains disinterred. It is not known why he did so. Health Department and Woodlawn Cemetery records indicate that the mostly decomposed, now over twenty-five-year-old remains were removed to Evergreen Cemetery in North Plainsfield, Connecticut. While there is a Jordan lot at Evergreen, Evangeline is not among those indicated as buried there, and none of the headstones in the cemetery bears her name.

At some point Jordan re-married, and died of pneumonia on November 3, 1967, almost exactly forty-five years after his first wife had passed, having suffered from emphysema and heart problems for years. He left his rights to *Astrology, Your Place Among the Stars* and *Astrology, Your Place in the Sun* to the Society for the Preservation of New England Antiquities.

Frank McDonough, a New Jersey businessman, read *The Bowl of Heaven* in the 1950's and became obsessed with finding Evangeline's library. After searching used bookstores in Boston and New York for three years, he finally found her collection of nearly 400 books.

His daughter, later the astrologer Margot Mason, became immediately attracted to the books and spent the rest of her short life in study and practice. She, in fact, believed herself to be the reincarnation of Adams, as their horoscopes had some important correlations. She hadn't much time to develop her astrological expertise, however, as she died in 1976, a victim of cancer at the age of forty.

Norman Winski, a Chicago Board Options Exchange floor trader, financial consultant and astrologer, learned from a friend that Evangeline Adams had been an advisor to famed financier J.P. Morgan and that she had forecast the 1929 crash. Upon hearing this, Norman thought that if Evangeline Adams' library or papers were still in existence, perhaps he could learn some stock market forecasting techniques. Coincidentally, Norman was going through some old papers in his office several months later when he came across an astrology newsletter with an article written by Margot Mason. The introduction included a biography on the author that said that Mason owned the Evangeline Adams library. Winski tried to find Margot, but discovered that she had died the previous year. Her parents, however, were by that time ready to let the astrological library go, and sold it to Norman. It included many old and rare volumes such as an original copy of *Christian Astrology* by famed seventeenth century astrologer William Lilly.

After his purchase, Winski heard that Adams' great-niece, Evangeline Adams Curry Elmore, was alive. He met her at her home in Decatur, Illinois, where he learned that she was Evangeline Adams' last known close relative and had all the family memorabilia related to Adams. A few years later, upon Mrs. Elmore's death, her husband gave Winski all of the Adams memorabilia. Some items of note are the *bas-relief* of Evangeline Adams that she had sent to Gertrude in 1931, an original cartoon from the *New Yorker* magazine, and Evangeline's letters. The library and other information are still with Norman in his home in Naples, Florida.

The Bowl of Heaven was reprinted by Dodd, Mead & Co. in 1970. *Astrology, Your Place in the Sun* and *Astrology for Everyone* had been reprinted throughout the 'forties and 'fifties. These two, in addition to *Astrology, Your Place Among the Stars*, were all reprinted in the early seventies, thus introducing Evangeline's work to a whole new generation of astrologers.

After buying up the copyrights to *Your Place in the Sun* and *Your Place Among the Stars*, the O.T.O. and other supporters of Aleister Crowley wanted his contribution to be known and planned on publishing the works under both his and Adams' names.

Evangeline Adams continues to be a well-known figure within the astrological community. Carroll Righter, whom she had advised to study astrology at the age of fourteen, became a famous popular astrologer in Hollywood. Adams' students Iris Vorel and Katherine Q. Spencer Young went on to write articles, books, and columns on astrology (Vorel had fictionalized Adams' legal difficulties, while in an odd twist, Young was herself arrested and acquitted of fortune telling in Washington, D.C. in 1959). Grant Lewi, later one of the foremost professional astrologers of the twentieth century, was influenced by Adams when he first began to study. His two popular astrology books have introduced countless numbers to the subject.

Adams wrote her books not only to gain publicity and prestige, but also to educate the public about her favorite topic. She popularized astrology in America. There were very few astrology books published in the United States before the twenties, compared with a great proliferation after Evangeline had made the public astrology-conscious. Newspaper and magazine horoscopes as we know them didn't exist until the 1940's and although Adams never wrote one, she paved the way for all popular astrologers who followed her. A 1991 Gallup poll concluded that one in four

Americans believe in astrology and that three in four occasionally read their horoscopes. Such was certainly not the case before Evangeline Adams came along.

Sadly, though, Evangeline never produced the major astrology books that she had talked about for so many years. The book she wrote with Aleister Crowley was only a beginning and barely scratched the surface of what real astrology was all about. While Adams used traditional astrology techniques developed over thousands of years, the simplified astrology that she'd popularized was what remained in vogue. Gaining momentum in the 1960's and 1970's it developed into a modern, psychological approach, which eschewed prediction in favor of better understanding the psyche. Today's astrology students are much more likely to read contemporary works that reflect this modern approach, rather than looking back to the traditional techniques Evangeline herself utilized.

Most astrologers today embrace Evangeline Adams as one of the "greats" of the past. What's remembered is mainly what advertisers would call her "brand" – a few memorable catch phrases. Evangeline was a cultivated lady from a great American family who predicted the future. Some might add that she predicted the Windsor Hotel fire or that she made astrology legal in New York State. The first claim may not be true at all and the second is certainly inaccurate. Evangeline's reputation has both been exaggerated and forgotten – exaggerated through repetition of, and additions to, questionable claims; forgotten because no one really remembers anything else. Any survey of astrology in books or television programs mentions Adams, but all simply repeat the sketchy, frequently apocryphal stories that have already been reiterated many times before.

While Evangeline was once one of the most popular personalities in the U.S., outside of today's astrology enthusiasts, she is now virtually forgotten. Ultimately, Adams was a woman with a mission: to legitimize astrology. If she did not completely succeed in doing so, she did make people much more aware of astrology and what it could do. She was nothing if not sincere in her intentions, and combined a spiritual commitment to the astral arts with a practical approach toward disseminating knowledge. While she was not the most upfront and straightforward about herself, her belief in the efficacy of astrology always stood firm. In the final analysis, the details of her marriage and personal life are not what haunt us; rather it's the woman herself and her sense of determination.

Did Evangeline really predict the Windsor Hotel fire, the stock market crash of 1929 or World War II? It depends on how you look at things. We don't know what Adams forecast for the Windsor Hotel, and it's not documented by any other witnesses. We might be tempted to say that her forecast for financial difficulties for the United States from 1927 to 1929 was right on the money, were it not for the explosive growth of the market until the period she had specified was nearly at an end. Evangeline's prediction of U.S. involvement in a great war from 1942 to 1944 is certainly frightening to consider, particularly since it was made fifteen years in advance. Yet, for every hit there was, regrettably, a miss. As weather forecasters, political pundits and market mavens know, the future, certainly, is something very difficult to describe.

With the passage of time, it will become more and more difficult to find original source material to either prove or disprove any of the Adams tales; much of this material is already gone. In another twenty or thirty years, newspaper morgues will disintegrate and other primary sources will be lost. In fifty years, microfilms will break and not be replaced. By the next century, new technologies will not keep up with older material that is rarely called for. Eventually, Evangeline Adams will simply be a legend, a story, perhaps a myth. She'll be remembered as someone who touched people's imaginations in a unique way, glittering in the heavens like one of the stars she was so enamored of.

She probably would have wanted it just that way.

Evangeline's Birth Chart

Evangeline Adams
Natal Chart
Feb 8 1868
8:26:13 AM EST +5:00
Jersey City NJ
40N33 074W04
Geocentric
Tropical
Porphyry
True Node

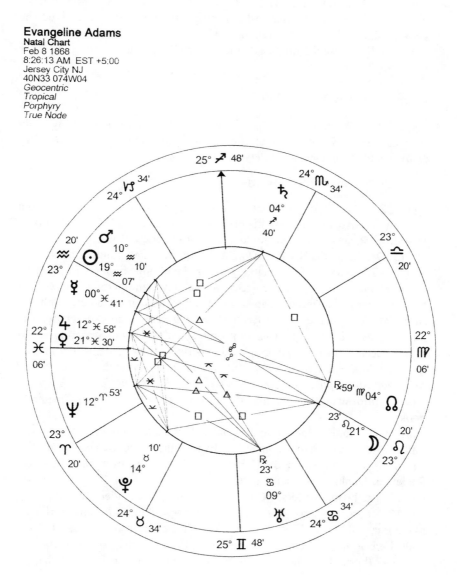

Notes

Material quoted is from *The Bowl of Heaven* unless specified otherwise. I've occasionally removed ellipses in quotes for easier reading, but only when it does not alter meaning. I've also corrected punctuation and obvious misspellings from other sources included in my text.

Introduction

p. 5 Fred MacDonald in his *Don't Touch That Dial!* quotes *Radio Round-ups* for 1932 as saying that Adams' program "Your Stars" received the heaviest fan mail of any program in 1931.

p. 5 Judge Freschi's quote is from his trial summary in the *New York Criminal Reports*

Chapter 1: New York, 1899

pp. 7-11. *The New York Times* and *New York World* were my main sources on the Windsor Hotel fire. Adams' autobiography *The Bowl of Heaven* added some personal details.

Chapter 2: Looking Backwards

pp. 12-18. Most of the genealogical material in this chapter is from Andrew N. Adams' family history; some is courtesy of the Andover Historical Society and North Andover Historical Society.

p. 13. Details on the Battle of Dorchester are from Page Smith's book.

pp. 14-15. Some of the vital records involving Evangeline Adams' maternal ancestors contain incorrect information. I am therefore not certain that this particular Isaac Adams was Evangeline's grandfather. Both the *National Cyclopaedia of American Biography* and Adams' brochure, *The Law and Astrology* say he was an inventor, and the family certainly seems to have been well-to-do. Biographical material on Isaac Adams is primarily from the *National Cyclopaedia of American Biography*, the *Dictionary of American Biography*, and *Appleton's Cyclopaedia of American Biography*.

p. 15. Information on the history of printing is from Warren Chappell's book.

pp. 16-17. Some information on Adams' father and brothers is courtesy of Phillips Academy Archives, including Evangeline's letter to Mr. Eaton.

pp. 16-17. Information on Dunkirk, New York is from the Historical Society of Dunkirk and their Centennial publication.

p. 17. The history of Jersey City is described by Alexander McLean.

p. 17. Andrew Adams' *Geneaological History* includes Adams' birth date as February 8, 1868. This date was also on her death certificate and the 1900 Census for Boston. However, in the 1910 Census, Adams claims an age of 47 (born 1863); in the 1920 Census, she is 49 (born 1861). Perhaps secretaries completed these forms. On her marriage certificate, Evangeline gave age 50 (born 1873; her husband also lied about his age). Various library and biographical sketches suggest 1859 or 1872.

pp. 17-18. James White's book provided information on the paper car wheel.

Chapter 3: Andover Days

pp. 19, 21-22. Much of the descriptive information on Andover at the time is from Elizabeth Stuart Phelps' autobiography, *Chapters from a Life*, and some from her biography of her father, Austin Phelps.

p. 19. A photo of the Adams' home appears in the *Woman's Home Companion* of June 1925.

pp. 22-23. Information on Elizabeth Stuart Phelps is from her autobiography and her biography of her father, as well as her novels and stories and Carol Farley Kessler's book.

p. 25. The quote from Phelps is from Michael Sartisky's notes to the 1987 edition of *Dr. Zay*, citing Mary Angela Bennett's 1939 biography of Phelps.

p. 25. Information on homeopathy is from Phelps' *Dr. Zay*, the Hahnemann University Archives and Martin Kaufman's book, although I found some of his statements about the history of homeopathy incorrect in light of documentation I turned up.

p. 25. Biographical information on Dr. Whiting is from the Hahneman University archives.

Chapter 4: A Whole New World

Evangeline Adams' quotes are all from *The Bowl of Heaven* unless otherwise noted.

p. 26. Adams' address is given on Harriet's death certificate.

p. 27. Adams mentions her inventor grandfather in her brochure, "The Law and Astrology."

p. 27. Phelps' quote is reiterated from Kessler's biography, citing a Phelps story.

pp. 28-30. I have pieced together the story of Mr. Lord from several different anecdotes in Adams' autobiography, but it is still somewhat speculative.

pp. 29-30. Details on Dr. Smyth's trial were provided by the Andover Newton Theological School Archives and Smyth's book.

pp. 30-32. Biographical information on Dr. Smith is from *The Bowl of Heaven*, Boston University Library Archives, Daniel Marsh's *Bostonia* article, scrapbooks in the Hahnemann University Archives, and Ellen McCaffery's book.

p. 31. The existence of 18th century medical astrology in academe is mentioned by Jim Tester; Galileo's astrological duties are noted in Dava Sobel's book.

p. 32-35. Dr. Smith's and Evangeline's quotes are from *The Bowl of Heaven.*

pp. 35-36, 40. Information on Catherine Thompson is from Marie Louise Clemens' book, with some details from Ellen McCaffery's history and W.H. Chaney's article.

p. 36. Biographical information on Dr. Adams is from the Westborough State Hospital and Hahnemann University Archives.

p. 37. Medical information on Harriet Adams is from her death certificate.

p. 38. The Phelps quote is from Perley in *The Silent Partner.*

p. 38. Adams listed "teacher" as her profession in the 1900 Census, but unfortunately, I've been unable to find out any more about this work. Considering that she said she was a "scientist" in the 1910 Census, she might not necessarily have been employed by an established school on a regular basis.

p. 39. Information on Dr. Savage is from the *Dictionary of American Biography*; his letter is quoted from *The Bowl of Heaven.*

p. 39. Clemens and McCaffery both tell us that Adams studied with Thompson.

p. 40. The quote from Thompson is from her "Speculums" article.

p. 40. The quote from Sepharial is taken from Kim Farnell's book, citing the *British Journal of Astrology*, August 1925.

p. 42. Evangeline's feelings for Dr. Smith are in a letter of hers dated April 6, 1930, now in Norman Winski's collection.

p. 42. The biographical information on Franklin Simmons is from *Appleton's Cyclopaedia, Who Was Who in American Art*, and the *New York Historical Society Dictionary of Artists in America.*

Chapter 5: The Lure of the Occult

pp. 44-45. My source on the Columbian Exposition is primarily Hubert Howe Bancroft's book.

p. 45. *Shepard's Encyclopedia* mentions Adams' studies with Vivekenanda, with no source given.

p. 46. Dr. Broughton's observation is from his book.

p. 47. The account of the Boston occult scene is taken from Evangeline's friend Lilian Whiting's book.

pp. 47-48. See Cheiro's biographies for his sensational life story. Other details are from *Who Was Who*, David Wallechinsky's book, and of course, *The Bowl of Heaven.*

p. 48. Cheiro includes his press reviews in his 1896 book, but does not include their year of publication, so these are somewhat speculative.

p. 49. Bacon and Kepler, while having an essential belief in astrology, felt much of the practice inaccurate. See Jim Tester for more.

pp. 50-51. My account of Harriet Adams' illness is from the typical case outlined in W.G. MacCallum.

p. 51. See Minot J. Savage's article for details on his explorations of spiritualism.

p. 52. See W.J. Colville's book for more on his work.

Chapter 6: On Her Own

p. 54. Information on Harriet's death is from her death certificate.

p. 54. See Elizabeth Hawes on the history of apartment life.

p. 55. Information on Copley Hotel residents is from the 1900 Census.

p. 56. Compare this excerpt from Evangeline's brochure to Smith's writing in *The Arena* magazine, which is quoted in part on page 141.

p. 58. Evangeline's list of clients is primarily from *The Bowl of Heaven*.

p. 58. Biographical information on Thomas Lawson is from the *Dictionary of American Biography*.

p. 60. I examined *The Arena* from around 1898 to 1900.

p. 60. See Edward J. Renehan on John Burroughs.

p. 61. Louise Chandler Moulton's biographical sketch can be seen in *Appleton's Cyclopaedia* and *Who Was Who*.

p. 61. Biographical information on Rabbi Fleischer is from his *New York Times* obituary, "Dr. Charles Fleischer..." on July 3, 1942.

p. 61. Norman Winski has pictures of Adams on horseback in his collection.

p. 61. Andrew N. Adams' genealogy gives Evangeline's grandmother's date of death.

Chapter 7: New York, New York

p. 64. Evangeline tells us of her referral to Warren Leland in Allison Gray's *American Magazine* article.

p. 64. The identity of Evangeline's secretary, Emma Brush, is in Windsor Hotel fire accounts and her will. Other details are from Census records and the New York City Directory.

p. 64. Much of Leland's biography is from the *New York Times* and the *New York World*.

p. 65. The *New York World* quote is from "Foretold the Calamity" on March 20, 1899. Evangeline repeats her story of the Windsor Hotel in many magazine articles.

pp. 65-66. The *American Magazine* excerpts and Evangeline's quote about Leland reporting her prediction are from Allison Gray's article. Much of the account of the Windsor fire is taken from the *New York Times* and the *New York World*. There were many dailies in New York City at that time and I also consulted the *Brooklyn Daily Eagle*, *Evening Journal*, *Evening Post*, *Evening World*, *Herald*, *Journal-American*, *New York Daily Commercial Advertiser*, *New York Sun*, *Press*, *Town Topics*, and *Tribune*. I could find no quotes from Leland about Evangeline in any of these papers. Judith Werner, an intrepid researcher, checked many of them in her own research on Adams as well. Of course, this does not assure us that Leland's quote never appeared; there are many papers from the time that are no longer available.

p. 66. The *New York Evening Journal* article was "Warren Leland Prostrated by Shock." The *Herald* quotes from Leland are in "Leland Crazed by Deaths in Family." The *Tribune's* interview with Dr. Pitkin was "Mr. Leland Not Insane."

p. 67. Evangeline's Windsor Hotel story was recounted in *Modern Astrology* in November 1899, though she would've been disappointed that they didn't actually mention her name.

pp. 68-71. The New York City forecast in the *Journal* was called "The Horoscope of Greater New York."

p. 69-70. The history of Jerome and Low is taken from the *Encyclopedia of New York City*. The railroad story is in James J. Hill's sketch in the *Dictionary of American Biography*. The Triangle Shirtwaist strike is described in Nell Irvin Painter's book. The actual stock market movements can be found in John Dennis Brown's book. Climatic information for October through December of 1899 is from the National Climatic Data Center's Data time series in the Global Historical Climatological Network.

p. 70. Adams' quote on being besieged is from Allison Gray's article.

p. 70. Alexander Bryan Johnson, a descendant of John Quincy Adams and thus a distant cousin of Evangeline's, died in the Windsor Hotel fire; but he'd been born in Utica, New York in 1848 and I've never been able to establish a connection with Adams.

pp. 71-72. The story of King Edward VII is from *The Bowl of Heaven*.

p. 72. Much on Alan Leo can be found in Patrick Curry's book. Al H. Morrison owned Evangeline's copies of Alan Leo's books, which had her signature, date and "London" indicated on the flyleaf.

p. 74. Information on the Carnegie Hall Studios is from the website *www.CarnegieHall.org* and the Carnegie Hall Archives.

p. 75. Evangeline's brother William's death certificate is in Norman Winski's collection.

pp. 75-76. The account of Richard Harding Davis is from *The Bowl of Heaven*.

Chapter 8: Problems and Publicity

p. 77. Evangeline quotes the old legal statute in *The Bowl of Heaven*. Adams' following quotes, are, as usual, from *The Bowl* unless otherwise specified.

p. 77. Mrs. Reed's address is from Evangeline's will.

pp. 77-81. The newspaper articles, "More Palmists Arrested," "Society Palmist Seized" and "War on Palmists" were all sources for the 1911 arrest and trial.

p. 79. A.J. Pearce's forecast for King Edward is given in Patrick Curry's book.

pp. 81-82. Evangeline tells us, herself, about most of her clients. Whenever I have found outside corroboration, I mention it. Many of the biographical sketches of Adams' clients are taken from the *Dictionary of American Biography*.

p. 81. Charles W. Ferguson quotes Adams predicting the Panic of 1907 in "Superstition in Cellophane."

p. 83. Norman Winski's collection has photos of Adams on horseback, as well as detailed pictures of her home.

p. 83. Those who gave Evangeline elephant figurines are from the article, "Beware of Market..." although some sound fictitious to me.

p. 83. Documents on Charles Adams' death are in Norman Winski's collection.

p. 84. Information on Gertrude's involvement with Adams' office is from her daughter, Evangeline Adams Curry, via Norman Winski.

p. 84. Information on Arnold Genthe is from Annette Melville's book and the *Dictionary of American Biography*.

Chapter 9: Evangeline and the Law

p. 85. Lynn Wells, in her introduction to the 1970 edition of *The Bowl of Heaven*, mentions Adams' 1910 prediction for the defeat of Theodore Roosevelt in 1912.

pp. 85-86. Evangeline's brochure, "The Law and Astrology" contains the repetition of her 1912-1915 forecast that appeared in the *American Club Woman's Magazine* – after the fact. Ed Dearborn was extremely helpful in providing me with this and many other Adams documents.

p. 86. The 1913-1915 historical events are described in Bernard Grun's book and *The Chronicle of America*.

p. 86. Evangeline tells us of her prediction for George V in *The Bowl of Heaven*, but I have not found the original source. Maurice McCann was kind enough to search the likeliest English papers of the time, but could find nothing.

p. 87. The excerpt from the *Paris Herald* is also from Adams' brochure, "The Law and Astrology."

p. 88. More on Alan Leo can be found in Patrick Curry's book.

p. 88. The quote from the psychic to Goodwin is from the *New York Times* report, "Fortune Tellers Trapped by Women," as is the following excerpt.

p. 90. The *Journal-American* morgue clipping is entitled, "Descendant of John Quincy Adams Held on Bail."

p. 90. Biographical material on Freschi is from his obituary in the New York Times, "J.J. Freschi Dead..."

pp. 98-99. Al H. Morrison quoted David Champlain Brooks, an astrologer and attorney who had been around at the time of Adams' trial, on his opinion of the Adams trial in his letter of September 15, 1993 and further personal communication. This informed my analysis, but I've never found any original documentation or reports to substantiate Adams' claims.

p. 99. The producer of the cable television program featuring Adams was Filmroos in Los Angeles.

Chapter 10: The Magician

pp. 101-104. Crowley's quotes are from his *Confessions* unless otherwise stated. Information on Crowley is primarily taken from his titles in the bibliography, with additional information from the occult reference works I've also listed and Hymenaeus Beta's introduction to *The General Principles of Astrology* which reproduces Crowley and Adams' original work with many excellent notes from Beta.

p. 103. The article mentioning Professor Seabury is Allison Gray's *American Magazine* piece; biographical information on Seabury is from the Brooklyn Public Library Catalog.

p. 103. Adams' quote is from the Court Report of her trial.

pp. 104-109. "A Treatise on Astrology" and "How Horoscopes are Faked" are both included in *Aleister Crowley: the Complete Astrological Writings,* but also see Crowley and Adams' *The General Principles of Astrology* for more in-depth and up-to-date information.

p. 109. Information on Mary C. Scheinman is from her niece, Adele Stein, who lived with her during the years she worked for Adams and seemed more like a sister.

p. 109. Gertrude Adams' wedding date is from her marriage certificate.

p. 110. Information on Carroll Righter is from James Holden and Robert Hughes' book and a *Current Biography* profile.

p. 110. Ella Wheeler Wilcox's profile is taken from the *Dictionary of American Biography.*

Chapter 11: Here Comes Mr. Jordan

p. 112. Adams' death certificate and Jordan's birth and death certificates reveal their true ages.

p. 112. The *New York Mirror* article is by Mary Phelps, from February 7, 1932.

pp. 112-113. Biographical information on George E. Jordan, Jr. is from his printed press statement and Irene Kuhn's article in the *New York Herald.*

p. 113. The picture of Jordan and Adams appeared with Phelp's *New York Mirror* story, in the *New York Sun* morgue.

p. 114. Information on Adams' house in Yorktown Heights is from *The Bowl*, and its description from an anonymous magazine spread in Norman Winski's collection.

p. 114-115. The *American Magazine* piece is by Allison Gray.

p. 116. The *Fortune* article is "Adamses Alive."

p. 116. Allene Talmey had the griddle cake remark in her magazine article.

p. 118. The *Boston Herald* article is by Carl Warton.

p. 119. Adams' arrest in 1923 is described in "Fortune Teller is Held," January 25, 1923. Vorel's fictional account is *Ad Astra.*

pp. 119-120. The statements on George Jordan, (from Adele Stein, who lived with her aunt Mary Scheinman, and from Norman Winski, who interviewed Evangeline Adams Curry Elmore, Adams' great-niece), were unusually consistent, even though they were from quite different and indirect sources.

p. 122. Irene Kuhn wrote the *New York Herald* article.

p. 122. The *Brooklyn Eagle* article is "Miss Adams, Noted Astrologist..."

pp. 122-123. The source for the actual stock market fluctuations in 1923 is once again John Dennis Brown's book.

Chapter 12: Big Business

p. 124. The Columbia Pictures article is an anonymous clipping in Norman Winski's collection.

p. 124. The Carnegie Hall Archives has rent rolls for both Adams and Jordan.

p. 124. *The Outlook* article is by Allene Talmey

pp. 124-125. Photos of Adams' office are in Norman Winski's collection and the July 1925 *Woman's Home Companion*.

pp. 125-126. Information on Adams' fees and business practices can be found in Charles Ferguson's article in *Christian Century*, Allene Talmey's article in *Outlook* magazine, "Adamses Alive" from *Fortune*, "Evangeline Adams in Death..." from the *New York World-Telegram*, "The Star Gazer," from *Review of Reviews*, and "Thirty Years of Star Gazing" from the *Woman's Home Companion.*

pp. 125-126. The description of Evangeline Adams' written reports is from Allene Talmey's article, quoting Adams' leaflet.

p. 126. Descriptions of Adams are from Adele Stein, Allene Talmey's article, and photographs.

pp. 126-127. The McCaffery quote is from *Astrology, Its History and Influence....*

p. 127. The Iris Vorel quote is from *Be Your Own Astrologer.*

p. 127. Adams' daily schedule is described in *The Bowl of Heaven*, as is the anecdote about the big response to her magazine article. The following quotes are also from *The Bowl of Heaven*.

p. 128. The *Eagle* piece is by Helen Hubert Foster.

p. 130. J. Bryan III and Charles J.V. Murphy in *The Windsor Story* misquote the Duchess of Windsor's autobiography, where she tells of a visit to "the favorite pupil" of Evangeline Adams (possibly Iris Vorel). They erroneously attribute the visit to Adams herself.

pp. 129-130. Adams' client list is culled from a wide variety of sources. Many of the thumbnail client sketches are from the *Dictionary of American Biography*.

p. 131. The *New York Telegram* report on Adams' incorrect forecast for President Harding was from the article, "Beware of Market..."

p. 131. Adams' erroneous prediction for Al Smith is from James Holden's *A History of Horoscopic Astrology*.

p. 131. I consider the Tokyo and Lindbergh predictions questionable reporting. They are quoted from *The Day the Bubble Burst*, which I discuss at length in a note on page 197.

pp. 131-132. The Tunney-Dempsey prediction was afterwards reported in "The Star Gazer," *Review of Reviews*, November 1930.

p. 132. The Jordan accident story and the cow forecast are from *The Bowl*, as are the remaining death predictions excepting Valentino's which appears in *The Day the Bubble Burst*, and the divorce story, which is from Frederick Collins' article.

p. 133. The trial quote is from the *New York Criminal Reports*.

p. 133. See Robert Zoller's book for more on fate and free will.

p. 134. Norman Winski now has Gertrude's scrapbook in his collection. Unfortunately, the newspaper's name is not included and I have been unable to identify it.

pp. 137-138. I could not find Arthur Hopkins' book; the quotes are from its excerpts in the *Ladies Home Journal*. His biographical information is from *The Almanac of Famous People* and *Dictionary of American Biography*.

p. 141. The quote from J. Heber Smith is from his article in *The Arena* magazine.

p. 141. The quote on Eugene O'Neill is from Louis Sheaffer's book, *Eugene O'Neill: Son and Artist*, as is the additional information on his finances.

Chapter 13: Onward and Upward

pp. 143-145. Quotes are from *The Bowl of Heaven*.

p. 144. Adele Stein quoted her aunt Mary Scheinman in an interview of June 29, 1994.

pp. 145-146. Adams' book reviews appeared in the *Book Review Digest* for 1926.

p. 146. Jordan's article, "In Memoriam" in *The Best of the Illustrated National Astrological Journal* can be compared to these excerpts.

p. 146. Rabbi Joel Dobin in his 1994 letter talks about Mankiewicz working with his mother for Evangeline sometime between late 1918 and July 1924.

p. 146. The quotes from Mankiewicz are in Kenneth L. Geist's book.

p. 149. Evangeline's letters are from Norman Winski's collection.

p. 151. The review of *Astrology, Your Place in the Sun* is from the *Book Review Digest* for 1927.

Chapter 14: Boom and Bust

p. 153. Adams' thoughts on Neptunian people are from *Astrology, Your Place in the Sun* and Vorel's *Be Your Own Astrologer*.

p. 154. My source for the actual stock market swings is once again John Dennis Brown's book.

p. 154. Carl Warton's article in the *Sunday Boston Herald* of April 27, 1930 unfortunately does not give us any more details on the "well-known magazine" from September 1928 that he quotes. The prediction was made two years before, but I have noted a similar forecast elsewhere.

p. 154. Adams speaks of her various ailments in her letters; her death certificate offers other clues to her health concerns, as do photos from the time. Adele Stein remembered that Evangeline gave the two necklaces to Mary.

pp. 155-157. Gordon Thomas and Max Morgan-Witts' *The Day the Bubble Burst* is a comprehensive book put together by a large team of researchers. Nevertheless, they fail to annotate even direct quotes, making it impossible to confirm or deny much of what is said about Evangeline Adams. Generalized chapter sources cover a wide variety of periodicals, and my search in many of the likeliest references listed proved fruitless. In addition, many personal interviews and unpublished material is cited, but the authors have chosen not to identify these sources.

Unfortunately, the authors also show a clear bias against Adams and sensationalized her story. They don't understand exactly what an astrologer does, and, at times, refer to Adams as using a crystal ball, tarot cards, or being a medium, all of which are incorrect. Other details seem to fictionalize her account, for example, a reference to "the admiring young men who surrounded her like acolytes" which does not sound right at all. I have thus included from this text only what I feel is realistic or supportable from other sources, but even this remains questionable.

It is curious that the authors quote Adams as saying the Dow could "climb to Heaven" when she had for many years been warning of market disaster for this period. Perhaps this was a shorter-term forecast, or maybe, as I suspect, *The Bubble Burst* account is more fiction than fact. Thomas and Morgan-Witts seem to think that Evangeline lied to the public about stocks going up so she could safely sell out her own holdings before the panic, knowing all the while that prices would continue to drop. Unless they interviewed her broker or husband (which is not disclosed), I can't imagine how they would know about this alleged transaction. Their conclusion incongruously suggests that Adams was indeed infallible in her forecasts. We have seen, of course, that she was not.

p. 156-159. The actual market swings are from John Dennis Brown's book.

Chapter 15: Superstar

p. 161. The quotes are all from Evangeline's letters.

p. 161. I am indebted to Norman Winski for the observation of dog versus husband.

p. 161. Uncle Edward's death date is recorded in Andrew N. Adams' book.

p. 162. The 150,000 figure is from Evangeline, repeated in many sources.

p. 163. Value-for-money figures are based on newspaper and magazine advertisements of the time.

p. 165. The Aquarian Age quote is from p. 17 of *The Bowl of Heaven* (1926 edition).

p. 165. Evangeline's bas-relief quote is from a letter dated April 13, 1931.

pp. 165-166. The observations of George Jordan are from Mary Scheinman, via Adele Stein.

p. 166. Fred McDonald in *Don't Touch That Dial!* quotes *Radio Roundups.*

pp. 166-168. Much of the information on early radio is from McDonald's book.

p. 167. Information on the history of the First Amendment in regard to radio is from Robert J. Wagman and Erick Barnouw's books. Susan Luck Hooks and Professor Wesley Wallace were very helpful in providing much additional information.

p. 168. Allene Talmey and other features from the time describe Adams' show, with additional information given in her newspaper features, such as the one that appeared in 1931 in the *New York Evening Journal*, "Expert Links Stars to Destiny."

p. 168. William Engles quotes the incorrect Lindbergh baby prediction in his *New York World-Telegram* obituary of Adams.

p. 168. Some of the references to other radio shows are from Charles W. Ferguson and Travis Hoke's articles; others are from my reading of daily radio schedules published in the *New York Times* and *Brooklyn Eagle* at the time.

pp. 169-170. The FRC's press release was included in Elizabeth Aldrich's *New York Astrologer* article as were her conclusions about the situation.

pp. 169. The *Harper's* quote is from Travis Hoke's article.

pp. 169-170. I owe the reasons Adams' show was cancelled to Elizabeth Aldrich's article, written shortly thereafter. Ed Dearborn also provided some background from Marion Mayer Drew.

16. Fading Light

pp. 171-172. Information on Adams' trips is from her letters.

pp. 172-173. The Sydney K. Bennett incident is described in Carl Payne Tobey's book.

p. 172. Information on Evangeline's donation to the Astrologer's Guild is from Ed Dearborn, who has the documentation in his collection.

pp. 173-174. Mr. Martin's quote about Chenko is from Mary Phelp's *New York Mirror* article. Evangeline's quotes are from an anonymous clipping in the *New York Sun* morgue, "Evangeline Adams Unperturbed..." The other articles I've drawn upon for the Jordan suit are Alfred Abbell's article in the *New York News*, "Evangeline Adams' Husband Accused..." from the *New York Sun* morgue and "Seeress' Husband Sued" from the *New York Times*. The threats are reported by Phelps in the *New York Mirror*, as is the following Martin quote.

p. 175 The *Herald Tribune* article, "Astrological Piracy," describes the chart suit and also quotes Jordan.

p. 175. The settlement quote is from Iris Vorel's *Ad Astra*.

p. 177. Details on Adams' health are from her death certificate.

p. 177. William Engle's obituary of Adams in The *New York World-Telegram* quotes Jordan as saying she predicted her own death.

p. 177. The cancellation of Adams' lecture tour is mentioned in the *Encyclopedia of Occultism and Parapsychology*, with no source noted. Ellen McCaffery mentions Adams' lack of astrological aspects that autumn in her article in *The Best of the Illustrated National Astrological Journal*.

p. 178. The World War II forecast is from the *Brooklyn Eagle* obituary, "Miss Adams, Noted Astrologer..." It was also reiterated in William Engle's *New York World-Telegram* obit.

p. 178. Dr. Ray's quote at the services is from the *New York Herald-Tribune* article, "Adams' Funeral Service is Held..."

pp. 178-179. Many newspaper articles filled in details on Adams' funeral services.

p. 179. Evangeline's will is available in New York City Surrogate's Court.

p. 179. Norman Winski's collection has a copy of Jordan's mailing.

p. 180. Jordan's piece appears in *The Best of the National Astrological Journal*.

Chapter 17: Epilogue

p. 181. The Eagle obit is called "Miss Adams, Noted Astrologist..."

p. 181. Some of O'Neill's prospective works are described in the Gelb's book; others are from O'Neill's book of play ideas. His penchant for the occult is mentioned in both of Louis Schaeffer's books.

p. 181. See Carol Farley Kessler's biography on Elizabeth Stuart Phelps.

pp. 181-182. See the *New York Times* articles, "Astrologer Figures in Suit" and "Believer in Stars..." for the quote about Thompson and more information. Thompson's letter to the editor of *Modern Astrology* appeared in the July-August 1933 issue. The remainder of Thompson's story is from Marie Louise Clemens' book.

p. 182. Cheiro's story is from *Who Was Who* and the *Encyclopedia of the Unexplained*.

p. 182. See "J.J. Freschi Dead" for Freschi's biographical information. His quotes are once again from the *New York Criminal Reports*. The New York City penal code was quoted in the *New York Times'* "It Seems the Cards Do Lie" on June 30, 1999.

pp. 182-183. Crowley's end is described in the *Encyclopedia of the Unexplained*.

p. 183. Woodlawn Cemetery records show that Evangeline's body was moved to the North Plainsfield Cemetery, but unfortunately they claim to have no records of burials. I searched the entire graveyard and could find her nowhere.

p. 183. Jordan's death information can be found in Social Security records.

p. 183. Hymenaeus Beta, in his introduction to Crowley's *General Principles of Astrology* tells about Jordan's will.

p. 183. Margot Mason's story is from Ruth Montgomery's book.

pp. 183-184. Norman Winski told me his story in interviews on October 9, 1993 and May 20, 2000.

p. 184. Kathy Fleck and *The Thelema Lodge Newsletter* provided the information on the O.T.O.'s purchase of Adams' copyrights.

p. 184. See James Holden and Robert Hughes' book for short bios of the astrologers Evangeline influenced. In her letter of November 23, 1993, Frances McEvoy reported that her teacher Grant Lewi was influenced by Adams.

Bibliography

Books

Adams, Evangeline. *Astrology for Everyone*. New York: Dodd, Mead & Co., 1931.

_____. *Astrology, Your Place Among the Stars*. New York: Dodd, Mead & Co., 1930.

_____. *Astrology, Your Place in the Sun*. New York: Dodd, Mead & Co., 1927.

_____. *The Bowl of Heaven*. New York: Dodd, Mead & Co., 1926.

_____. *The Bowl of Heaven*, with an Introduction by Lynn Wells. New York: Dodd, Mead & Co., 1970.

_____. *The Evangeline Adams Guide for 1933*, ed. George E. Jordan, Jr. New York: Dodd, Mead & Co., 1933.

Adams, Andrew N., ed. *A Geneaological History of Henry Adams of Braintree, Massachusetts and His Descendants*. Rutland, VT: The Tuttle Co., 1898. Reprinted by Parker River Researchers, Newburyport, MA, 1984.

Adams, James Truslow. *The Adams Family*. New York: The Literary Guild, 1930.

Bancroft, Hubert Howe. *The Book of the Fair*. New York: Bounty Books, Crown Publishers, 1894.

Bankhead, Tallulah. *My Autobiography*. New York: Harper & Brothers, 1952 .

Barnouw, Erick. *A Tower of Babel, A History of Broadcasting in the U.S. to 1933*. New York: Oxford University Press, 1966.

Black, Mary. *Old New York in Early Photographs*. New York: Dover Publications, 1973.

Britt, Albert. *Turn of the Century*. Barre, MA: Barre Publishers, 1966.

Broughton, Luke D., M.D. *Elements of Astrology*. New York: L.D. Broughton, 1898.

Brown, John Dennis. *101 Years on Wall Street, An Investor's Almanac*. Englewood Cliffs, NJ: Prentice Hall, 1991.

Browning, Norma Lee. *Sydney Omarr, Astrology and the Man*. Englewood Cliffs, NJ: Signet, 1978.

Bryan, J. III and Murphy, Charles W. *The Windsor Story*. New York: William Morrow & Co., 1979.

Byron, Joseph. *New York Life at the Turn of the Century in Photographs*. New York: Dover Publications, Inc., in cooperation with the Museum of the City of New York, 1985.

Cavendish, Richard. *A History of Magic*. London and New York: Arkana, The Penguin Group, 1990.

Chappell, Warren. *A Short History of the Printed Word*. Boston: Nonpareil Books, 1980.

Cheiro (Count Louis Hamon). *Confessions: Memoirs of a Modern Seer*. London: Jarrods Publishers, 1932.
_____. *Cheiro's Language of the Hand*. Chicago and New York: Rand, McNally & Co., 1896.
_____. *Cheiro's Memoirs: The Reminiscences of a Society Palmist*. London: William Rider and Son Ltd., 1912.
_____. *Palmistry for All*. New York: Prentice Hall Press, 1988 (reprint of original edition).

Clemens, Marie Louise. *The Autobiography of Marie Louise Clemens*. Boston: Bruce Humphreys Publishers, 1953.

Coleman, Walter. *Astrology and the Law*. New York: Greenlawn, Casa de Capricornio Publishers, 1977.

Colville, W.J. *Universal Spiritualism*. New York: R.F. Fenno & Co., 1906.

Crow, Duncan. *The Edwardian Lady*. New York: St. Martin's Press, 1978.

Crowley, Aleister. *The Complete Astrological Writings*, ed. John Symonds and Kenneth Grant. London: Tandem Publishing, Ltd., 1976.

_____. *The Confessions of Aleister Crowley*, ed. John Symonds and Kenneth Grant, London and New York: Arkana, 1969.
_____. *Eight Lectures on Yoga*. Phoenix, AZ: Falcon Press, 1987.
_____. Crowley, Aleister, with Evangeline Adams. *The General Principles of Astrology*, edited and with an introduction by Hymenaeus Beta. York Beach, ME: Redwheel/Weiser, 2002.

Curry, Patrick. *A Confusion of Prophets*. London: Collins & Brown, 1992.

Davis, Richard Harding. *Vera, The Medium*. New York: Charles Scribner's Sons, 1908.

Duncan, Isadora. *My Life*. New York: Boni & Liverwright, Inc., 1927.

Evans, Sara M. *Born for Liberty: A History of Women in America.* New York: The Free Press, a Division of Macmillan, Inc., 1989.

Farnell, Kim. *The Astral Tramp: A Biography of Sepharial.* London: Ascella Publications, 1998.

Flower, B.O. *Progressive Men, Women and Movements of the Past 25 Years.* Boston: New Arena, c. 1914.

Geist, Kenneth L. *The Life and Films of Joseph L. Mankiewicz.* New York: Charles Scribner's Sons, 1978.

Gelb, Arthur and Barbara. *O'Neill.* New York: Dell Publishing Co., 1965.

Grun, Bernard. *The Timetables of History based on Werner Stern's Kulturfahrplan.* New York: Simon & Schuster, 1975.

Guiley, Rosemary Ellen. *Encyclopedia of Witches and Witchcraft.* New York and Oxford: Facts on File, 1989.

Hawes, Elizabeth. *New York, New York: How the Apartment House Transformed the Life of the City 1869-1930.* New York: Holt & Co., 1993.

Holden, James Herschel. *A History of Horoscopic Astrology.* Tempe, AZ: American Federation of Astrologers, 1996.

Holden, James H. and Hughes, Robert A. *Astrological Pioneers of America.* Tempe, AZ: American Federation of Astrologers, 1988.

Holzman, Robert S. *The Romance of Firefighting.* New York: Bonanza Books, 1956.

Howard, Brett. *Boston, A Social History.* New York: Hawthorn Books, Inc., 1976.

Howard, Sidney. *The Late Christopher Bean.* New York: Samuel French, 1933.

Israel, Lee. *Miss Tallulah Bankhead.* G.P. New York: Putnam's Sons, 1972.

Jordan, George E., Jr. "In Memoriam, Evangeline Adams" in *The Best of the Illustrated National Astrological Journal,* ed. Edward A. Wagner, 1978.

Kaufman, Martin. *Homeopathy in America: The Rise and Fall of a Medical Heresy.* Baltimore: Johns Hopkins Press, 1971.

Kerr, Howard and Crow, Charles L., editors. *The Occult in America.* Urbana and Chicago: University of Illinois Press, 1986.

Kessler, Carol Farley. *Elizabeth Stuart Phelps*. Boston: Twayne Publishers, 1982.

Larsen, Stephen and Robin. *A Fire in the Mind, the Life of Joseph Campbell*. New York: Doubleday, 1991.

Lyman, Susan Elizabeth. *The Story of New York*. New York: Crown Publishers, Inc., 1975.

MacCallum, W.G. *A Textbook of Pathology*. Philadelphia: W.B. Saunders & Co., 1940

MacDonald, J. Fred. *Don't Touch That Dial! Radio Programming in American Life, 1920-1960*. Chicago: Nelson-Hall, 1979.

McCaffery, Ellen. *Astrology, Its History and Influence in the Western World*. New York: Charles Scribner's Sons, 1942.
_____. "Horoscope of Evangeline Adams" in *The Best of the Illustrated National Astrological Journal*, ed. Edward A. Wagner, 1978.

McLean, Alexander. *History of Jersey City, New Jersey*. Jersey City, NJ: Press of the Jersey City Printing Co., 1895.

Montgomery, Ruth. *Here and Hereafter*. New York: Ballantine Books, 1968.

Morris, Lloyd. *Postscript to Yesterday*. New York: Random House, 1947.

Nagel, Paul C. *Adams Women*. New York: Oxford University Press, 1987.

O'Neill, Eugene. *Eugene O'Neill at Work: Newly Released Ideas for Plays*, annotated and ed. Virginia Floyd. New York: Frederick Ungar Publishing Co., 1981.

Painter, Nell Irvin. *Standing at Armageddon*. New York: W. W. Norton & Co., 1987.

Parker, Derek and Julia. *The New Compleat Astrologer*. New York: Crescent Books, 1990 (orig. 1971).

Phelps, Elizabeth Stuart. *Austin Phelps: A Memoir*. New York: Charles Scribner's Sons, 1891.
_____. *Chapters from a Life*. New York: Houghton, Mifflin & Co., 1896.
_____. *Dr. Zay*. New York: The Feminist Press of the City of New York, 1987 (reprint of 1882 original).
_____. *The Gates Ajar*. Boston: Houghton, Mifflin & Co., 1868.
_____. *Men, Women and Ghosts*. New York: Garrett Press, Inc., 1969 (reprint of original stories published prior to 1869).

_____. *The Silent Partner*. Old Westbury, NY: The Feminist Press, 1983 (reprint of 1871 original).
_____. *The Story of Avis*, ed. Carol Farley Kessler New Brunswick and London: Rutgers University Press, 1988 (reprint of 1877 original).

Renehan, Edward J., Jr. *John Burroughs, An American Naturalist*. Post Mills, VT: Chelsea Green Publishing Co., 1992.

Savage, Minot J., D.D. *The Passing and the Permanent in Religion*. New York and London: G.P. Putnam's Sons, 1901.

Sheaffer, Louis *O'Neill: Son and Artist*. Boston: Little, Brown and Company, 1973.
_____. *O'Neill: Son and Playwright*. Boston: Little, Brown and Company, 1968.

Smith, Page. *A New Age Begins: A People's History of the American Revolution*. New York: Penguin Books, 1989

Smyth, Egbert Coffin. *In the Matter of the Complaint Against Egbert Coffin Smyth and Others...* Boston: Cupples, Upham & Co., 1887.

Sobel, Dava. *Galileo's Daughter*. New York: Walker & Co., 1999.

Tester, Jim. *A History of Western Astrology*. New York: Ballantine Books, 1987.

Thomas, Dana L. *The Plungers and the Peacocks*. New York: William Moran & Co., Inc., 1967.

Thomas, Gordon and Morgan-Witts, Max. *The Day the Bubble Burst*. Garden City, NY: Doubleday & Co., 1979.

Tobey, Carl Payne. *Astrology of Inner Space*. Tucson, AZ: Omen Press, 1972.

Tyl, Noel. *Prediction in Astrology*. St. Paul, MN: Llewellyn Publications, 1991.

Viault, Birdsall S. *American History Since 1865*. New York: McGraw-Hill, Inc., 1989.

Vorel, Iris. *Ad Astra*. New York: Uranian Press, 1933.
_____. *Be Your Own Astrologer*. New York: Wehman Brothers, 1935.

Wagman, Robert J. *The First Amendment Book*. New York: Pharos Books, 1991.

Wallechinsky, David. *The Book of Predictions*. New York: William Morrow & Co., 1981.

Washington, Peter. *Madame Blavatsky's Baboon*. New York: Schocken Books, 1993.

White, James H. *The American Railroad Passenger Car*. Baltimore: Johns Hopkins University Press, 1978.

Whitehill, Walter Muir. *A Topographical History of Boston*. Cambridge: Harvard University Press, 1959, 1968.

Whiting, Lilian. *Boston Days*. Boston: Little, Brown & Co., 1911.

Wilson, James. *Dictionary of Astrology*. Boston: A.H. Roffe & Co., 1885 (reprint of 1819 edition).

Windsor, Duchess of. *The Heart Has its Reasons*. New York: David McKay, 1956.

Zoller, Robert. *Fate, Free Will and Astrology*. New York: Ixion Press, 1992.

Magazines

Adams, Evangeline "Find Birthdays in the Stars," *Pictorial Review*, October 1926.
_____. "Just How I Read Horoscopes," *Pictorial Review*, March 1927.
_____. "Thirty Years of Star Gazing," *Woman's Home Companion*, June, 1925.
_____. "Twelve Husbands," *Woman's Home Companion*, September 1930.
_____. "Twelve Wives," *Woman's Home Companion*, June, 1931.
_____. "What I Have Learned from Clients," *Woman's Home Companion*, August, 1930.
_____. "What Kind of Child Do You Want?" *Pictorial Review*, November 1926.
_____. "What Men Ask Me," *Woman's Home Companion*, August, 1925.
_____. "What Women Ask Me," *Woman's Home Companion*, July, 1925.

Aldrich, Elizabeth. "Is Astrology Prohibited on the Radio?" *New York Astrologer*, September 1935.

Chaney, W.H. "The Astrologer's Vade Mecum," *The Sphinx*, February 1900.

Collins, Fred L. "They Hitched Their Wagons to the Stars," *Colliers*, May 15, 1926; May 22, 1926; May 29, 1926.

Ferguson, Charles W. "Superstition in Cellophane," *The Christian Century,* February 17, 1932.

Gallup, George H., Jr., and Newport, Frank. "Belief in Paranormal Phenomena Among Adult Americans," *The Skeptical Inquirer,* Winter, 1991.

Gray, Allison. "People Who Try to Get Tips from the Stars," *American Magazine,* December 1921.

Hoke, Travis. "The Heyday of the Fortune Tellers," *Harper's Monthly Magazine,* January 1932.

Hopkins, Arthur. "Letters to a Lonely Boy," *Ladies Home Journal,* August 1937.

Marsh, Daniel L. "All Noisy on the Medical Front," *Bostonia, The Boston University Alumni Magazine,* April 1940.

Mason, John. "Evangeline Adams," *Yankee,* November 1966.

Savage, Rev. M.J. "A Reply to Mr. Hawthorne," *The Arena,* Volume 3, 1889.

Smith, J. Heber, M.D. "Man in His Relation to the Solar System," *The Arena,* Volume 15, December 1895.

Talmey, Allene. "Evangeline Adams and Her Stars," *Outlook,* February 18, 1931.

Thompson, Catherine V. H. "Speculums," *The Sphinx,* January 1900.
_____. "To the Editor," *Modern Astrology,* July-August, 1933.

"Adamses Alive," Anon. *Fortune,* October 1930.

"Evangeline Adams," Anon. (obituary), *Publisher's Weekly,* November 26, 1932.

"Modern Prophecies Which Have Come to Pass," Anon. *Modern Astrology and Occult Astronomy,* ed. Alan Leo November 1899.

"A Place in the Stars,"Anon. *Saturday Review of Literature,* January 14, 1933.

"The Star Gazer," Anon. *The Review of Reviews,* November, 1930.

General Magazine References

The Arena, ed. B.O. Flower, Boston, 1890-1909.

The Sphinx, ed. Catherine H. Thompson, Pyramid Publishing Co., Boston, July 1899-May 1901.

Newspaper Articles

Adams, Evangelina S. "Horoscope of Greater New York," *New York Journal and Advertiser Sunday Supplement*, April 30, 1899.

Albelli, Alfred. "Evangeline Adams Mate Involved in Love Theft," *New York News,* December 31, 1931.

Currie, George. "Astrology, Your Place in the Sun," *The Brooklyn Eagle Book Review,* January 22, 1928.

Engle, William. "Evangeline Adams in Death Joins the Prophets of the Ages," *New York World-Telegram*, November 11, 1932.

Garrison, Rev. Webb. "She Made Astrology Respectable in 1914 by Demonstrating her Talent in Court," *National Enquirer*, September 24, 1972.

Foster, Helen Herbert. "Seeks Wisdom Among the Stars," *Brooklyn Eagle Sunday Magazine,* April 24, 1927.

Keating, Isabelle. "Did Auto-Suggestion Kill Astrologer who Forecast Own Death?" *The Brooklyn Eagle,* November 13, 1932.

Kuhn, Irene. "Astrologers Mate as Stars Dictated," *New York Herald*, April 7, 1923.

Phelps, Mary. "What Happened When the Stars told a Wife What the Moon Saw," *New York Mirror*, February 7, 1932.

Pogrebin, Robin. "It Seems the Cards Do Lie," *New York Times*, June 30, 1999.

Sherwood, M.E.W. "After a Great Fire," *New York Times Saturday Review*, June 3, 1899.

Warton, Carl. "Predicts War in U.S. Within 15 Years," *The Boston Herald*, April 27, 1930.

"300 at Funeral of Miss Adams," Anon. *New York World-Telegram*, November 14, 1932.

"$83,911 Left by Miss Adams," Anon. *New York Sun*, August 30, 1933.

"Adams Funeral Service is Held at Little Church," Anon. *New York Times*, November 15, 1932.

"Adams Funeral Service is Held at Little Church," Anon. *New York Herald-Tribune,* November 15, 1932.

"Arriving Astrologist Sees New World War Due in 1942," Anon. *The Brooklyn Eagle*, June 14, 1923.

"Astrologer Again Freed," Anon. *New York Tribune*, December 12, 1914.

"Astrologer's Body to Lie in State," Anon. *New York Times*, November 13, 1932.

"Astrological Piracy Charged to Miss Adams," Anon. *New York Herald-Tribune*, January 8, 1932.

"Astrology Figures in Suit" Anon. *New York Times*, June 7, 1922.

"Believer in Stars Loses $100,000 Suit" Anon. *New York Times*, June 13, 1922.

"Beware of Market, for Hostile Uranus is in Control, Noted Astrologist Warns," Anon. *New York Telegram*, February 4, 1930.

"Church Filled at Evangeline Adams Rites," Anon. *New York American*, November 15, 1932.

"Descendant of John Quincy Adams Held on $500 Bail," Anon. May 21, 1914 clipping from the *New York Journal-American* morgue.

"Dr. Charles Fleischer, Editor and Lecturer" Anon. (obituary) *New York Times*, July 3, 1942.

"Evangeline Adams," Anon. (obituary) *New York Sun*, November 11, 1932.

"Evangeline Adams, Astrologer, Dead," Anon. *New York Times*, November 11, 1932.

"Evangeline Adams' Funeral," Anon. *New York Sun*, November 14, 1932.

"Evangeline Adams' Husband Accused in Love Case," Anon. *New York Sun*, December 31, 1931.

"Evangeline Adams Tells Why She Became an Astrologer," Anon. *The Boston Herald*, December 5, 1930.

"Evangeline Adams Unperturbed by Alienation Suit," Anon. December 31, 1931 clipping from the *New York Sun* morgue.

"Evangeline Adams' Will," Anon. *New York Times*, November 18, 1932.

"Expert Links Stars to Destiny," Anon. *New York Evening Journal*, April 4, 1931.

"Fire Destroys Windsor Hotel," Anon. *New York World*, March 18, 1899.

"Foretold the Calamity," Anon. *New York World*, March 20, 1899.

"Fortune Teller is Held," Anon. *New York Times*, January 25, 1923.

"Fortune Tellers Trapped by Women," Anon. *New York Times*, May 15, 1914.

"J.J. Freschi Dead; A Jurist 34 Years," Anon. *New York Times*, July 30, 1944.

"Jacob Stout," Anon. (obituary), *New York Times*, July 9, 1907.

"Leland Crazed by Deaths in Family," Anon. *New York Herald*, March 18, 1899.

"Many at Funeral of Evangeline Adams," Anon. *New York Times*, November 15, 1932.

"Miss Adams, Noted Astrologist, is Dead; Proves her Prediction," Anon. *The Brooklyn Eagle,* November 11, 1932.

"Modest Windsor Hero," Anon. *New York Times*, April 26, 1899.

"More Palmists Arrested," Anon. *New York Tribune*, January 13, 1911.

"Mr. Leland Not Insane," Anon. *New York Tribune*, March 18, 1899.

"Puts Blame on Planets," Anon. *New York Herald,* December 12, 1914.

"St. Patrick Honored," Anon. *New York Times*, March 18, 1899.

"Searching Windsor Ruins," Anon. *New York Times*, March 20, 1899.

"Seeress' Husband Sued," Anon. *New York Times*, December 31, 1931.

"Services for Evangeline Adams," Anon. *New York Times*, November 12, 1932.

"Seymour Cromwell Dead After Fall," Anon. *New York Times*, September 17, 1925.

"She is Astrologer, Not Fortune Teller," Anon. *The World*, *New York*, December 12, 1914.

"Society Palmist Seized in a Raid," Anon. *The World, New York,* January 13, 1911.

"Strange Man in the Halls," Anon. *New York World*, March 20, 1899.

"Stroke Fatal to Astrologer of Radio Fame," Anon. *New York American*, November 11, 1932.

"War on Palmists," Anon. *New York Herald*, January 13, 1911.

"Wills of Hotel Fire Victims," Anon. *New York Times*, September 14, 1899.

"Warren F. Leland Dead," Anon. *New York Times*, April 5, 1899.

"Warren F. Leland Follows His Wife," Anon. *New York Journal-American*, April 5, 1899.

"Warren Leland Prostrated by Shock," Anon. *New York Evening Journal*, March 18, 1899.

"Windsor Hotel Disaster Grows," Anon. *New York Times*, March 19, 1899.

"Windsor Hotel Lies in Ashes," Anon. *New York Times*, March 18, 1899.

"Windsor Hotel Verdict," Anon. *New York Times*, April 25, 1899.

Reference Works

A Thousand and One Notable Nativities, Alan Leo's Astrological Manuals, No. 11. London: L.N.Fowler & Co, c. 1910.

Almanac of Famous People, 6th Edition. Detroit: Gale Research, 1999.

Appleton's Cyclopaedia of American Biography. New York: D. Appleton & Co., 1886, 1888 (facsimile edition).

Biographical Cyclopaedia of American Women, ed. Mabel Ward Cameron. New York: Halvord Publishing Co. Inc., 1924.

Biographical Dictionary of American Business Leaders, ed. John H. Ingham. Westport, CT: Greenwood Press, 1983.

Book Review Digest, ed. Marion A. Knight, Mertice James, Matilda L. Berg and Dorothy Brown. New York: H.W. Wilson & Co., 1926, 1927, 1928, 1933.

Brooklyn Eagle Almanac, Brooklyn, NY, 1901.

Chronicle of America, ed. Clifton Daniel and John Kirshon. Mount Kisco, NY: Chronicle Publications, c. 1989.

Current Biography Yearbook. New York: H.W. Wilson Co., 1972, 1973.

Dictionary of American Biography. New York: James T. White & Co., 1936.

Dictionary of American Biography. New York: Charles Scribner's Sons 1964.

Dictionary of Mysticism and the Occult, ed. Nevill Drury. San Francisco: Harper & Row, 1985.

Encyclopedia of New York City, ed. Jackson, Kenneth T. New Haven: Yale University Press, 1995.

Encyclopedia of Occultism and Parapsychology, ed. Leslie Shepard. Detroit: Gale Research Co., 1984.

Encyclopedia of the Unexplained, ed. Richard Cavendish. London: Arkana, Penguin Books, 1994.

National Cyclopaedia of American Biography, Vol. 25 reprint. Ann Arbor, MI: University Microfilms, 1967.

National Cyclopaedia of American Biography. Clifton, NJ: James T. White & Co., 1979.

New York Criminal Reports, Volume XXXII, 1914, ed. Charles N. Mills. Albany, NY: W.C. Little & Co., 1915.

New York Historical Society Dictionary of Artists in America 1564-1880, ed. Grace C. Groce and David H. Wallace. New Haven, CT: Yale University Press, 1957.

Notable Names in the American Theater, Clifton, NJ: James T. White & Co., 1976.

Special Collections in the Library of Congress, by Annette Melville. Washington, DC: Library of Congress, 1980.

This Fabulous Century Volumes II-IV. New York: Time-Life Books, 1969.

Twentieth Century Biography of Notable Americans, Boston: The Biographical Society, 1904. Republished in Detroit by Gale Research Co., 1968.

Who Was Who, Volumes I-III. London: Adam & Charles Black, 1967.

Who Was Who in American Art, ed. Peter Hastings. Madison, CT: Sound View Press, 1985.

Other Sources

Evangeline Adams' sales brochure, "*Astrology and Palmistry*" c. 1900.

Evangeline Adams' sales brochure, "*The Law and Astrology*" c. 1915.

Scrapbook of Gertrude Adams Curry and Evangeline Adams Curry Elmore (Norman Winski Collection).

Biographical profile of George E. Jordan, Jr., National News Association, 1934.

Carnegie Hall's website, "*Carnegie Then & Now*," *www.carnegiehall.org.*

Federal Census of 1900, 1910 and 1920.

History and Program commemorating the Centennial of the City of Dunkirk, NY, August 1980.

National Climatic Data Center's Data time series from their Global Historical Climatological Network, *www.ncdc.noaa.gov.*

Thelema Lodge Newsletters of September 1992 and October 1992.

Trow's *New York City Directories*, 1899 to 1935.

Brooklyn Eagle morgue at the Brooklyn Public Library, Grand Army Plaza.

New York Journal-American morgue at the Harry Ransom Humanities Research Center, University of Texas at Austin.

New York Sun morgue at the New York Public Library Newspaper Division.

T.L. Bradford Scrapbooks at the Hahnemann University Library, Philadelphia, PA (obituaries of homeopaths).

Various catalogs from the Boston University School of Medicine, 1897-1911.

Adams, Evangeline.
Horoscopes of Beatrice Cameron Mansfield and Richard Mansfield, Jr.
Letter to Mr. Eaton at Phillips Academy, November 18, 1908.
Letters to "Everybody": June 25, 1927; July 1, 1927; April 9, 1928; April 16, 1928; May 1, 1928, January 26, 1929; April 6, 1930; August 22, 1931; August 26, 1931, August 30, 1931.
Letters to Gertrude: May 1, 1928; January 7, 1929; December 19, 1929; April 13, 1931; November 3, 1932.

Adams, George. Letter to Dr. Paine January 14, 1903.

Dearborn, Edward L. Letters of March 5, 1993; March 25, 1993; April 12, 1993; February 6, 1994; April 18, 1994; October 7, 1994; February 8, 1995; March 1-2, 1995.

Dobin, Rabbi Joel C. Letter of November 11, 1994.

Fleck, Kathy. Letters of February 2, 1996 and April 23, 1996.

McEvoy, Frances. Letter of November 23, 1993.

Morrison, Al H. Letters of September 15, 1993; October 9, 1993; November 3, 1993.

Stein, Adele. Interview of June 29, 1994.

Winski, Norman. Evangeline Adams' library and memorabilia collection; Interviews of October 9, 1993, June 4-5, 1994, and May 20, 2000.

The collections of the New York and Brooklyn Public Libraries were indispensable, and provided much of the core of the research.

Photo Credits

Cover Photo - Norman Winski Collection
George and Harriet Adams - Norman Winski Collection
Evangeline as a little girl - Author Collection
Elizabeth Stuart Phelps - Haverford College Library, Haverford PA
Evangeline at 19 - Norman Winski Collection
House on Chestnut Street - Author photo
Dr. Smith - Boston University Archives
Cheiro - Brooklyn Public Library; Aime Dupont photo
Warren Leland - New York Public Library
Adams in 1904 - Norman Winski Collection
King Edward VII - Princess Lazarovich-Hrebelianovich; J.W. Adams drawing
NYC Directory ad - Brooklyn Public Library
Adams in 1912 - Norman Winski Collection; Arnold Genthe photo
George Jordan - Norman Winski Collection
Adams on stoop - Norman Winski Collection
Adams' office - Norman Winski Collection
Portrait of Adams from the 1920's - Carnegie Hall Archives
Adams in 1930 - Carnegie Hall Archives
Jordan Lot at the North Plainsfield Cemetery Association, CT - Author photo
Back Cover - Michelle Hannay photo

Index

Adams, Abigail Smith 16
Adams, Benjamin 14
Adams, Charles Francis (Evangeline's
    brother) 17-19, 21, 83
Adams, Elizabeth Horne 14
Adams, Evangeline
    advertisements 82, 148
    appearance 28, 113
    arrests 77-79, 88-90, 119, 135
    autobiography 19, 24, 145-147
    beliefs 34, 38, 143-145
    birth 17
    Carnegie Hall 74, 75, 77, 88, 124
    childhood 19-25
    clients 58, 60, 65, 69, 75, 81, 82,
        110, 114, 116, 127-131, 138, 139
    Copley Street studio 54 ff.
    death 177 ff.
    education 21
    engagement 28, 30, 35, 37
    estate 179
    fees 55, 81, 125, 126
    health 25-26, 154, 155, 160, 171 ff.
    legal difficulties 81, 82, 85-100, 108,
        109, 119, 120, 174, 175, 184
    library 62, 103, 183, 184
    mail-order horoscopes 71, 73,
        108-109, 124, 125
    marriage 112, 119-122
    miniature elephant collection 83
    monthly forecast service 108
    palmistry 49, 56, 57, 79
    personal characteristics 20, 26, 27
    pets 19, 82, 83, 161
    predictions 65-71, 79-81, 85, 86, 95,
        100, 114, 115, 122, 123, 141, 142,
        152, 154, 156-159, 168, 177, 186
    promotion 67, 132, 134, 147, 160
    promotional brochures 56, 97, 103
    radio show 5, 160-163, 166-170
    recreation and hobbies 82, 83
    spiritualism 24, 46, 51, 52, 143
    standardized forecasts 107
    stock market crash 156-159
    trial -- See legal difficulties
Adams, George (Evangeline's father) 14
Adams, Dr. George S. 36
Adams, Gertrude (Evangeline's niece) 75,
    84, 109, 120, 134, 149, 153, 155,
    158, 165, 175 ff., 184

Adams, Harriet Smith (Evangeline's
    mother) 6, 14, 16-19, 20, 26, 27,
37, 38, 50, 54
Adams, Henry 12
Adams, Isaac 14-16. 26, 27
Adams, John (b. 1750) 13, 14
Adams, John III (b. 1803) 14
Adams, John, Jr., (b. 1774) 13
Adams, John D. (Evangeline's brother)
    17-19, 21, 26, 35, 44, 83, 179
Adams, John Quincy (President) 5, 16,
    97, 118, 178
Adams, Joseph (b. 1688) 12
Adams, Ralph 75, 179
Adams, Seth 15
Adams, Stella 75, 84
Adams, Captain William (b. 1725) 13
Adams, William Lincoln (Evangeline's
    brother) 17-18, 26, 44, 75, 84
Alsey, Alexa See Chenko, Muriel
Andover Theological Seminary 19, 29
Andover (Massachusetts) 14, 16, 19 ff.
Aquarius, Age of 165
Arena (magazine) 60, 141
Arnold, Sir Edwin 178
astrology
    and Christianity 133
    and colors 141
    and free will 10, 110, 132-145
    legal ordinances 77, 87, 89 ff., 96,
        97, 124, 169, 170, 182
    popularity 46, 72, 184, 185
Bankhead, Tallulah 135, 136
Barrymore, John 138
Belmont, Mrs. August 82, 130
Bennett, Sydney K. 172, 173
Besant, Annie 47, 51
Bishop, Washington Irving 130
Brooks, Phillips 55
Broughton, Luke D., Dr. 31, 36, 46
Brush, Emma 7 ff., 64, 70, 179
Bryan, William Jennings 86, 131
Bull, Mrs. Ole 47, 53
Burroughs, John 60
Campbell, Joseph 139, 140
Carnegie Hall 74, 75, 77, 88, 124
Carter, Mrs. Leslie 130
Caruso, Enrico 74, 114-117
Chaney, W.H. 46
Chaplin, Charlie 130

Cheiro 47-51, 182
Chenko, Leo 173, 174
Chenko, Muriel 173
Claire, Ina 130
Cleveland, Grover (President) 83
Cochran, Charles 135, 136
Collins, Frederick 174
Columbian Exposition of 1893 44, 45
Colville, William Wilberforce J. 52, 53
Congregationalism 29, 34, 39, 122, 143
Coolidge, Calvin (President) 131
Copley Hotel 54, 55
Cromwell, Seymour 81, 154
Crowley, Aleister 101-108, 150, 164,
    182-184
Curry, Claude 109
Curry, Evangeline Adams 148ff., 184
Davis, Richard Harding 75, 76
Dempsey, Jack 131, 132
Douglas, Governor 82
Dryden, John P. 82
Du Maurier, Sir Gerald 135, 136
Dudley, David 8
Duncan, Isadora 9, 74
Dunkirk (New York) 16, 17
Edward VII, King 71, 72, 79, 80
Fairbanks, Douglas 83
Farrar, Geraldine 130
Federal Radio Commission 166-170
Fifth Avenue Hotel 6-7, 63
Fleischer, Rabbi Charles 61, 134, 178
Flower, B.O. 60
Freschi, Magistrate John J. 90-100, 182
Garden, Mary 130
Garth, Metta and Franklin 171
Genthe, Arnold 84
George V, King 86
Gibbons, Cardinal 131
Goodwin, Isabella 77, 78, 88, 93
Goold, Oliver Ames 60, 61
Gould, Helen 7, 8
Grant, Kenneth 103, 105
Hall, Mrs. 161
Hamon, Count Louis See Cheiro
Harding, Warren G. (President) 130
Harriman, Mrs. Oliver 130
Heinze, Fritz 81, 154
Hill, James J. 69, 131, 154
Hindu Vedanta 45
Homeopathy 25, 31
Hopkins, Arthur 137-140
Hyslop, Professor 51
Israel, Lee 135-137
Jefferson, Joseph 132
Jones, Robert Edmund 138, 141, 142

Jordan, Clark 89, 90, 99, 181
Jordan, George E., Jr. 112-121, 124ff.,
    132, 134, 145, 149, 153, 158, 160,
    164-166, 169, 173, 177, 179, 183
Jupiter (planet) 63, 79, 83, 121, 122
Lawlor, Mariska 89, 90, 114, 119, 121,
    137, 170, 175
Lawson, Thomas 58, 154
Le Gallienne, Eva 130
Leland, Helen 10
Leland, Warren F. 6 ff., 64-68, 70, 80
Leo, Alan 72, 73, 88
Lockhart, L.S. 92-95
Long, Ray 130
Loos, Anita 130
Magnetik Manufacturing Co. 175
Manchester, Duchess of 82
Mankiewicz, Joseph L. 146
Mansfield, Richard 130
Marbury, Elizabeth 130
Martin, Riccordo 130
Mason, Margot 183
McDonough, Frank 183
Modern Astrology (magazine) 67, 72, 182
Morgan, J. Pierpont 69, 81, 117
Moulton, Louise Chandler 61
Mundy, Talbot 130
Murphy, Charles F. 132
Mussolini, Benito 134
Nordica, Lillian 130
Northcliffe, Lord 130
O'Neill, Eugene 128, 141, 142, 181
Paget, Lady Minnie 79, 80, 130
Pallas, Lord Chief Justice 82
Payne, Philip 133
Pearce, A.J. 79
Phelps, Elizabeth Stuart 22-25, 181
Pickford, Mary 83, 130
Priess, Adele D. 88-92, 133
Radio Industry Production Code 167.
Reed, Mrs. Melvin D. 77, 179
Rich, Isaac B. 58
Righter, Carroll 110, 184
Robson, May 124
Roosevelt, Theodore (President) 85
Roosevelt, Theodore, Jr. 131
Ross, David 162, 163
Russell, Lillian 82
Saturn (planet) 85, 86
Savage, Minot J. 39, 51
Scheinman, Mary C. 109, 144, 146, 149,
    165, 179
Schwab, Charles 154
Seabury, David 103
Sepharial 40

Siam, King of 83
Simmons, Franklin 42, 43
Smith, Al 131
Smith, Dr. J. Heber 30-36, 41, 60ff., 103
Smyth, Professor Egbert Coffin 29, 30
Society of Psychical Research 39, 51
Sphinx (magazine) 40, 41, 157
Spiritualism 23, 46, 51, 52, 111, 143
Stevens, Elizabeth Allen 14
Stout, Jacob 70, 154
Symonds, John 103, 105
Taylor, Laurette 130
Theosophical Society 88
Theosophy 46, 47, 88, 110, 111
Thomas, August 130
Thompson, Catherine 35, 36, 39-41, 46,
        61, 157, 181, 182
Tunney, Gene 131
Unitarianism 38, 39, 122, 143
Valentino, Rudolph 132
Vanderbilt, Gloria Morgan 130
Vanderbilt, Reggie 131
Vivekenanda, Swami 45 ff.
Vorel, Iris 89, 90, 99, 107, 119, 121
Wagner, Charles 130
Warner, William See Cheiro
Weeks, John W. 130
Wells, H.G. 61
Whiting, Dr. Lewis 25, 30
Wilcox, Ella Wheeler 110
Wilson, James 46
Windsor Hotel 6 ff., 64-68, 70, 185
Winski, Norman 183

Also Available from *One Reed Publications*

The Circuitry of the Self: Astrology and the Developmental Model
by Bruce Scofield
2001, ISBN 0-9628031-7-0, 192 pages, paperback $12.95
Presents a theoretical model and conceptual framework for astrology,
placing it in the context of developmental biology and psychology.

Day-Signs: Native American Astrology From Ancient Mexico
by Bruce Scofield
1991, ISBN 0-9628031-0-3, 220 pages, paperback, $11.95.
This book contains the first practical delineations ever published for the
day-signs used by the Maya and Aztecs of ancient Mexico.

Signs of Time: An Introduction to Mesoamerican Astrology
by Bruce Scofield
1993, ISBN 0-9628031-1-1, 220 pages, paperback, $11.95
This companion volume to *Day-Signs* covers the entire spectrum of Maya
and Aztec astrology, including the 260-day tzolkin, the cycle of Venus, and
the Mayan calendar.

User's Guide to Astrology **by Bruce Scofield**
1997, ISBN 0-9628031-3-8, 144 pages, paperback, $10.00
An essential reference and guidebook to the entire field of astrology,
providing basic information on the history and practice of this ancient
discipline, and explaining the symbolism, philosophy, and scientific proofs.
Includes useful sections on astrological software, how to choose a personal
astrologer, plus how to do "amateur" astrology and calculate a horoscope.

Persephone is Transpluto **by Valerie Vaughan**
1995, ISBN 0-9628031-2-X, 256 pages, paperback, $12.95
Astronomers have long suspected the existence of a planet beyond Pluto.
This book is a pioneering and scholarly investigation into the astrology,
mythology, history and scientific evidence of this "undiscovered" planet.
Includes a 115-year ephemeris for Transpluto.

Astro-Mythology: The Celestial Union of Astrology and Myth
by Valerie Vaughan
1998, ISBN 0-9628031-5-4, 176 pages, paperback $11.00

The ancient star legends are brought to life and revealed as the source of
astrological symbolism. Presents instructive stories of the gods we call
planets and their adventures in the celestial lands we know as the signs of
the Zodiac, and offers directions on how to use astro-mythology to interpret
birth charts and discover personal myths.

One Reed Publications
PO Box 561, Amherst, MA 01004-0561
413-253-9450
Visit our Web site   www.onereed.com